THE
LOST LANGUAGE
OF SYMBOLISM

AN INQUIRY INTO THE ORIGIN OF CERTAIN LETTERS, WORDS, NAMES, FAIRY-TALES, FOLKLORE, AND MYTHOLOGIES

BY

HAROLD BAYLEY

"The English mind, not readily swayed by rhetoric, moves freely under the pressure of facts."
E. B. TYLOR.

"One may, for a moment, arouse interest by a new hypothesis, but it is only by the accumulation of facts that public opinion is perceptibly influenced in the end."
WALTER JOHNSON.

A CITADEL PRESS BOOK
PUBLISHED BY CAROL PUBLISHING GROUP

Carol Publishing Group Edition - 1993

A Citadel Press Book
Published by Carol Publishing Group
Citadel Press is a registered trademark of Carol Communications, Inc.

Editorial Offices: 600 Madison Avenue, New York, NY 10022
Sales & Distribution Offices: 120 Enterprise Avenue, Secaucus, NJ 07094
In Canada: Canadian Manda Group, P.O. Box 920, Station U, Toronto, Ontario, M8Z 5P9, Canada

Queries regarding rights and permissions should be addressed to: Carol Publishing Group, 600 Madison Avenue, New York, NY 10022

Manufactured in the United States of America
ISBN 0-8065-1100-1

14 13 12 11 10 9 8 7 6 5 4 3

Carol Publishing Group books are available at special discounts for bulk purchases, for sales promotions, fund raising, or educational purposes. Special editions can also be created to specifications. For details contact: Special Sales Department, Carol Publishing Group, 120 Enterprise Ave., Secaucus, NJ 07094

CONTENTS

CHAPTER I

INTRODUCTORY

CHAPTER II

THE PARABLE OF THE PILGRIM

CHAPTER III

THE WAYS OF ASCENT

v

CHAPTER VII

KING SOLOMON

CHAPTER VIII

THE FAIR SHULAMITE

CHAPTER IX

CINDERELLA

CONTENTS

CHAPTER XIII

THE PRESIDENT OF THE MOUNTAINS

THE LOST LANGUAGE OF SYMBOLISM

CHAPTER I

INTRODUCTION

" There can be no question that an enormous number of these water-marks had a religious significance, but we are asked to believe, on the ground that the same symbol was used contemporaneously in various parts of Europe, that these symbols formed a means of intercommunication and spiritual encouragement between all those who had been admitted to the secrets of the sect. The suggestion has many points to recommend it, but it requires a prolonged and scholarly analysis before it can rank as an acceptable hypothesis. . . .

" In all justice to Mr Bayley, let us admit that he is not arrogant or dogmatic. He has put forth a theory on somewhat insufficient grounds, and has evidenced some over-anxiety to expand that theory beyond reasonable limits. But he is ready to confess that his own work is one of suggestion rather than of proof, and he has undoubtedly established a claim to further consideration. His hypothesis is ingenious, and up to a point seems tenable ; but at present we must regard it as ' not proven.' "—*Westminster Gazette*, 12th May 1909.

THIS book, though not written specially with that end, substantiates the tentative conclusions formulated three years ago in *A New Light on the Renaissance*. I then said : " The facts now presented tend to prove that—

" 1. From their first appearance in 1282, until the latter half of the eighteenth century, the curious designs inserted into paper in the form of water-marks constitute a coherent and unbroken chain of *emblems*.

" 2. That these emblems are thought-fossils or thought-crystals, in which lie enshrined the aspirations and traditions of the numerous mystic and puritanic sects by which Europe was overrun in the Middle Ages.

" 3. Hence that these paper-marks are historical documents of high importance, throwing light, not only on the evolution of European thought, but also upon many obscure problems of the past.

" 4. Water-marks denote that paper-making was an art introduced into Europe, and fostered there by the pre-Reformation Protestant sects known in France as the Albigeois and Vaudois, and in Italy as the Cathari or Patarini.

" 5. That these heresies, though nominally stamped out by the Papacy, existed secretly for several centuries subsequent to their disappearance from the sight of history.

" 6. The embellishments used by printers in the Middle Ages are emblems similar to those used by paper-makers, and explicable by a similar code of interpretation.

" 7. The awakening known as the Renaissance was the direct result of an influence deliberately and traditionally exercised by paper-makers, printers, cobblers, and other artisans.

" 8. The nursing mother of the Renaissance, and consequently of the Reformation, was not, as hitherto assumed, Italy, but the Provençal district of France."

There is curious and direct proof of Vaudois influence at the end of one of the earliest editions of the Bible (that of

1535, known to collectors as the Olivetan), where the following claim is cunningly concealed in cipher :

> "Les Vaudois, peuple évangélique,
> Ont mis ce thrésor en publique."

The vehicle in which this interesting cryptogram was concealed from the world at large is the stanza found at the end of the volume. The *first letters of each word* of these verses, as will be seen, spell out the secret message :

> "*L*ecteur *e*ntends, *s*i *v*erité *a*ddresse
> *V*iens *d*onc *o*uyr *i*nstamment *s*a *p*romesse
> *E*t *v*if *p*arler : *l*equel *e*n *e*xcellence
> *V*eult *a*sseurer *n*ostre *g*relle *e*sperance
> *L*esprit *i*esus *q*ui *v*isite *e*t *o*rdonne
> *N*oz *t*endres *m*eurs, *i*ci *s*ans *c*ry *e*stonne
> *T*out *h*ault *r*aillart *e*scumant *s*on *o*rdure.
> *P*renons *v*ouloir *b*ienfaire *l*ibrement.
> *I*esus *q*uerons *v*eoir *e*ternellement."

In the following studies I have taken all symbolism to be my province, but the subjects illustrated are, as before, hitherto-uninterpreted printers' marks and paper-marks. Most of these signs have entirely lost their primitive significance, and are now used purely for commercial purposes ; but there was a time when they were not only trade signs, but were also hieroglyphics, under which the pearl of great price was revered.

The extraordinary tenacity with which the Vaudois or Albigeois maintained their traditions will to some extent account for the apparition of their mystic tenets in the form of paper-marks, and it is possible to trace faintly the course of this tradition link by link.

The paper-mills of Europe have, in the main, always been situated in heretical districts—in Holland, for instance, which Bayle described as a "great ark of heresy," and Lamartine as " the workshop of innovators " and " the asylum and the arsenal of new ideas."

But the technical terms of paper-making — such as " retree," a corruption of the French " retiré "—imply that paper-making was primarily a *French* art, and, as is well known, the introduction of paper-making into England was due to *French* refugees. Wherever these sufferers landed they acted as missionaries of skilled labour, and the records of the Patent Office show clearly the activity of the exiles, not only in manufacture, but also in invention. Numerous patents were taken out by them for paper-making, printing, spinning, weaving, and other arts. In 1686 there is reference to a patent granted for making writing- and printing-paper, the patentees having " lately brought out of France excellent workmen, and already set up several new-invented mills and engines for making thereof, not heretofore used in England."

At the present day the paper-makers of Scotland enjoy a deserved pre-eminence, and it is interesting to find that their industry likewise owes also its introduction to the same source. " At Glasgow," says Smiles, " one of the refugees succeeded in establishing a paper-mill, the first in that part of Scotland. The Huguenot who erected it escaped from France, accompanied only by his little daughter. For some time after his arrival in Glasgow, he maintained himself by picking up rags in the streets. But, by dint of thrift and diligence, he eventually contrived to accumulate means sufficient to enable him to start his paper-mill, and thus to lay the foundation of an important branch of Scottish industry."[1]

The present makers of the paper used for the Bank of England's notes are descendants of the De Portal family of Provence, many of whose members are recorded as " amongst

[1] *The Huguenots*, p. 338.

the most active of the leaders of the Albigeois."[1]   After the Revocation of the Edict of Nantes, the founder of the present business fled to England, where he died in 1704.   In his will, which is written in French, he says : " In the first place, I thank my God without ceasing, for having put it in my heart to escape from persecution, and for having blessed my project in my own person and in that of my children. I regard my English refuge as the best heritage which I can bequeath to them."[2]

The headquarters of the Huguenots were Auvergne, Angoumois, and the Southern Provinces of France, where, in Angoumois alone, according to Smiles, they owned six hundred paper-mills.[3]

The Revocation of the Edict of Nantes ostensibly wiped the Huguenots—whom Pope Clement XI. identified with " the execrable race of the ancient Albigenses "—completely out of France ; yet it is characteristic of the spirit of the Southern Provinces that one hundred years after that disastrous event it was the progress to Paris of a battalion of Marseillais, marching as they believed to support the tottering statue of Liberty, that turned the scale of the French Revolution.[4]

The historian of paper-making at Arches, in the South of France, states that secret organisations, dating from immemorial antiquity, existed among the paper-making workmen, and that these "solidly organised associations of comradeship" endured for long after the Revolution. "One is struck," says he, "by the general spirit of insubordination which from all time under the ancient regime

---

[1] *Library Association Record*, iv. p. 129.
[2] *Ibid.*, p. 129.
[3] *The Huguenots*, p. 158.
[4] There is a graphic presentment of this episode in *The Reds of the Midi*, by Félix Gras. See also *Secret Societies and the French Revolution*, Una Birch.

animated the paper-making workmen. Collaborating in the propagation of written thought, which, during the eighteenth century, was the main destructive agent of the existing state of affairs until then respected, it would appear that the paper-making workmen had a foreknowledge of the social upheavals that were about to take place, and of which they were the obscure auxiliaries."[1]   Heckethorn devotes a chapter of his *Secret Societies* to these guilds or corporations, which existed not only among the paper-makers, but also among other French artisans and journeymen. Freemasonry was early mixed up with this *compagnonnage*, and the various sections of it were known by titles such as the "Sons of Solomon," the "Companions of the Foxes," the "Foxes of Liberty," the "Independents,"[2] and so forth.

The preliminary chapters of the present book—which I have cut to their lowest limits—will, I am afraid, read somewhat wearily, but in Chapter VIII. the reader will be introduced to some of the hitherto unappreciated beauties underlying fairy-tales, and in the later chapters we shall reach a group of facts that must, I think, undoubtedly have formed part of the Gnosis or secret Wisdom of the Ancients. It is common knowledge that during the early centuries of Christianity there existed certain "Gnostics" who claimed supernatural wisdom and an "ability to restore to mankind the lost knowledge of the true and supreme God."[3]

The Gnostic, unlike the modern *agnostic* or avowed *non-knower*, claimed to be *gnostikos* or "good at knowing," and

---

[1] " On est frappé de l'esprit général d'insubordination qui, de tout temps, sous l'ancien régime, a animé les ouvriers papetiers. Collaborant à la propagation de la pensée écrite, qui, pendant le xviiie siècle, a été le grand agent destructeur de l'état de choses, jusque-là respecté, il semble que les ouvriers papetiers avaient conscience des bouleversements sociaux, qui allaient survenir et dont ils étaient les obscurs auxiliaires."—H. Onfroy, *Histoire des Papeteries à la Cuve d'Arches et d'Archettes*, p. 35. Paris, 1904.

[2] Vol. i. pp. 317-24.

[3] Mosheim, *Eccles. Hist.*, part ii. ch. v.

to be the depositary of *Gnosis*, a term defined by modern dictionaries as meaning "philosophic insight," "illumination," "intuition," and "a higher knowledge of spiritual things."

The chief function of Gnosticism was moral salvation, but it also claimed to get behind the letter of the written word, and to discover the ideal value of all religious histories, myths, mysteries, and ordinances. Mythologies were held to be popular presentments of religious ideas originally revealed, and Christianity was believed to be the full revelation of the deeper truth embedded more or less in every religion. The faith of Christianity was indeed treated as if it had little or no connection with historic fact, and almost as though it were an ideal system evolved from the brain of a philosopher.

The Gnostic claimed to be not only the philosophical Christian who evolved truth out of thought, but also to be the depositary of a secret tradition, upon which his system was primarily constructed.

Prior to about the middle of the second century the Gnostics were not considered heretical,[1] but the subsequent history of Ecclesiasticism unhappily resolves largely into a record of the ghastly and protracted struggle between the spirituality of Gnosticism and the literalism of official Christianity. It was a contest in which Gnosticism in its varied phases was nominally extinguished and Ecclesiasticism was ostensibly triumphant.

By the end of the sixth century Gnosticism disappears from history, being supposedly crushed out of existence; seemingly, however, it simply dived underground and continued to flourish *sub rosâ*.

It is in the ancient cemeteries of Provence that one still finds the greatest number of Gnostic medallions.

---

[1] Mead (G. R. S.), *Fragments of a Faith Forgotten*, p. 418.

"Gnosticism," says King, "early took root and *flourished in Southern Gaul*, as the treatise of Irenæus directed against it attests."

In 1135–1204 materialistic rationalism attained probably its climax in the system of MAIMONIDES, who recognised only the primary or literal sense of the Scriptures, and dismissed as a fantastic dream all existing allegorical interpretations.   Mr Bernard Pick states : "A reaction came and the Kabala [1] stepped in as a counterpoise to the growing shallowness of the Maimunist's philosphy.   The storm against his system *broke out in Provence* and spread over Spain." [2]

The extended Hand marked FOY (see fig. 1327), the symbol of Fidelity or faith maintained, is a sixteenth-century *Provençal* paper-mark, and it is logical to surmise that the Faith there maintained was the traditional faith of that long-suffering, blood-sodden district, and that the marks put into paper were a continuance of the traditional Gnostic system of intercommunication.   "Their ideas," says King, "were communicated to those initiated by composite figures and *siglæ* having a voice to the wise, but which the vulgar heareth not."

Many of these Gnostic symbols figure at the present day among the insignia of Freemasonry, and it is probable that Freemasonry is the last depositary of traditions that were

---

[1] Like its forerunner the Gnosis, the Kabala of the Middle Ages was the secret Science of Wisdom, and its adherents delighted in terming themselves "intelligent" and "connoisseurs of secret wisdom."—*The Cabala*, Bernard Pick.   *The Open Court*, 1910, p. 146.   "The Kabala," said REUCHLIN, "is nothing else than symbolic theology, in which not only are letters and words symbols of things, but things are symbols of other things."   This Kabalistic method of interpretation was held to have been originally communicated by revelation, in order that persons of holy life might by it attain to a mystical communion with God, or deification.—Inge (W. R.), *Christian Mysticism*, p. 269.

[2] *The Open Court*, 1909, p. 148.

taken over by them from the secret societies of the Middle Ages. The course of these traditions was not improbably by way of the Templars and the Rosicrucians. De Quincey maintained that the latter when driven out of Germany by persecution reappeared in England as Freemasons, and Elias Ashmole recorded it in his Diary that the symbols and signs of Freemasonry were borrowed partly from the Knight-Templars and partly from the Rosicrucians. It is claimed for Freemasonry that it is a beautiful system of morality veiled in allegory and illustrated by symbols, and, according to Dr Oliver, "The noble and sublime secrets of which we (Freemasons) are possessed are contained in our traditions, represented by hieroglyphic figures and intimated by our symbolic customs and ceremonies." "Again," says Dr Oliver, "we have declared over and over again that the great secret of Christian Freemasonry is the practice of morality and virtue here as a preparation for happiness in another world."

Whatever may have been its origin and purpose, Freemasonry spread rapidly over Europe, notwithstanding the bitter opposition of the Church of Rome. In 1738, at the instigation of the Inquisition, terrible anathemas were fulminated against it, all Freemasons were excommunicated and the penalty of death was decreed against them.

Many of the trade-marks illustrated in the following pages are obviously Masonic emblems, whence it may be inferred that among the initiates of Freemasonry were numerous working and wayfaring men. The ramifications of the mediæval secret societies upon which Freemasonry was built, the amazing vitality of tradition added to the disseminating powers of itinerant apostles and wandering minstrels, all no doubt served to keep alive the smouldering embers of what at one time must have been a brilliant and highly developed philosophy.

The aim and intention of the famous printer whose mark is reproduced herewith was evidently to carry on the traditional Great Wisdom, whose emblem, the serpent, surrounds a pair of storks.

These birds symbolised "filial piety" by reason of the care and solicitude which they were supposed to exercise towards aged storks, and "filial piety" as defined by Confucius—an expert on that subject—means "carrying on the aims of our forefathers." [1]

But after making all reasonable allowance for the force of tradition, it is still exceedingly difficult to account for the recondite knowledge unquestionably possessed by the mystics of the Dark Ages. It will be evident that not only the meanings of Egyptian symbols, such as the scarab, the sail, and the buckle, were perfectly understood, but also that

[1] Giles (H. A.), *Religions of Ancient China*, p. 32. It is not improbable that this notion of doing as our fathers have done is the explanation of the nursery lore that it is the storks who bring the babies.

the intimate relation between symbolism and word origins
was correctly appreciated.

Although etymologists are agreed that language is fossil
poetry and that the creation of every word was originally a
poem embodying a bold metaphor or a bright conception,
it is quite unrealised how close and intimate a relation
exists between symbolism and philology. But, as Renouf
points out, " It is not improbable that the cat, in Egyptian
Mau, became the symbol of the Sun-God or Day, because
the word *Mau* also means light." [1] Renouf likewise notes
that not only was RA the name of the Sun-God, but that
it was also the usual Egyptian word for *Sun*. Similarly the
Goose, one of the symbols of SEB, was called a *Seb* ; the
Crocodile, one of the symbols of SEBEK, was called a *Sebek* ;
the Ibis, one of the symbols of TECHU, was called a *Techu* ;
and the Jackal, one of the symbols of ANPU (ANUBIS), was
called an *Anpu*.

Parallels to this Egyptian custom are also traceable in
Europe, where, among the Greeks, the word *Psyche* served
not only to denote the Soul but also the Butterfly, a symbol
of the Soul ; and the word *Mylitta* served both as the name
of a Goddess and of her symbol the Bee. Among the
ancient Scandinavians the Bull, one of the symbols of THOR,
was named a *Thor*, this being an example, according to
Dr Alexander Wilder, " of the punning so common in those
times, often making us uncertain whether the accident of
similar name or sound led to adoption as a symbol or was
merely a blunder." [2]

I was unaware that there was any ancient warrant for
what I supposed to be the novel supposition that in many

---

[1] *On the Origin and Growth of Religion as Illustrated by the Religion of
Ancient Egypt*, p. 237 ; *Hibbert Lectures*, p. 879.

[2] *Symbolical Language of Ancient Art and Mythology*, R. Payne-Knight,
p. 124.

instances the names of once-sacred animals contain within
themselves the key to what was originally symbolised.
The idea that identities of name were primarily due to
punning, to blunder, or to accident, must be dispelled when
we find that—as in most of the examples noted by myself
—the symbolic value of the animal is not expressed by a
homonym or pun, but in monosyllables that apparently are
the debris of some marvellously ancient, prehistoric, almost
extinct parent tongue.   Modern language is a mosaic in
which lie embedded the chips and fossils of predecessors in
comparison with whose vast antiquity Sanscrit is but a
speech of yesterday.   In its glacier-like progress, Language
must have brought down along the ages the detritus of
tongues that were spoken possibly millions of years before
the art of recording by writing was discovered, but which,
notwithstanding, were indelibly inscribed and faithfully
preserved in the form of mountain, river, and country
names.   Empires may disappear and nations be sunk into
oblivion under successive waves of invasion, but place
names and proper names, preserved traditionally by word
of mouth, remain to some extent inviolate ; and it is, I
am convinced, in this direction that one must look for
the hypothetical mother-tongue of the hypothetical people,
known nowadays as " Aryans."

The primal roots which seem to be traceable in directions
far wider than any yet reconnoitred are the Semitic EL,
meaning God and Power ; the Semitic UR, meaning Fire or
Light; the Semitic JAH, YAH, or IAH, meaning "Thou art"
or the Ever-existent; the Sanscrit DI, meaning Brilliant ; and
the Hindoo OM or AUM, meaning the Sun.   It is also
evident that PA and MA, meaning a Parent, were once widely
extensive, and in addition to the foregoing I have, I believe,
by the comparative method, recovered from antiquity the
root *ak*, apparently once meaning *great* or *mighty*.

The syllable AK first came under my attention in connection with HACKPEN Hill at Avebury in Wiltshire. On a spur of this hill stood the ruined remains of the Head of the colossal Rock-temple that once stretched in the form of a serpent over three miles of country. As *Pen* notoriously meant *Head*, it occurred to me that HACKPEN might originally have been equivalent to " Great Head," a supposition that derived some support from the names CARNAC in Brittany and KARNAK in Egypt. At both these spots, as at AVEBURY, are the ruins of prodigious temples, and the usual rule that temple sites were primarily burial sites seemed easily and legitimately to resolve the two KARNACS into *KARN AK*, the great *CARN* or heap of stones covering a grave. One of the greatest stones at CARNAC in Brittany is known as MENAK, and one of the Longship Rocks lying off Land's End is named MENAK. As *men* was Celtic for *stone*, the name MENAK in both these instances seemingly meant *Great Stone*. There is also at CARNAC a gigantic tumulus named THUMIAC, seemingly a combination of *tum*, the Celtic for *hillock*, and *ac*, great. The irresistible children of ANAK are mentioned in Deuteronomy [1] as " great and tall," and they " were accounted giants." CASTOR and POLLUX, whose appellation in certain places was *Great Gods*, were in Greece denominated ANAKES. *Anak* was the Phœnician term for a Prince, and *anax* is the Greek for " prince." One of the Sanscrit words for King is *ganaka*, and we find *ak* occurring persistently and almost universally in divine and kingly titles, as, for example, in AKBAR, still meaning " the Great "; in CORMAC [2] the Magnificent—the " High King " of Ireland ; in BALAK, King of Moab ; in SHISHAK, who deposed Rehoboam ; in

[1] xi. 10 ; ix. 2.

[2] This name is supposed to mean " son of a chariot," which is very unconvincing. I have not thought it necessary everywhere to contrast current opinions with my own suggestions.

Z<small>TAK</small>, the Chaldean "great messenger"; in O<small>DAKON</small>, a form of the Babylonish D<small>AGON</small>; and in H<small>AKON</small>, the name of the present King of Norway. H<small>AKON</small> or H<small>AAKON</small>, cognate with the German name H<small>ACO</small>, which is defined by dictionaries as meaning "High Kin," must be allied to the Greek word *archon*, now meaning "supreme ruler," but primarily, I think, "great one." The *arch* of *archon* survives in our English *monarch* and *archangel*; it occurs in the royal names A<small>RCHELAUS</small>, A<small>RCHIDAMUS</small>, and A<small>RCAS</small>, and may probably be equated with the guttural *ach* of the fabulous "G<small>WRNACH</small> *the Giant*," who figures in Arthurian legend. The Greek words for a "chief" are *archos* and *aktor*, and these, like *anak*, a "prince," and *archon*, a "ruler," meant once, in all probability, "great one." In our *major* and *mayor* we have parallel instances of titles primarily traceable to "great," and in the centre of *magnus* there is recognisable the primordial <small>AK</small> blunted into <small>AG</small>.

The word *maximus* is phonetically "ma*k*simus." The nobles or great men of P<small>ERU</small> were known as *Curacas*. The ancient name for M<small>EXICO</small> was A<small>NAHUAC</small>, and in the time of C<small>ORTEZ</small> there was a native tradition that A<small>NAHUAC</small> was originally "inhabited by giants." The Giant Serpent of South America is known as the *anaconda*, and the topmost peak of the Andes is named A<small>CONCAGUA</small>. In P<small>ERU</small>, according to Prescott, the word *capac* meant "*great or powerful*," and the Supreme Being, the Creator of the Universe, was adored under the name P<small>ACHACHAMAC</small>. The triple *ac* occurring in this word suggests that it was equivalent to Trismegistus or Thrice Great. One of the appellations of J<small>UNO</small> was A<small>CREA</small>, *i.e.* the Great R<small>HEA</small>, the Magna Mater of the Gods. The Assyrian J<small>UPITER</small> was entitled M<small>ERODACH</small>, and the radical *ac* is the earliest form of our English *oak*, sacred to J<small>UPITER</small>, and once worshipped as the greatest and the strongest of the trees. The East

Indian *jak* fruit is described in Dr Murray's *New English Dictionary* as "enormous" and "monstrous." The giant ox, the largest animal of Tibet, is named a *yak* ; the earliest form of BACCHUS, who was symbolised by an ox, was IAKCHOS, and we again meet with *AK* in the hero-names HERAKLES and ACHILLES. At ACHILL Head in IRELAND a giant hill, upwards of two thousand feet high, presents to the sea a sheer precipice from its peak to its base ; and the most impressive, if not actually the loftiest, of the cliffs around Land's End is still known locally as PORDENACK. In *Zodiac*, the Great Zone of DI, the Brilliant Light, and in other instances noted hereafter, we again meet seemingly with the prehistoric AK used in the sense I have suggested.

These and kindred inferences may be due to fantasy or "coincidence," but the validity of some of my philological conclusions is strengthened, if not verified, by the fact that they were formulated almost against my common-sense and before I had any conception that there was ancient warrant for them. It is said that the Devil once tried to fathom the Basque language, and at the end of six months had successfully mastered one word : this was written NEBU-CHADNEZZAR and pronounced something like SENNACHERIB. I am, of course, fully aware how dangerous a ground I am treading and how open many of my positions are to attack ; yet it has seemed to me better to run some risk of ridicule rather than by over-caution to ignore and suppress clues which, under more accomplished hands, may yield discoveries of high and wide interest, and even bring into fresh focus the science of Anthropology.

The singularity, the novelty, and the almost impregnable strength of my position lies in the fact that every idea which I venture to propound, even such kindergarten notions as the symbolism of rakes, snails, cucumbers, and sausages, is based upon material evidence that such were unquestionably once prevalent. The printers' emblems are reproduced in facsimile from books mostly in my possession. The outline drawings are half-size reproductions of water-marks, some from my own collection, but mainly from Mons. Briquet's monumental *Les Filigranes : Dictionnaire historique des Marques du Papier dés leur apparition vers* 1282 *jusqu'en* 1600 *; avec* 39 *figures dans le texte et* 16,112 *facsimiles de filigranes* (4 vols., folio, Bernard Quaritch, 1907).

CHAPTER II

THE PARABLE OF THE PILGRIM

> " Give me my scallop shell of quiet,
>   My staff of faith to walk upon,
>   My scrip of joy, immortal diet,
>   My bottle of salvation,
>   My gown of glory, hope's true gage ;
>   And thus I'll take my pilgrimage."
>   SIR WALTER RALEIGH.

THE notion that Life is a pilgrimage and Everyman a pilgrim is common to most peoples and climes, and Allegories on this subject are well-nigh universal. In 1631 one of them was written in BOHEMIA under the title of *The Labyrinth of the World and the Paradise of the Heart.* Its author was John Amos Komensky (1592–1670), a leader of the sectarians known among themselves as the " Unity " or " Brethren," and to history as the " Bohemian Brethren " or the " Moravian Brothers." These long-suffering enthusiasts were obviously a manifestation of that spirit of mysticism which, either active or somnolent, is traceable from the dawn of History, and will be found noted under such epithets as Essenes, Therapeutics, Gnostics, Montanists, Paulicians, Manichees, Cathari, Vaudois, Albigeois, Patarini, Lollards, Friends of God, Spirituals, Arnoldists, Fratricelli, Anabaptists, Quakers, and many others.

The Labyrinth of the World was condemned as heretical, and, until 1820, was included among the lists of dangerous and forbidden books. Count Lutzow—to whom English readers are indebted for an admirable translation—states that so congenial was its mysticism, that the many Bohemian exiles who were driven on account of their faith from their beloved country carried the *Labyrinth* with them, and that it was often practically their sole possession. In Bohemia itself, the book being prohibited, the few copies that escaped destruction passed from hand to hand secretly, and were safely hidden in the cottages of the peasants.[1]

The author of *The Pilgrim's Progress* was a persecuted Baptist tinker, and among the pathetic records of Continental Anabaptism will be found the continually expressed conviction : " We must in this world suffer, for Paul has said that *all that will live godly in Christ Jesus must suffer persecution*. We must completely conquer the world, sin, death, and the devil, not with material swords and spears, but with the sword of the Spirit, which is the Word of God, and with the shield of faith, wherewith we must quench all sharp and fiery darts, and place on our heads the helmet of salvation, with the armour of righteousness, and our feet be shod with the preparation of the Gospel. Being thus strengthened with these weapons, we shall, with Israel, get through the wilderness, oppose and overcome all our enemies." [2] In 1550 another obscure Anabaptist under sentence of death for heresy exclaimed : " It is not for the sake of party, or for conspiracy, that we suffer : we seek not to contest with any sword but that of the Spirit—that is, the Word of God." [3]

These pious convictions are to be seen expressed in the

[1] *The Labyrinth of the World and the Paradise of the Heart*, edited and Englished by Count Lutzow (The Temple Classics), p. 266.

[2] *A Martyrology of the Churches of Christ commonly called Baptists*, translated from the Dutch by T. J. Van Braaght, and edited for the Hanserd Knollys Society by E. B. Underhill, vol. i. p. 376. London, 1850.

[3] *Ibid.*

trade-mark emblems herewith, representing the sword of the Spirit and the helmet of salvation.

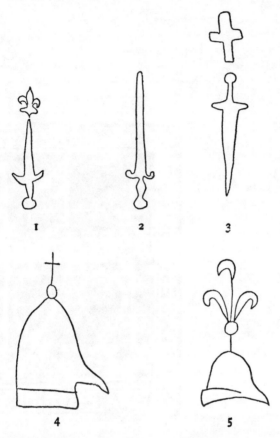

Almost equally familiar are the pilgrim symbols here below. Fig. 6 is the scourge of discipline, fig. 7 the girdle of righteousness,[1] fig. 8 the staff of faith, fig. 10 the scallop shell, figs. 12 and 13 the bottle of salvation, and fig. 14 the well of salvation, wherefrom " with joy shall ye draw water."

[1] " Righteousness shall be the girdle of his loins and faithfulness the girdle of his reins."—Isaiah xi. 5.

[2] Isaiah xii. 3.

6

7

8

9

10

12

11

13

14

In *The Labyrinth of the World* Komensky furnishes his pilgrim with certain implements in addition to the conventional equipment, and among them are the wings of aspiration, herewith represented. He makes Christ to say, " My son, I dwell in two spots, in heaven in My glory, and on earth in the hearts of the humble. And I desire that henceforth thou also shouldst have two dwelling-places : one here at home, where I have promised to be with thee ; the

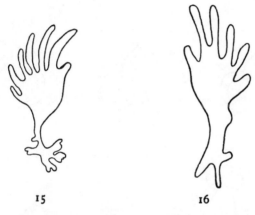

15   16

other with Me in heaven. That thou mayst raise thyself thither, I give thee these wings (which are the desire of eternal happiness and prayer). If thou dost will it, thou shalt be able to fly upward unto Me, and thou shalt have delight in Me, and I in thee."

When Komensky's hero started on his quest through the City of Queen Vanity, his guide Falsehood endeavoured to blind him to true reality by fitting him with certain falsifying glasses. " These spectacles, as I afterwards understood, were fashioned out of the glass of Illusion, and the rims which they were set in were of that horn which is named Custom." These distorting glasses of Conventionality showed everything in sham colours, foul as fair, and black as white, and it was only when the pilgrim emerged from Vanity Fair and turned towards Christ that he rid himself of his misleading encumbrances. Then, in lieu of the spectacles of Custom, Christ bestowed upon him certain Holy Spectacles, of which "the outward

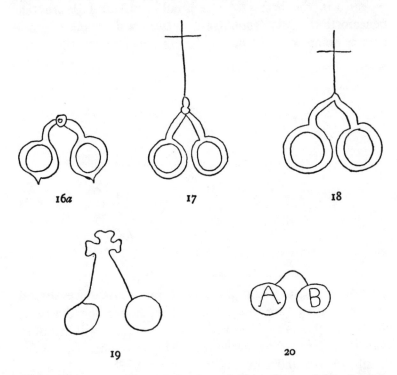

16a   17   18

19   20

border was the Word of God, and the glass within it was the Holy Ghost."

These sacred spectacles, of which some are illustrated herewith, possessed a fairy-like faculty to reveal surprising wonders. Among others, they enabled the pilgrim to perceive and recognise hitherto unseen fellow-Puritans dwelling here and there, dispersed and unsuspected in the World.

In early Christian and pre-Christian times the symbol

of purity was the Unicorn,[1] and this trade-mark had an extensive vogue, M. Briquet registering 1133 examples among paper-makers alone.   Even to-day an ancient unicorn, which has evidently drifted down with the tide of time, may be seen in use as a sign outside a druggist's shop in Antwerp ; and a well-known firm of English chemists employs the same emblem as its trade-mark—once,

21   22   23   24   25

evidently, a mute claim to purity of drugs.   In each case the sign, having outlived its century, has survived as a mere convention, a form from which the spirit has long since flown.   Among the Puritan paper-makers and printers of the Middle Ages the unicorn served obviously as an emblem, not of material but of moral purity.   As a rule, the animal is found without any tell-tale indications of its meaning, but the few examples here reproduced betray their symbolic character.

[1] *Christian Symbolism*, Mrs H. Jenner, p. 148.

One of the generic terms under which the Puritans of the Middle Ages were designated was *Cathari*, *i.e.* the pure ones.

In fig. 25 the Puritan Unicorn is represented as feeding upon a Fleur de Lys, which, as an emblem of the Trinity, is one of the few survivals still employed in Christian ecclesiology. In fig. 26 it is sanctified by a cross, and in fig. 27 is lettered with the initials I S, standing for Jesus Salvator, the Way, the Truth, and the Life. The possible

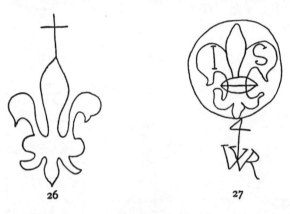

26   27

objection that Latin was a language above the comprehension of the artisan classes may be discounted by the testimony of De Thou,[1] who wrote in 1556 with reference to the Vaudois, " Notwithstanding their squalidness, it is surprising that they are very far from being uncultivated in their morals. *They almost all understand Latin*, and are able to write fairly enough."

The motto of the Italian Vaudois was *Lux lucet in tenebris*,[2] and this light shining uncomprehended in the darkness was like Christ, the Light of the World, symbolised by the Fleur de Lys. In fig. 27a the Flower de Luce or Flower of Light

[1] *The Huguenots in France*, S. Smiles, p. 330.
[2] *Narrative of an Excursion to the Valleys of Piedmont*, Wm. Gilly, p. 257.

27a   27b   28

29

is represented flaming with a halo, and in figs. 27*b* and 28 it is shown budding and extending in all directions.

The English printer JOHN DAY comparing the darkness of the preceding period with his own times of purer enlightenment, adopted as a trade-mark the pithy insinuation to the reader, " Arise, for it is Day " ; and in a similar spirit the printer JOHN WIGHT employed as his device the portrait of himself carrying *Scientia*, with the motto, " Welcome the Wight that bringeth such light."

Sometimes the Light was symbolised by a candlestick, as in the examples herewith.

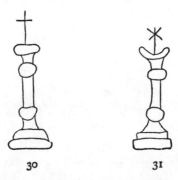

30   31

Fig. 30 is surmounted by a cross, and in fig. 31 the Light is represented by a Star-cross or letter X. Into the form of this X the mystics read the letters L V X so that it formed an ingenious rebus or monogram of the word " lux."

The following designs represent Jesus Christ, the "Anointed of the Light." Mons. Briquet has collected many specimens of these effigies, all of which are distinguished by *three* locks of hair, the three evidently being intended to symbolise Christ's oneness with the Trinity. In figs. 33 and 34 Light—denoted by the Lux cross—is proceeding out of the mouth, and the " anointing " of the Light is unmistakably indicated in fig. 33 by the position of the Lux on the locks of hair. There is a size of paper known to this day as JESUS ;

and as most of the technical terms of the paper trade owe their origin to primitive water-marks, it may safely be inferred that the designs now under consideration are the source of the term " Jesus."

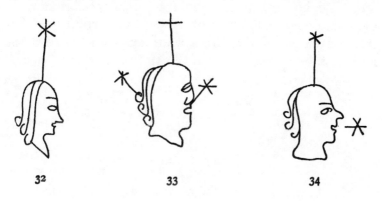

32   33   34

" God," says Komensky, " is our Shield," and the designs herewith represent this invulnerable Shield and Buckler.

35   36   37

The letters I H S on fig. 35 are the well-known initials usually misread to indicate *Jesus Hominum Salvator*. On fig. 36 is the Fleur de Lys and I S of Jesus Salvator ; and on figs. 38 and 39 Christ is represented by a Fish. This was a symbol much used by the primitive Christians in the Catacombs, and its popularity was due partly to the fact that the letters of the Greek word for "fish" yielded the initials of the sentence, "Jesus Christ, Son of Man, Saviour."

38   39

The Fish often takes the form of a Dolphin, which was anciently regarded as the special friend of man. Among the Greeks the Dolphin was venerated as the Saviour of the shipwrecked, and this special quality as a Saviour made it a favourite fish-emblem with the Christians.

40   41   42   43

A Dolphin was the arms of the French province of DAUPHINEY, which district was the headquarters of the Vaudois.

The designer of the candlestick below has adopted the motto, "I am spent in others' service," and the aim of the mystic has always been to lead his fellows from the bondage

of corruption into the liberty of the children of Light. The
emblem of the Italian Vaudois was a burning candle standing
in a candlestick surmounted by seven stars and lettered
underneath, *Lux lucet in tenebris.*[1]   " Men can only be happy,"
says Eckartshausen, " when the bandage which intercepts
the true light falls from their eyes, when the fetters of
slavery are loosened from their hearts. The blind must see,

Alteri feruiens confumor.

44

the lame must walk, before happiness can be understood.
But the great and all-powerful law to which the felicity of
man is indissolubly attached is the one following : ' Man,
let reason rule over your passions.' "   " Where," he asks,
"is the man that has no passions ? Let him show himself.
Do we not all wear the chains of sensuality more or less
heavily ? Are we not all slaves, all sinners ? This realisation
of our low estate excites in us the desire for redemption ;
we lift our eyes on high." [2]

The designs herewith portray Everyman as this dolorous
slave. In fig. 45 he is seen languishing in the bonds of

[1] Bompirni (S. V.), *A Short History of the Italian Waldenses*, p. 1.
[2] *The Cloud upon the Sanctuary*, Karl von Eckartshausen, p. 62.

wretchedness towards a Perfection that is symbolised by the circle over his head.

"Only the perfect can bring anything to perfection," continues Eckartshausen. There is "but One who is able to open our inner eyes, so that we may behold Truth ; but One who can free us from the bonds of sensuality. This

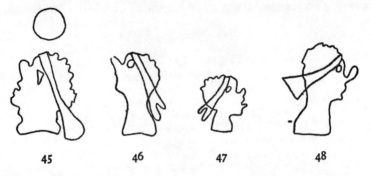

45   46   47   48

one is Jesus Christ the *Saviour of Man*, the *Saviour* because he wishes to extricate us from the consequences which follow the blindness of our natural reason." By the power of Jesus Christ "the hoodwink of ignorance falls from our

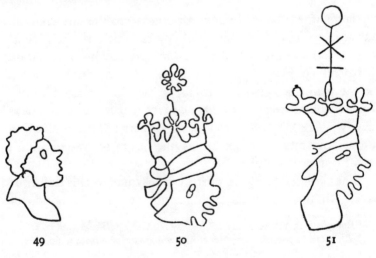

49   50   51

eyes ; the bonds of sensuality break, and we rejoice in the liberty of God's children." [1]   It will be noticed that in all these slave designs the bandage has been pushed up from over the eyes.   In fig. 49 the hoodwink of ignorance has completely disappeared, and the enlightened slave is gaping with an expression of astonishment and wonder.   In figs. 50 and 51 the disbanded figure, now weeping apparently with joy, is crowned, in one case with the Rose of Bliss, in the other with the Cross of Salvation, the Crown of Lux, and the Circle of Perfection.

Doubtless these emblems represent the fulfilment of the promise : " And the glory which thou gavest me I have given them ; that they may be one, even as we are one : I in them, and thou in me, that they may be made perfect in one." [2]

[1] *The Cloud upon the Sanctuary*, Karl von Eckartshausen, p. 60.
[2] St John xvii. 22, 23.

CHAPTER III

THE WAYS OF ASCENT

" My soul, like quiet palmer,
    Travelleth towards the land of heaven ;
  Over the silver mountains,
  Where spring the nectar fountains.'
                            SIR WALTER RALEIGH.

" And many people shall go and say : ' Come ye, and let us go up to the
mountain of the Lord.' "—ISAIAH.

ONE might indefinitely multiply the symbols under which
Allegory has veiled the Quest of the Ideal, and almost
as multifarious are the forms under which the symbolists
expressed their conceptions of the Vision Beautiful.

The accompanying designs represent the ascent of the
soul by means of the Ladder of Perfection, the time-
honoured *Scala Perfectionis* of Mysticism. From PLOTINUS
downward there has been a persistent preaching of this
Ladder of the Virtues. " Our teaching," says PLOTINUS,
" reaches only so far as to indicate the way in which the
Soul should go, but the Vision itself must be the Soul's
own achievement." [1]

The Ladder was a favourite emblem of the roadway of
the Gods, because it depicted a gradual ascent in goodness,
a progress step by step and line upon line towards Perfection. Dante records the vision :

[1] Cf. *Studies in Mystical Religion*, R. M. Jones, p. 76.

> " I saw rear'd up
> In colour like to sun-illumined gold
> A ladder, which my ken pursued in vain,
> So lofty was the summit." [1]

The sanctity of the emblems herewith is indicated by the Angel on the top of fig. 53, and by the cross surmounting fig. 52. The goal of ascent is expressed in fig. 54 by the Fleur de Lys of Light, and in fig. 55 by a Star, the Vision of Christ the Bright and Morning Star.

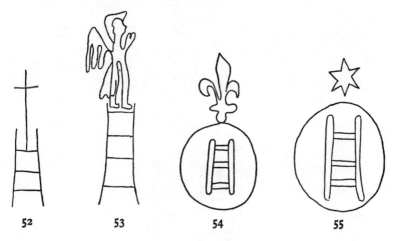

52   53   54   55

It was a Vaudois tenet that " Jesus Christ, whom all things obey, is our Pole Star, and the only star that we ought to follow," which idea is doubtless expressed in the crowned and long-tailed star herewith.

The Vaudois also regarded Christ as a Stag, and their pastors as Chamois who leaped from virtue to virtue.[2] The letters I.S. imply that the meaning of the design herewith is to be found in the passage, " The day starre arises in men's hearts ; yea, the day breaks and the shadows flee away ; and

---

[1] *Paradiso*, Canto xxi.
[2] Ed. Montet, *Histoire Littéraire des Vaudois*, p. 65.

Christ comes as a swift Roe and young Hart upon the mountains of Bether."[1]

Mons. Briquet reproduces upwards of three hundred devices (dating from 1318) which he describes as "Mounts, Mountains, or Hills." They are emblems of what Bunyan terms the Delectable Mountains—in other words, those

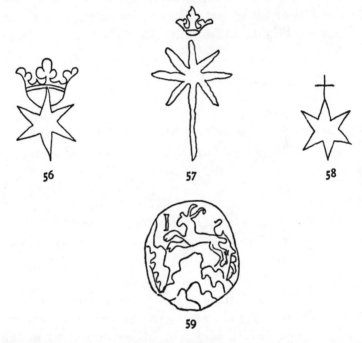

56   57   58

59

Holy Hills to which the Psalmist lifted his eyes, and which, according to Obadiah, "dropped sweet wine." The mystics gloried in the belief that they "walked with the Lord, treading and tripping over the pleasant mountains of the Heavenly Land," and their eyes were strained perseveringly eastward in expectation of Christ's speedy coming over the hills of Bether.

[1] *Cf.* S. Fisher, *Baby Baptism meer Babism,* London, 1653, p. 512.

In Allegory, hills or mountains very frequently imply Meditation and Heavenly Communion, and for this reason the legend runs that the Holy Grail was preserved on the summit of *Montsalvat*, the Mountain of Salvation.

The Mountains of Myrrh and the Hills of Frankincense, to which the writer of The Song of Solomon[1] says he will

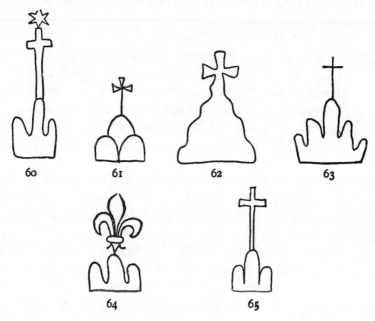

retreat, are ideally the same as those "silver mountains" over which, according to Sir Walter Raleigh—

> "My soul, like quiet palmer,
> Travelleth towards the land of heaven."

In Emblem they were represented as three, five, or six, but most usually as three. Among the Jews the *three*-peaked Mount Olivet was esteemed to be holy, and accounted to be the residence of the Deity. Mount Meru, the Indian

[1] iv. 6.

holy mountain, was said to have three peaks composed of gold, silver, and iron ; and by Hindoos, Tartars, Manchurians, and Mongols, Mount Meru was venerated as the dwelling-place of the Trinity, Brahma, Vishnu, and Siva.   The Fleur de Lys of Light poised over fig. 64 is an ideograph of the words, " As a spirit before our face is Christ the Lord, who will lead us to the tops of the mountains in the bonds of Charity."

This passage is from *The Holy Converse* of St Francis of Assisi.   If, as is supposed, Francis was the son of a Vaudoise, it will account for his ardent practice of the Waldensian tenet, " Work is Prayer."   " I was ever," said he, " in the habit of working with mine own hands, and it is my firm wish that all the other brethren work also." Francis reversed the traditional idea that the Church alone could save men's souls, by acting on the belief that the Church itself was to be saved by the faith and work of the people.   A subsequent development of the movement was the formation of the allied order of Tertiaries, *i.e.* working men and women who maintained the spirit of his rule, at the same time carrying on their worldly occupations.   The most important feature of this movement, says Dr Rufus M. Jones, was the cultivation of a group spirit, and " the formation of a system of organisation among the artisans and working men, which developed into one of the powerful forces that finally led to the disintegration of the feudal system." [1]

There is thus an obvious probability of meeting with Franciscan mysticism expressed in the marks and ciphers of contemporary craftsmen.   Fig. 65a is a printer's device, and figs. 67, 83, and 84 are copied from examples of seventeenth-century domestic stained glass exhibited in the Musée Cluny at Paris.

[1] *Studies in Mystical Religion,* p. 162.

In fig. 66 the circle is again the symbol of Perfection. The mystic loved to meditate upon the supreme point of perfection, and to the best of his ability followed the

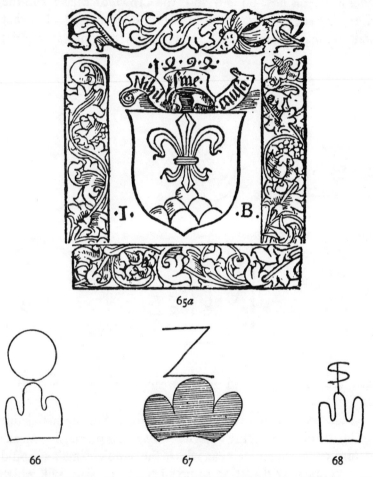

65a

66   67   68

injunction, "Be ye perfect, as your Father in Heaven is perfect." The initial Z surmounting fig. 67 here stands for Zion, the "Beauty of Perfection," and the monogram I.S. in fig. 68 represents Jesus Salvator, the promised

Deliverer. "There shall come out of Zion the Deliverer, and shall turn away ungodliness from Jacob."[1]

Over fig. 60 was the Star and Cross of the expected Messiah ; on figs. 69 and 70 is the Crown of Bliss ; and the fluttering eagle in fig. 71 represents the promise, "They that wait upon the Lord shall mount up with wings as eagles ;

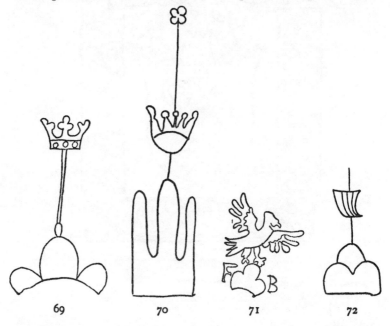

| 69 | 70 | 71 | 72 |

and they shall run and not be weary ; and they shall walk, and not faint."[2]

The sail surmounting fig. 72 is a rare but unmistakable emblem of the Holy Spirit. *Spiritus* primarily means breath or wind, an element which the emblem-maker could only express by depicting some such object as a sail, which catches and enfolds the wind.[3]

---

[1] Romans xi. 26.   [2] Isaiah lx. 31.

[3] Since writing, I find that the sail was an Egyptian symbol for Spirit. F. E. Hulme states : "The Egyptian symbol for breath is the sail of a

To convey this same idea of the Spirit dwelling on the mountain-tops, the deviser of figs. 73 and 74 has employed the familiar symbol of the Dove.

The followers of the Holy Spirit were themselves considered to be Doves ; an idea fostered by the injunction, " Be ye harmless as doves." In the *Holy Converse* between St Francis and the Lady Poverty it is recorded that certain men "all began at once to follow after the blessed Francis, and whilst with most easy steps they were hastening to the heights, behold the Lady Poverty standing on the top of that self-same mountain looked down over the steeps of the

73   74

hill, and seeing those men so stoutly climbing—nay, *flying* up, ['winged' by aspiration]—she wondered greatly, and said : 'Who are these who come flying like clouds and like doves to their windows ?' And behold a voice came to her and said : 'Be not afraid, O daughter of Zion, for these men are the seed whom the Lord hath blessed and chosen in love unfeigned.' So, lying back on the throne of her nakedness, did the Lady Poverty present them with the blessings of sweetness, and said to them : 'What is the cause of your coming ?—tell me, my brothers. And why hasten ye so from the Vale of Tears to the Mount of Light ?' "

In figs. 75 and 76 is shown the Mount of Light with

vessel : a happy and expressive idea, as the sail is inert and useless till quickened by the breath of the wind, but springs beneath its influence into movement and service."—*Symbolism in Christian Art*, p. 102.

the Cross of Lux upon its summit, and surmounting fig. 77 is the device of a dove flying heavenward.

" We come to thee, our Lady (Poverty)," continues the writer of *The Holy Converse*, " and we beseech thee receive us unto thee in peace ; we desire to become bondservants of the Lord of Virtue because He is the King of Glory. We have heard that thou art Queen of Virtue, and in some wise have learned it by trial. Wherefore, fallen at your feet, we entreat thee humbly to deign to be with us and to be unto us a way of attaining unto the King of Glory.

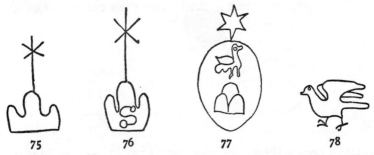

75   76   77   78

. . . Only admit us to thy peace and we shall be saved, that through thee He may receive us who through thee has redeemed us."[1]

The expression " redeemed " has always possessed among mystics a meaning somewhat different from that which popularly obtains. Redemption was believed to be not an act of unconditional mercy or an immediate losing of one's guilty stains by a sudden plunge into " the fountain of Emmanuel's blood," but rather a gradual and progressive process, a slow growth and expansion of man's spiritual faculties. " That man is no Christian," wrote a well-known mystic, " who doth merely comfort himself with the suffering, death, and satisfaction of Christ, and doth impute it to himself as a gift of favour, remaining himself still a wild

[1] *Sacrum Commercium*, Temple Classics, pp. 44–45.

beast and unregenerate. If this said sacrifice is to avail for me, it must be wrought *in* me. The Father must beget His Son in my desire of faith."[1]

Mysticism has universally taught that every man has within himself the germs or seeds of Divinity, and that by self-conquest these sparks of Heaven may be fanned into a flame, the flame into a fire, the fire into a star, and the star into a sun.

The spirit of Christ was regarded as a star dawning in the darkness of the soul, "a light that shineth in a dark place, until the day dawn and the day-star arise in your hearts."[2] The ideal of Paul and of his mystic followers in general was "Christ *in* you," and "every man perfect *in* Jesus Christ,"[3] and this ideal was fostered by mysticism centuries before Paul was born or Christianity dawned upon the world. "Ye are *gods*, and all of you are children of the Most High," says the poet who wrote the 82nd Psalm, and he prefaces the assertion by the lament, "They know not, neither will they understand ; they walk on in darkness : all the foundations of the earth are out of course."

No one knows when or where the idea of Re-Birth had its origin. Forty centuries ago it was current in India, whither it had probably travelled from Chaldæa. In an Egyptian document assigned to the third century before Christ there occurs the question and the answer, "Who is the author of Re-Birth ?" "The Son of God, the One Man, by God's will." The same document teaches that no one can be saved without Re-Birth ; that the material body perceived by the senses is not to be confused with the spiritual and essential body ; that to reach Re-Birth one

[1] Wm. Law, quoted in *Christian Mysticism*, Inge, p. 280.
[2] 2 Peter i. 19.
[3] 1 Colossians i. 27, 28.

must conquer the bodily senses, develop the inward faculties, and resolutely exert one's will power, whereupon " Divinity shall come to birth." " Dost thou not know," continues the Egyptian philosopher, " thou hast been born a God, Son of the One ? " This ancient hymn of the Re-Birth was to be recited in the open air, facing south-west at sunset and towards the east at sunrise, and the doctrine was to be kept secret or esoteric.[1]

One of the first experiences of Komensky's Pilgrim is his instruction by Christ upon the necessity of being born again. On being equipped with the spectacles of the Holy Spirit he is told to pass by again the spots where previously he had gone astray. He enters " a church that was named ' Christianity,' " and, seeing within its innermost portion what seemed to be a curtained or screened chancel, he immediately approached it, " heeding not those sectarians who were wrangling in the aisles." From within the veiled shrine which he perceived was " the truth of Christianity," there flashed light and was wafted fragrance ; yet to the Pilgrim's astonishment thousands of men passed by the sanctuary and did not enter it. " I saw also that many who were learned in scripture—priests, bishops, and others who thought highly of their holiness — went around the sanctuary ; some, indeed, looked in, but did not enter ; and this also appeared mournful unto me." [2]

The Egyptian philosopher already quoted wrote of the Re-Birth : " Whenever I see within myself the sincere vision brought to birth out of God's mercy, I have passed through myself into a body that can never die, and now *I am not what I was before*, but I am born in Mind." [3] This is paralleled by Komensky's assertion, " He, however, who has

---

[1] *Personal Religion in Egypt*, W. M. Flinders Petrie, pp. 94, 98.
[2] Pp. 214, 215.
[3] *Personal Religion in Egypt*, W. M. Flinders Petrie, p. 94.

passed through the innermost portal *becomes somewhat different* from other men : he is full of bliss, joy, and peace." [1]

To attain to this beatitude of Renaissance or Regeneration was the world-old goal of mysticism. "To be reborn," says Eckartshausen, "means to return to a world where the spirit of wisdom and love governs, where animal-man obeys." [2] The Gothic " R " poised on the mountains, in

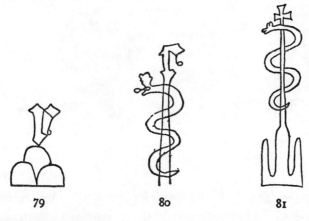

79   80   81

fig. 79, was the initial and the symbol of *Regeneratio*. The serpent coiled upon the cross, as in figs. 80 and 81, was also a symbol of regeneration or salvation, from the fact that this reptile periodically sloughs its skin and is born anew. The meaning of the serpent symbol is clenched in fig. 80 by the addition of the letter R—this being one of those cases where "inscriptions are placed above the pictures in order that the letter may explain what the hand has depicted." [3]

The trefoil surmounting fig. 82 is a widely acknowledged

[1] P. 215.
[2] *Cloud upon the Sanctuary*, p. 77.
[3] Cf. *The Romance of Symbolism*, S. Heath, p. 15.

emblem of the Trinity. Placed thus upon the summit of
the Holy Hills it indicates "the three loaves of the
knowledge of the Trinity, in which consists the final felicity
of every sojourner below."[1] The morning star and Christ
the Fish need no elucidation. The crescent moon surmounting figs. 84 and 85 was a symbol of the Land of
Heaven, and was used with this import by the early
Christians in the catacombs.[2]

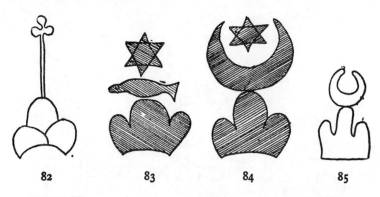

82   83   84   85

But emblems of the contemplative life are relatively
infrequent in comparison with those representing the active
virtues. Each of the various Virtues and Graces had its
own distinctive symbol, by means of which were expressed
the several ways of ascent.

The first of the Ways was purity and aspiration. "Who
shall ascend the Hill of the Lord?" asks the Psalmist, and
the condition follows, "He that hath clean hands and a pure
heart."[3] The Way of Solitude and Purity was symbolised
by the Stag, which was also regarded as a type of religious
aspiration, probably from the passage in the Psalms, "Like
as the hart panteth for the water brooks." There was an

---

[1] *Philobiblon*, Richard de Bury.
[2] *The Word in the Pattern*, Mrs G. F. Watts.
[3] Psalm xxiv. 3, 4.

old belief that the stag, though a timorous creature, had a
ruthless antipathy to snakes, which it laboured to destroy ;

86   87   88

hence it came to be regarded as an apt emblem of the
Christian fighting against evils.[1]

A second Way was Justice. "The just Lord loveth
Justice," and the path of the just "as a shining Light

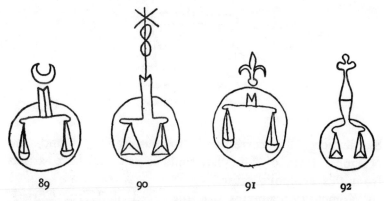

89   90   91   92

shineth more and more unto the Perfect Day." The reader
will be familiar with the emblems surmounting the Scales
of Justice, here illustrated. Note how ingeniously the

[1] *Symbolism in Christian Art*, F. E. Hulme, p. 176.

Spirit of Love has been indicated by the heart shape of the Dove's Wing in fig. 93. The number 8 surmounting fig. 90 has from most ancient times been the emblem of regeneration. In Egypt it was one of the symbols of Thoth, the reformer and regenerator who poured the waters of purification on the heads of the initiated. According to

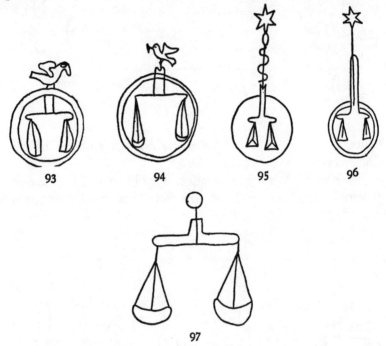

93   94   95   96

97

Swedenborg, 8 "corresponds to purification,"[1] and the octagonal form of Christian fonts is said to have arisen from this symbolic cause.[2]

Komensky maintains that the creed of "True Christianity" is summed up in two words, that everyone should love God above all things that can be named, and that he should

[1] *Arcana Celestia*, n. 2044, 2633.
[2] Cf. *The Science of Correspondence*, E. Madeley, p. 363.

sincerely wish well to his fellow-men as to himself.[1] This Way of Love was symbolised by the heart, which in fig. 68 is portrayed flaming with the ardent fire of charity. The flowers blossoming from the heart in fig. 104 were the emblems of good works ; flowers, as DURANDUS says, being " portrayed to represent the fruit of good works springing from the roots of Virtue." [2]

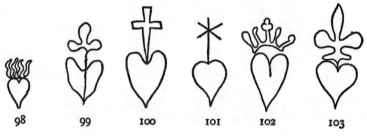

98   99   100   101   102   103

A fourth Way was Humility. " He hath shewed thee, O man, what is good ; and what doth the Lord require of

[1] The following expressions of this golden rule prove that it is universal, and belongs to no time or sect :—
" Do as you would be done by."—*Persian.*
" Do not that to a neighbour which you would take ill from him."—*Grecian.*
" What you would not wish done to yourself, do not unto others."—*Chinese.*
" One should seek for others the happiness one desires for oneself."—*Buddhist.*
" He sought for others the good he desired for himself. Let him pass on."—*Egyptian.*
" All things whatsoever ye would that men should do to you, do ye even so to them."—*Christian.*
" Let none of you treat his brother in a way he himself would dislike to be treated."—*Mohammedan.*
" The true rule in life is to guard and do by the things of others as they do by their own."—*Hindu.*
" The law imprinted on the hearts of all men is to love the members of society as themselves."—*Roman.*
" Whatsoever you do not wish your neighbour to do to you, do not unto him. This is the whole law. The rest is a mere exposition of it."—*Jewish.*   (From *The Swastika.*)
[2] *The Symbolism of Churches and Church Ornaments,* p. 51.

thee but to do justly, and to love mercy, and to walk humbly
with thy God?"[1] The symbol of humility and patient
endurance was the Ass, and by the cross of Lux on its
forehead was implied, " It is humility that must fasten you

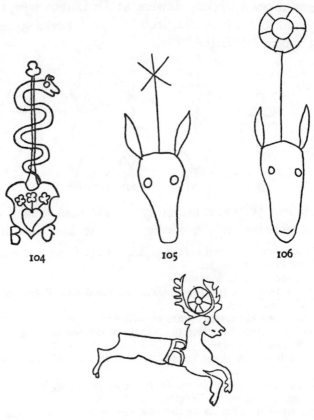

104   105   106

107

to God, and that will keep you in a constant adherence
to Him."

The wheel surmounting figs. 106 and 107 was the
emblem of Divine reunion. As the innumerable rays of a

[1] Micah vi. 8.

circle are united in a single centre, so, as the mind mounts
upward, do differences of sect lose their bitterness and merge
into the axle-tree of Christ.

A fifth Way was Hope, the Anchor of the Soul.   The

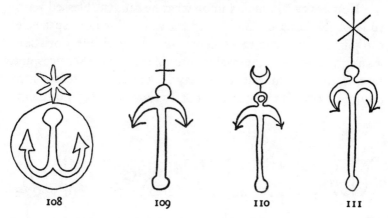

| | | | |
| 108 | 109 | 110 | 111 |

designers of figs. 108 to 115 probably had in their minds
the words of Paul : "we might have a strong consolation, who
have fled for refuge to lay hold upon the hope set before us :

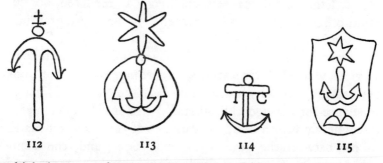

| | | | |
| 112 | 113 | 114 | 115 |

which hope we have as an anchor of the soul, both sure
and stedfast, and which entereth into that within the veil ;
whither the forerunner is for us entered, even Jesus, made
an High Priest for ever after the order of Melchisedec."[1]

[1] Hebrews vi. 18–20.

The initials I.C. on fig. 114 signify Jesus Christ, who was regarded not only as The Way, but also as the goal of attainment.   In fig. 115 the anchor and star appear in this latter sense surmounting the Holy Hills.

Komensky comments upon what he calls the blessed servitude of the Sons of God.   By the aid of his holy spectacles the pilgrim was able to perceive that the invisible Christians willingly took upon themselves humble and mean services, and that, if they could but see a way in which their fellow-men might be benefited, they did not hesitate and did not delay.

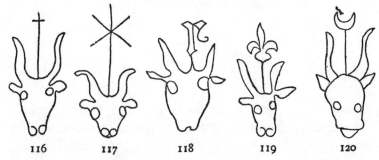

116   117   118   119   120

Nor did they extol the services they had rendered, nor remind others of them, but, whether they met with gratitude or ingratitude, continued " serving quietly and gaily." [1]

The symbol of disinterested toil and indefatigable fellow-service was the Ox, which, according to Hulme, was emblematic " of all who patiently bear the yoke and labour in silence for the good of others." [2]   Mons. Briquet reproduces nearly fifteen hundred varieties of the Ox water-mark, in use between the years 1321 and 1600 ; and, commenting upon its strange multiplication in Italy, France, and Germany, observes : " The fact of its wide popularity is real, but its cause is unknown." [3]

[1] *Labyrinth*, p. 224.
[2] *Symbolism in Christian Art*, F. E. Hulme, p. 277.
[3] *Les Filigranes*, vol. iv. p. 716.

The sign of the Ox occurs not infrequently unadorned, when it may be read, like the motto in fig. 44, " I am spent in others' service " ; but as a rule it is combined with some supplementary symbol or symbols of the Vision.

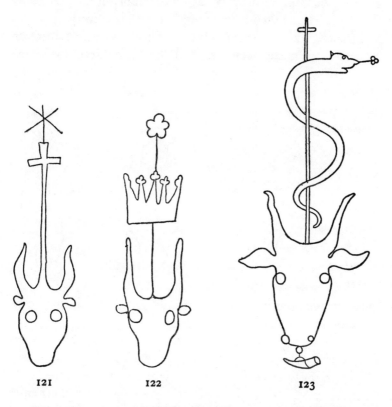

121   122   123

The object surmounting fig. 127 is the Sangraal, which, according to tradition, was the cup used at the Last Supper, and subsequently by Joseph of Arimathea to catch the blood flowing from the crucified Saviour's side. Mr A. E. Waite considers the various versions of the quest for the lost Grail as mirrors of spiritual chivalry, mirrors of perfection, pageants of the mystic life, as the teaching of the Church spiritualised, and as offering in romance form a presentation of all-souls' chronicle.[1]

In the example of the Grail here illustrated, the New Wine of God's kingdom is symbolised by the clustering grapes ; but the variety of St Grail emblems is practically endless, each symbolist depicting his Vision according to his preference. The mystics beheld themselves as an unbroken procession of human temples, and the Holy Grail for which

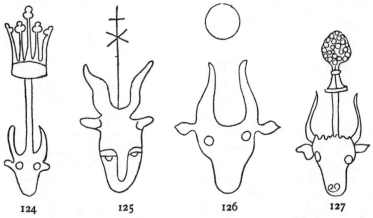

<table>
<tr><td>124</td><td>125</td><td>126</td><td>127</td></tr>
</table>

each strove was the ever-expanding ideal of his own aspirations.

The roadways to the Quest thus far illustrated have been Purity and Aspiration, Justice, Charity, Humility, Hope, and Unselfish Service. There are still one or two others yet to be considered, but symbols of the more conventional schemes of salvation are noticeably absent. The crucifix does not occur in water-mark,[2] nor do any emblems that can be read to imply justification by Faith, salvation by Blood, or, indeed,

[1] A. E. Waite, *The Hidden Church of the Holy Grail : Its Legends and Symbolism considered in their affinity with certain Mysteries of Initiation and other traces of a secret tradition in Christian Times.*

[2] Among the 15,112 examples illustrated by Mons. Briquet there is *one* exception to this statement.

by anything in the nature of a vicarious atonement. The cause lies in the fact that these popular paths were regarded by the mystics as misleading, and for that reason were not mapped out in emblems. King Arthur says :

> " Spake I not truly, O my knights ?
> Was I too dark a prophet when I said
> To those who went upon the Holy Quest,
> That most of them would follow wandering fires
> Lost in the quagmire ? "

Dr Patrick (1626–1707) expresses the traditional doctrine of mysticism in his once popular but now neglected *Parable of the Pilgrim*, where he says that the only Faith which will carry us to Jerusalem is conformity to the ethics of Jesus. " But, if I may be so bold as to interpose a question," said the inquirer, " I pray satisfy me why you call this the pilgrim's faith : is there any else besides ? " " There is," replied his teacher ; " we meet in this world with a faith more gallant, fine, and delicate, than the plain and homely belief which I have described ; a modish and courtly faith it is, which sits still, and yet sets you in the lap of Christ. It passes under so many names, that I cannot stand to number them all now. It is called a casting of ourselves upon Christ, a relying on his merits, a shrouding ourselves under the robes of His righteousness : and though sometimes it is called a going to Him for salvation, yet there is this mystery in the business, that you may go, and yet not go ; you may go, and yet stand still ; you may cast yourself upon Him, and not come to Him ; or if you take one little step, and be at the pains to come to Him, the work is done, and you need not follow Him. It is indeed a resting, not a travelling grace.

" I hope your soul will never enter into this secret, nor follow the rabble in these groundless fancies. But you will rather put to your hands to pull down that idol of faith which hath been set up with so much devotion, and religiously worshipped so long among us ; that dead image of faith, which so many have adored, trusted in, and perished ;—I mean the notion which hath been so zealously advanced, how that believing is nothing else but a relying on Jesus for salvation ; a fiducial recumbency upon Him ; a casting ourselves wholly upon His merits ; or an applying of His righteousness to our souls. And if you throw all those other phrases after them, which tell us that it is a taking of Christ, a laying hold of Him, a closing with Him, or an embracing of Him, you shall do the better, and more certainly secure yourself from being deceived." [1]

[1] *The Parable of the Pilgrim*, London, 1840, pp. 96, 97.

CHAPTER IV

THE MILLENNIUM

" Thou hast destroyed it,
The beautiful world,
With powerful fist :
In ruin 'tis hurled,
By the blow of a demigod shattered !
The scattered
Fragments into the void we carry,
Deploring
The beauty perished beyond restoring.
Mightier
For the children of men,
Brightlier
Build it again,
IN THINE OWN BOSOM BUILD IT ANEW ! "

GOETHE.

A CARDINAL doctrine among the mystics was the imminence of the Millennium ; not the material notion of Christ's
descent upon a cloud, the catching upward of 144,000
Christians, and the destruction of this wicked world, but the
opinion of Origen that, instead of a final and desperate conflict between Paganism and Christianity, the Millennium
would consist of a gradual enlightenment, and in voluntary
homage paid by the secular powers to Christianity.[1]

The anticipated reign of God was expressed by a cross-

---

[1] Gibbon observes that the doctrine of Christ's reign upon earth, treated
at first as a profound allegory, was considered by degrees as a doubtful and
useless opinion, and was at length rejected as the absurd invention of heresy
and fanaticism. (*Decline and Fall*, xv.)

surmounted sphere, and this emblem has been found in paper made as early as 1301.   In the course of later centuries the primitive and simple forms were gradually embellished with supplementary symbols, evidence that the spirit underlying these trade-marks was not mere mimicry, but a living and intelligent tradition.   In fig. 128 the ball and cross of

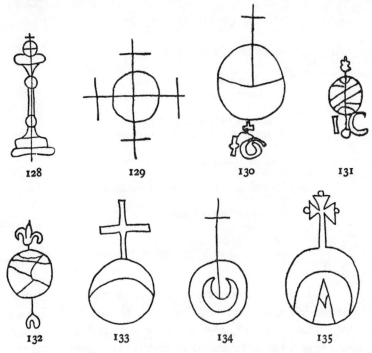

gradual enlightenment appears in place of the cross of Lux at the summit of a candlestick.

The deviser of fig. 129 expressed the universal spread of Christianity by extending a cross to each of the four quarters of the globe.   The initials I.C. obviously imply Jesus Christ, and in fig. 132 the eagerly expected reign of Sweetness and Light is indicated by the Heart and the Fleur de Lys.   The Kingdom of Heaven was frequently pointed by the introduction of a Crescent into the circle. The capital A, if with a V-shaped cross-stroke, stood frequently for Ave ;[1] and thus fig. 135 may be read as *Ave Millenarium*, an old-world mode of expressing the aspiration, " Thy Kingdom come."

With the globe and cross of the Millennium are frequently associated the Holy Hills, as in the examples below. These emblemise the prophecy : " It shall come to pass, that the mountain of the house of the Lord shall be estab-

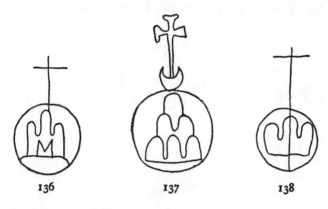

136   137   138

lished in the top of the mountains, and it shall be exalted above the hills ; and the people shall flow unto it. And many nations shall come, and say, Come, and let us go up to the mountain of the Lord, and to the house of the God of Jacob ; and he will teach us of his ways, and we will walk in his paths : for the law shall go forth of Zion, and the word of the Lord from Jerusalem. And he shall judge among many people, and rebuke strong nations afar off ; and they shall beat their swords into plowshares, and their spears into pruning-hooks : nation shall not lift up a sword

---

[1] Over the altar to the Virgin in the Church of St Gudule, Brussels, there appears the cipher herewith. It reads, forward and backward, AV MARIA.

against nation, neither shall they learn war any more.   But
they shall sit every man under his vine and under his fig
tree ; and none shall make them afraid : for the mouth of
the Lord of hosts hath spoken it.   For all people will walk
every one in the name of his god, and we will walk in
the name of the Lord our God for ever and ever.   In
that day, saith the Lord, will I assemble her that halteth,
and I will gather her that is driven out, and her that I
have afflicted ; and I will make her that halted a remnant,
and her that was cast far off a strong nation : and the

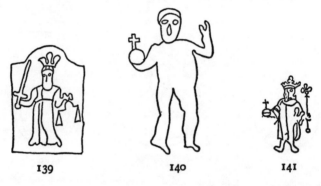

139   140   141

Lord shall reign over them in mount Zion from henceforth,
even for ever." [1]

In the above marks is portrayed the eagerly expected
King who was to rule in Zion.   Fig. 139, carrying the scales
of Justice and the sword of the Spirit, is crowned with a
trefoil ; and fig. 140, bearing the globe and cross, is apparently extending one hand in benediction.   The sceptre borne
by fig. 141 is tipped significantly with the Fleur de Lys
of Light.

The deviser of fig. 142 has indicated the reign of Light
by the extension, high and low, of the *Lux* cross.   The
letter R within the circle was the sign of the City of Re-

[1] Micah iv. 1–7.

generation, and the initials I.R. stood in all probability for
Jesus Redemptor. This combined I.R. (in fig. 144 it is
hallowed by a cross) may be seen carved on a fragment of
stone tracery lying to-day in the garden of the Musée
Cluny at Paris, a relic from some ancient rood-screen or
balustrade. Fig. 145 shows the two initials combined into

142   143   144

145   146   147   148

a monogram, and fig. 146 (which is taken from a specimen
of seventeenth-century domestic stained glass) shows a
variation of this monogram.

An eighteenth-century Italian antiquary surmised that
the capital M found frequently on ancient gems and signets
may have stood for the word *Millenarium* ;[1] and the fact
that this letter is combined frequently with water-marked

[1] *Gemmæ Antiquæ Litteratæ*, Francisci Ficoronii, Rome, 1757, p. 21.

emblems of the Millennium tends to support the supposition. The capital M occurs in paper as early as 1296 ; at times it was distinguished by a cross, it figures frequently as the goal of ascent, and occasionally it was curiously interblended with the globe and cross and the letter A as in figs. 154 and 155.

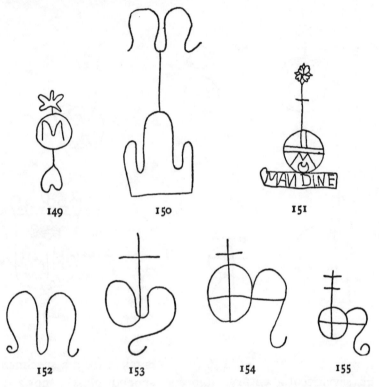

The prevalence of Millennium emblems proves how rife were Millenarian ideas. The ambition of mediæval mysticism to bring about a purified Christian Commonwealth, and to overturn what it believed to be the dominion of Antichrist, is emphatically expressed in the *Romance of the Rose*, where the poet writes :—

"No one apart,
Should claim the fulness of thy heart,
But every living man should be
Joined in one vast fraternity;
Loving the human race as one,
Yet giving special love to none :
Mete out such measure as ye fain
From others would receive again.

. . . . .

It is because unrighteous folk
Refuse to bear the gentle yoke
Of this fair love, that it hath been
Needful to set the judge as screen
To shield the weak against the strong,
Uphold the right, and quell the wrong."

These socialistic and Utopian ideas were held very widely among "the common man" of mediæval Europe, and it was the attempt of our English Lollards to carry them into practical effect that brought down upon Lollardy such disastrous and protracted persecution. On the Continent it is surprising that history records no attempt to enforce the Millennium by the sword until 1524, when there broke out the abortive revolution known as the Peasants' War. The figure most prominently associated with this movement is Thomas Munzer, a Master of Arts, who "founded a secret society at ALLSTATT, pledged by a solemn oath to labour unceasingly for the promotion of the new Kingdom of God on earth, a Kingdom to be based on the model of the primitive Christian Church."[1] Munzer, whose ideas were largely derived from an itinerant weaver who, in the course of his travels, had come under the influence of the Bohemian Brethren, established a special printing press for the dissemination of his views. Inflamed by the preaching of Munzer's apostles, and goaded by the

[1] E. Belfort Bax, *The Peasants' War*, London, 1899, p. 239.

oppression of their feudal superiors, the peasantry of Central Europe rose in insurrection and established among themselves an "Evangelical Christian Brotherhood." In their *Twelve Articles* they announced the rights of "the common man," condemning the abuses of the times as "unbecoming and unbrotherly, churlish and not according to the word of God." "Christ," they contended, "hath purchased and redeemed us all with His precious blood, the poor hind as well as the highest, none excepted. Therefore do we find in the Scripture that we are free, and we will be free. Not that we would be wholly free as having no authority over us, for this God doth not teach us. We shall live in obedience, and not in the freedom of our fleshly pride ; shall love God as our Lord ; shall esteem our neighbours as brothers, and do to them as we would have them do to us."

For six months the ignorant and misguided peasantry held their own, sacking and destroying castles and convents, and committing deplorable excesses. Upon feudalism regaining the upperhand, "of hanging and beheading there was no end," or, as another contemporary expressed it : "It was all so that even a stone had been moved to pity, for the chastisement and vengeance of the conquering lords was great."[1]

Within ten years of the suppression of the Peasants' rising, Europe witnessed another effort to impose forcibly a material Kingdom of Christ. A group of fanatics, reinforced by enthusiasts and political discontents from various parts of Europe, fortified themselves within the city of Münster, and proclaimed it "the new Jerusalem, the City of Regeneration, the thousand years' Kingdom, according unto His Holy pleasure."

[1] The number of victims to this tragical insurrection has been placed by some historians as high as 130,000.

It is needless to consider the sequent events in Münster, as, with the exception of a small but noisy minority, the mystics rigorously condemned the use of carnal weapons, and deprecated as "wild men" the advocates of physical force. The siege of Münster not only stands out, however, as one of the most remarkable and romantic episodes in history, but has an added interest in the probability that it was the basis and inspiration of John Bunyan's *Holy War*. In the eyes of Bunyan the Münsterists were the saints of God warring against the powers of this world and of Satan.

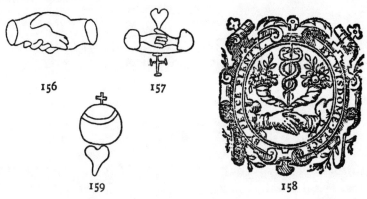

156   157

159   158

Among the royal insignia manufactured at Münster for the popularly elected King of Zion was a golden ball. "On the ball," says Mr Bax, "was a golden cross on which were the words, 'A King of Righteousness everywhere.'" On the fall of Münster, the leaders of the movement were skinned alive with redhot pincers, and the rank and file suffered the customary massacre.

History does not record any further attempts to impose the Millennium by the sword, but the evidence of trademarks proves how extensively during subsequent centuries Millenary notions were entertained.

The hands clasped in brotherly concord need no comment; and in fig. 157 their meaning is further pointed by the addition of the heart and cross.

The sympathies of Komensky leaned inevitably towards "the common man." He figures him in *The Labyrinth* as presenting a petition of his manifold grievances, showing his weals, stripes, and wounds, and begging for some remission of being so driven and harassed that bloody sweat ran down him. "The common man" is informed by the Council of Authority that, as he apparently does not appreciate the favour of his superiors, he must accustom himself

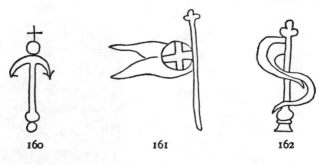

160   161   162

to their ferocity; but the "concession" is ironically granted that "if by willingness, compliance, and true attachment" to his superiors and rulers he can succeed in gaining their favour, he shall "be allowed to enjoy it."[1]

But the working men of the Middle Ages were indomitable optimists, and they continued to anchor their hopes upon the imminence of Christ's coming. In fig. 160 the Anchor of Hope points upward to the globe and cross, and the cross upon fig. 161 stamps it as the Banner of Christ and the sign of His triumph.

Both these standards are tipped with the trefoil, and the streamers in fig. 162 weave themselves into the form of an S. The letter S stood frequently for Spiritus, and in its

[1] Pp. 183-184.

present context may be read as an emblem of the passage,
" When the enemy shall come in like a flood the Spirit of
the Lord shall lift up a standard against him. And the
Redeemer shall come to Zion and unto them that turn from
transgression in Jacob, saith the Lord. Arise, shine ; for thy
light is come, and the glory of the Lord is risen upon thee.
For, behold, the darkness shall cover the earth, and gross
darkness the people : but the Lord shall arise upon thee,
and his glory shall be seen upon thee." [1] The Z of Zion is
seen on fig. 163, and the S of Spiritus on fig. 164.

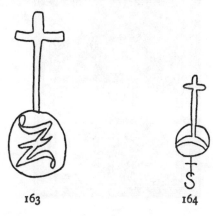

163   164

It is hard for us, living in these secure and comparatively enlightened days, to realise the wistfulness and
expectation with which the mediæval mystics yearned for
" the brightness of Thy rising." " Make haste," they said,
" make haste, my beloved, and be thou like to a roe or to a
young hart upon the mountains of spices. Until the day
break and the shadows flee away I will get me to the
mountains of myrrh and to the hill of frankincense." [2] The
enlightenment which the heretics of the Middle Ages understood as the Millennium is known nowadays as the Renais-

[1] Isaiah lix. 19, 20 ; lx. 1, 2.
[2] Song of Solomon viii. 14 ; iv. 6.

sance ; and it may be compared with that " Redemption "
for which, says the Apostle Paul, " all creation groans and
travails in the pain of desire."

The printers' mark herewith is a plant being watered
from the rose of a watering-pot, and the motto reads Donec
Optata Veniant, " Until the desired things come."   There
can be little doubt as to what was implied by *optata*, the
" desired-for things."   Before having met with this eloquent

165

device I wrote : " What we call the Renaissance was merely
the fruiting of a plant whose cult had been the cherished
work of centuries. . . . It was not an untended wild
flower, but rather a plant rare and exotic, cherished by
centuries of blood and tears." [1]

Prophecies of the expected Dawn were as plentiful as
were emblems illustrating it, and hopes of the blessed
Aurora seem never to have flagged.   Figs. 166 and 167
illustrate the Dawn approaching with her bright streamers,
the " forerunner of pleasant Phœbus, who, with her clear

[1] *A New Light on the Renaissance*, p. 212.

and glistening beams, brings forth that blessed day long wished for of many." [1]   Aurora of the Latins or Eos of the

166   167

Greeks is identical with the Hindoo Ushas, of whom three thousand years ago an Indian singer wrote :—

"Ushas ! Daughter of the sky,
Hold thy ruddy lights on high;
Bring us food with dawning day,
Riches with thy radiant ray;
White-robed nymph of morning sky,
Bring us light, let shadows fly !

.　　　.　　　.　　　.　　　.

Lo, she comes in crimson car,
Scattering splendour from afar;
From the realms beyond the sun
In her chariot comes the Dawn;
Ushas in her loveliness
Comes to rouse us and to bless!

[1] *Fama Fraternitatis*, R.C., anon. (1614–1616).

Mortals in devotion bend,
Hymns and songs of joy ascend;
Ushas in her radiant beauty
Comes to wake us to our duty;
Brings us blessings in her car,
Drives all evil things afar !

White-robed daughter of the sky,
Hold thy ruddy light on high,
Day by day with dawning light
Bring us blessings ever bright,
Bring us blessings in thy car,
Drive the shades of night afar ! " [1]

The keys surmounting the emblem of Love in fig. 168
were the symbols of Janus, the doorkeeper of Heaven,

168

whose name JANUS is a form of Dianus, and contains the
same root as *dies*, day. It was the rôle of JANUS to fling
open the portals of the sky and liberate the Dawn, sometimes represented by a wading bird.

The waders herewith (ibises,[2] cranes, or herons) symbolised the Morning, because, standing in water or at the
seashore, they were the first to welcome the Dawn as
she came up from the East. Either by intention or
intuition, Farquharson's well-known picture *Dawn* represents a waste of waters and a crane flapping upwards.

[1] *Rig Veda* ; Hymn to Ushas, the Dawn Goddess, from *Indian Poetry*,
Dutt, pp. 20, 22.
[2] The ibis was also reverenced as the destroyer of serpents and the
drinker of pure water. See Plutarch, *Isis and Osiris*.

Among the Egyptians, a bird known as the bennu—a sort of heron—was regarded as the emblem of Regeneration, and betokened the re-arising of the Sun, the return of Osiris to the light.[1]

169   170   171

The Baboon with uplifted paws was the emblem of wisdom hailing the uprising Dawn. The baboon was adopted as an emblem of wisdom from its serious expression and human ways, and its habit of chattering at the sunrise led to its being reverenced as the Hailer of the

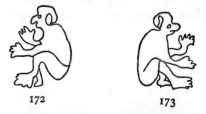

172   173

Dawn.[2] The baboon and the ibis were the emblems of Thoth, the reformer, the regenerator, and the God of writing and learning. The Egyptians called the ibis a *techu*, and TECHU was one of the names of Thoth ; the month Thoth, like our January derived from JANUS, was the first or opening month in the year.

[1] Cf. *The Romance of Symbolism*, S. Heath, p. 154.
[2] *Religion of Ancient Egypt*, W. M. Flinders Petrie, pp. 22, 32.

CHAPTER V

THE GOOD SPIRIT

"Before beginning and without an end,
   As space eternal and as surety sure,
   Is fixed a Power Divine which moves to good :
   Only its laws endure."
                                    The Light of Asia.

BELIEF in the existence of a beneficent, omnipotent, and omniscient Spirit is, and has been, more or less universal. The primitive religions of China, Egypt,[1] Mexico, and Peru all exhibit a pure monotheism and a high standard of ethics,[2] and Monotheism is similarly apparent in the venerable collection of Indian hymns and legends known as the Vedas (*circa* 1500 B.C.)—

"He the Father, made us all,
   He the Ruler, hears our call,
   He the Feeder, feeds each nation,
   Every creature in its station :
   Names of many Gods he bears,
   He is one—we seek by prayers." [3]

Elsewhere the *Rig Veda* affirms : "There is One Existence, sages call it by many names" ;[4] and there is reason

---

[1] Cf. *Egyptian Religion*, E. A. Wallis Budge.
[2] Cf. *The Original Religion of China*, John Ross.
[3] *Rig Veda*, x. 82, from *Indian Poetry*, trans. by Romesh Dutt, p. 34.
[4] *Brahma Knowledge*, L. E. Barnett, p. 14.

to believe that the numerous divinities of Egypt were originally local expressions of an underlying monotheism. Plutarch maintained that all the names of the gods referred to the same Essence : " Not different Gods for different peoples, not Barbarian and Greek, not southern and northern, but just as sun and moon and earth and sea are common to all, though they are called by different names among different peoples, so to the Logos that orders all things, and to one Providence that also directs powers ordained to serve under her for all purposes, have different honours and titles been given according to their laws by different nations." [1]

Although it was recognised among Grecian mystics that " Jove, Pluto, Phœbus, Bacchus, all are One," [2] and although MICAH depicts the Millennium as every man walking in the name of his God, adding " we will walk in the name of the Lord our God," [3] the official custodians of Christianity worked summarily to suppress what they condemned as heretical depravity of mind. If a Manichee passed over into the Christian system of Constantine he was required to forswear his late associates with the formula, " I curse those persons who say that Zoroaster, and Buddha, and Christ, and Manichaes, and the Sun are all one and the same." [4] The philosophic system known as the Kabbalah, which exercised a far-reaching influence upon the thought of Europe during the later Middle Ages, numbered seventy-two terms for the Godhead, and with many of these names we shall meet in the course of the present inquiries.

The characters within fig. 174 form the Hebrew Tetragrammaton or four-lettered mystery-name of the Creative Power. Derived from and combining within

---

[1] Cf. *Personal Religion in Egypt*, W. M. Flinders Petrie, pp. 122, 123.
[2] *The Gnostics and their Remains*, C. W. King, 2nd ed., p. 321.
[3] iv. 5.   [4] Cf. *Mystical Traditions*, I. Cooper-Oakley, p. 286.

itself the past, present, and future forms of the verb "to be," the Tetragrammaton was revered as a symbol of the immutable I AM. It is found in theologies other than the Hebrew, and in the triliteral form AUM was used as

174

a password in the Egyptian mysteries. It was regarded among Mohammedans as an omnific syllable whose efficacy cured the bites of serpents, and restored the lame, the maimed, and the blind. The Brahmins maintain that all rites, oblations, and sacrifices will pass away; "but that

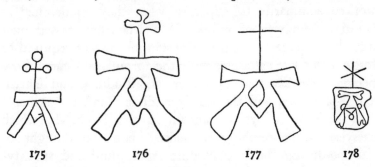

175   176   177   178

which passes not away is the syllable AUM, since it is a symbol of God, the Lord of created beings."[1]

The combination of A and T here illustrated is the Hebrew form of *Alpha* and *Omega*, T (*Tau*) being the last letter, and A (*Aleph*) the first in the Hebrew alphabet. The symbol of the *Alpha* and the *Omega*, the First and the

[1] Cf. *A Lexicon of Freemasonry*, A. G. Mackey (articles "Jehovah," "Name of God," "Tetragrammaton").

Last, was not restricted to Christianity, but has been found among Egyptian documents. The expression "last" is generally misunderstood in this connection, the truer implication being the end of the last days and the dawn of a new era or beginning.[1]

Related to the Alpha and Omega is the familiar Dove. The Dove was regarded as a symbol of the Good Spirit because of the circles on its throat, the colours of which were taken to represent the Seven Spirits of God or rays of the prism constituted by the Trinity.[2] It was also understood that the soft and insinuating "voice of the turtle"

179

was an echo on earth of the voice of God.[3] The Dove was considered to be an equivalent of the Alpha and Omega because the numerical value of the Greek word for Dove, 801, was the same as the numerical value of the letters AO written backwards.[4]

Fig. 181 is the well-known mark of Christopher Plantin, the great printer. The compasses, with or without the Hand of God, were the sign of "Him who fixed the earth and sky, and measured out the firmament." There is a

---

[1] Cf. *Encyclopædia of Religion and Ethics* (articles A and O).
[2] *Clothed with the Sun*, Anna Kingsford, p. 298.
[3] *Solomon and Solomonic Literature*, Moncure D. Conway, p. 123.
[4] *Fragments of a Faith Forgotten*, G. R. S. Mead, p. 371.

reference in Proverbs [1] to the Creator preparing the Heavens and setting a compass upon the face of the deep. It is said that the compasses' two points represent spirit and matter, life and form ; from these all the complexities of the fleeting, ever-changing mantle of the one-life are produced within the circle, self-imposed by the Being who has decreed the bounds of His Universe or His System.

180

The authors of *The Perfect Way* point out that among the symbols and insignia of the Egyptian Gods none is more frequently depicted than the Sphere. This Sphere—illustrated below—was the emblem of creative Motion, because Manifesting Force is rotatory ; being in fact the "wheel of the Spirit of Life" described by EZEKIEL as a "wheel within a wheel," the whole system of the universe from the planet to its ultimate particle revolving in the same manner.[2]

[1] viii. 27. [2] P. 167.

The insect illustrated in figs. 188 and 189 is the Egyptian Scarabæus, the symbol of self-existent Being. The scarabæus was worshipped and revered because of the iridescent beauty of its wing-sheaths, but more particularly

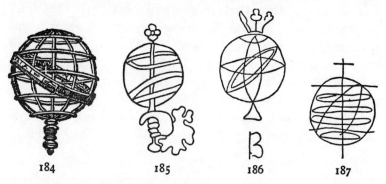

184   185   186   187

on account of its peculiar habit of moulding mud pellets. "There are many that to this day," says Plutarch, "believe that the beetle kind hath no female, but that the males cast out their sperm into a round pellet of earth, which they roll about by thrusting it backward with their hinder part—and this in imitation of the Sun which, while

188   189

it moves from west to east, turns the heaven the contrary way."[1] The Egyptians called the scarabæus *Chepera*, a word which is also the Egyptian for "Being."[2]

In fig. 190 the Scarab is associated with a two-headed Eagle—the symbol of Omnipotence.[3] The two-headed eagle was worshipped by the Hittites as the emblem of the

[1] *Isis and Osiris.*
[2] Renouf, *Hibbert Lectures,* p. 217.
[3] *The Migration of Symbols,* G. d'Alviella, p. 21.

King of Heaven, and the Hittite Bird of the Sun is said to be the magic Roc of Oriental mythology. It was a roc—the mortal enemy of serpents—that carried Sindbad the Sailor to an altitude so great that he lost sight of earth, and it was a Roc that transported him into the valley of diamonds.[1] Central American mythology records the existence of a great bird called "Voc," and associates it with a serpent-swallowing episode.[2] The Australian natives believe that birds were the original gods, and that the eagle especially is a great creative power.[3]

Mr Andrew Lang, who reproduces in *Custom and Myth* an illustration of the North American "Thunderbird,"

190

observes that Red Indians have always, as far as European knowledge goes, been in the habit of using picture writing for the purpose of retaining their legends, poems, and incantations.[4] The eagle was identified with ZEUS the Thunderer, and the European Spread-Eagle (see fig. 192) accords very closely with the Red-Indian Thunderbird as illustrated in fig. 191.[5]

During the Mosaic period the eagle was regarded as an emblem of the Holy Spirit, and its portrayal with two

[1] According to Swedenborg, precious stones signify spiritual truths, and the monuments of Egypt call precious stones hard stones of truth. Cf. *The Science of Correspondences*, E. Madeley, p. 363.
[2] *The Popol Vuh, the Mystic and Heroic Sagas of the Kiches of Central America*, L. Spence, p. 20.
[3] *Custom and Myth*, A. Lang, p. 54.
[4] P. 294.
[5] From *Custom and Myth*, p. 298.

heads is said to have recorded the double portion of Spirit miraculously bestowed upon Elisha. Dante refers to the

191   192

eagle as the Bird of God, and pictures the spirits of just princes as forming their hosts into the figure of an eagle.

"Lo! how straight up to Heaven he holds them reared,
Winnowing the air with those eternal plumes."[1]

In Heraldry one sometimes encounters an eagle on the

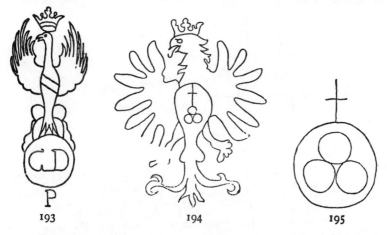

193   194   195

summit of a ladder. The Ladder is the *Scala perfectionis*, and the eagle is the goal of the Vision.

Occasionally the devisers of eagle emblems emphasised the purpose of their designs by adding a supplementary symbol of the Great Spirit. The Cross and Three Circles

[1] *Purgatory*, Canto ii.

in fig. 195, and on the breast of fig. 194 represent the threefold Deity, "that Trinitie and Unitie which this

196   197

globous triangle in a mortall immortall figure represents."[1] Note in fig. 196 the olive wreath of Peace and the heart of Love.

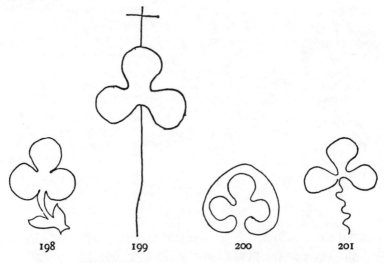

198   199   200   201

The modern pawnbroker's sign is a degraded survival of the arms of the Medici family and subsequently of Lombardy. The three golden spheres once represented

[1] *Microcosmus*, Purchas. London, 1619.

the triple Perfection, gold being the perfect metal, and the sphere or circle the perfect form. In fig. 178 (p. 72) these three circles of perfection are associated with the Aleph-Tau.

The three principles of the Divine Essence were also portrayed by a clover-leaf. There is a tradition that St Patrick, preaching the doctrine of the Trinity to the pagan Irish, plucked a shamrock and employed it as an object-lesson. But the word *shamrakh* is Arabic, and the trefoil or three-lobed leaf is a symbol more ancient and more widely spread than Christianity. The Deity has very

202

generally been conceived as Threefold, and in the ruined temples of both East and West the trefoil emblem is abundant.

The number *four* and the quadrifoil were held as sacred to the Supreme Spirit as was the number *three*. The potent Tetragrammaton was a *four*-lettered word, and almost all peoples of antiquity possessed a name for the Deity composed of *four* letters.[1] Among the Gnostics the Supreme Being was denoted by *four*.[2] On this sacrosanct figure the

---

[1] Assyrian ADAD; Egyptian AMUN; Persian SIRE; Greek THEOS; Latin DEUS; German GOTT; French DIEU; Turkish ESAR; Arabian ALLAH; cf. *Numbers: Their Occult Power and Mystic Virtue*, W. Wynn Westcott, p. 22.

[2] *The Gnostics*, C. W. King, 2nd ed., p. 307.

oath was administered among the Pythagoreans, an oath which is given by Jamblichus as follows :—

> " By that pure quadriliteral Name on high,
> Nature's eternal fountain and supply,
> The parent of all souls that living be—
> By it, with faithful oath I swear to thee." [1]

One reason for this reverence of the figure four was the perfect equality of the four sides of a square, none of

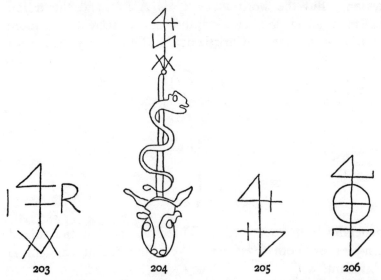

203   204   205   206

the bounding lines exceeding the others by a single point. [2] Hence it became a geometrical symbol of the Equity and Justice of the Divinity, " in whom nought unequal dwells." [3]

The geometrical 4 was used not infrequently to denote the supreme point and pinnacle of ascent. It is thus employed in figs. 204 and 203. In the latter the initials I.R. will denote Jesus Redemptor.

[1] Cf. *A Lexicon of Freemasonry*, Mackey, p. 348.
[2] *Isis Unveiled*, H. P. Blavatsky, i. 9.
[3] On an old house in Peebles is a carving of the numeral 4 supported by a male and female figure. The inscription reads : " We love Equity."

Sometimes the 4 is duplicated, so that it reads either upwards or downwards. A correspondent has suggested that the circle in fig. 206 represents the round world, and that the two fours symbolise the passage, "Whither shall I go from thy Spirit? or whither shall I flee from thy presence? If I ascend up into heaven, thou art there : if I make my bed in hell, behold, thou art there."[1] The Eagle herewith is marked with the upward and the downward 4.

Among the symbols of antiquity probably the most

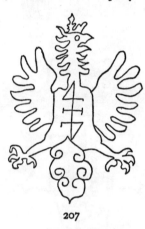

207

widely distributed is the *four*-limbed cross with lines at right angles to each limb, known as the *svastika*. It is found in Scandinavia, Persia, India, Mexico, Peru, Greece, Scotland, and in the prehistoric burial-grounds of North America, where it appears always to have been associated with sun-worship. The meaning most usually assigned to it is "It is well," the Sanskrit word having in it the roots "to be" and "well." Mrs G. F. Watts describes it as "a sign of beneficence indicating that the maze of life may bewilder, but the path of Light runs through it : 'It is well' is the name of the path, and the key to life

[1] Psalm cxxxix. 7-10.

eternal is in the strange labyrinth for those whom God leadeth."[1]

The *svastika* is to be seen woven into the centres of the labyrinthine designs illustrated in figs. 208 and 209. These

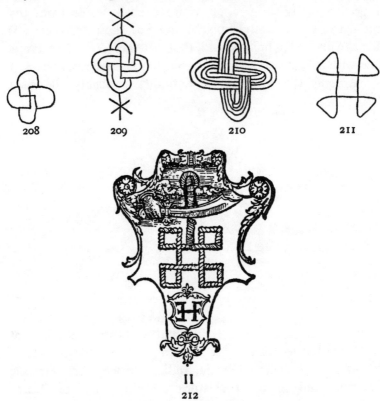

208   209   210   211

II
212

traceries, known in Italy as "Solomon's Knots," occur in more or less complicated forms, and are frequently to be seen on Celtic crosses. Without beginning and without an end, they were regarded as emblems of the Divine Inscrutability, and it was not unusual to twist them into specific forms so that they constituted supplementary symbols

[1] *The Word in the Pattern*, p. 15.

within symbols. As a rule they were traced in a three-
or fourfold form, but fig. 215—a peculiarly ingenious exception—is an unending tracing of three triplets of clover

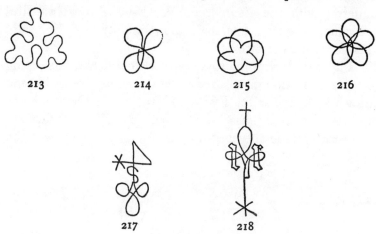

leaves, the centre is a five-rayed star, and the whole is in
the form of a flower. Fig. 216 also forms the flower and
star. Fig. 218 is a trefoil associated with the Lux cross
and the initials of Jesus Redemptor.

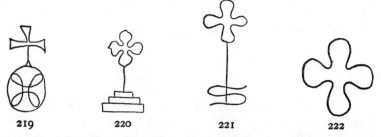

The fourfold meander in the centre of fig. 219 is
traceable to India, and is occasionally found as in fig. 220
in the form of a Calvary. Figs. 221 and 222 show variants
of the same idea. There is an interesting example of Knot
carving on the font in Dollon Parish Church, where the

architect has woven a series of figures eight—eight, as has been mentioned, being the symbol of Regeneration.

In *The Labyrinth* Komensky strengthens his fellow-sufferers with the assurance, "We have a most watchful guardian, protector, defender—the Almighty God Himself : therefore let us rejoice."[1]

Fig. 223 depicts the foreseeing, watchful, and unsleeping Eye of the Almighty, an emblem familiar to India and known in Egypt as the Eye of Horus or of OSIRIS. The watcher Himself was symbolised by the Panther or Leopard,[2] presumably because of the eye-like spots upon

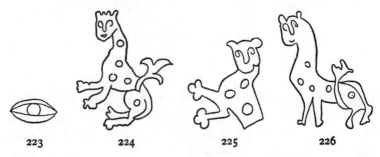

223   224   225   226

its skin. In Egypt the spotted skin of a leopard was always suspended near the images of OSIRIS, who was himself represented as a crouching leopard surmounted by an open eye. The name OSIRIS is said by Plutarch to have been understood as Os = many and IRI = eye, *i.e.* the "many-eyed."[3]

Figs. 224 to 226 portray "the Incomprehensible One furnished with innumerable eyes whom all nature longeth after in different ways,"[4] and the tail of fig. 224 is

[1] P. 234.
[2] The terms Leopard and Panther seem to have been used indifferently and indiscriminately. The "Leopards" of Heraldry are sometimes panthers or lions, and the panther's skin of Bacchus and Pan is spotted like a leopard's.
[3] *Isis and Osiris.*   [4] Cf. *The Gnostics*, King, p. 92.

conspicuously twisted into the form of a Fleur de Lys. It was a favourite device among the symbolists to utilise the tails of their symbolic creatures, and numerous examples of this custom are to be met with.[1] In the personality of Jesus Christ the mystics hailed the Divine culmination of all preceding types and Deities, hence Jesus was sometimes spoken of as Rabbi Ben Panther and He was said to have been the son of one Panther. Some mystics assume this to be a play upon the Greek words *pan* and *theos*, and to mean " all the Gods." [2]

The old superstition that the breath of the panther was so sweetly fragrant that it allured men, beasts, and cattle to inhale it, was in all probability due to a forgotten fable. Breath means spirit, and in the breath of the Panther was presumably figured the sweetness of the Breath of Life, or Holy Spirit. Air, breath, and wind were world-wide synonyms for *spirit*, and in many languages the words for soul, spirit, air, and breath, are identical.[3] The Supreme Spirit seems in many directions to have been originally conceived as Gentle Air and Mighty Wind. The South American Indians worshipped HURAKAN, " the mighty wind," whence our word " hurricane." JUPITER was the Deity of wind, rain, and thunder, and the natives of New Zealand regarded the wind as an indication of the presence of God.[4]

A hymn called " breath " or " *haha*," an invocation to the mystic wind, is pronounced by Maori priests on the initiation of young men into the tribal mysteries.[5] Among the religious rites of ancient nations none was more universal than the use of an implement known nowadays in England as a " swish," " buzzer," " whizzer," " boomer,"

[1] A well-known Mithraic symbol was a bull with the tuft of hair at the end of its tail twisted into three bearded ears of corn.
[2] *Clothed with the Sun*, Anna Kingsford, p. 134.
[3] Cf. *Religion: its Origin and Forms*, J. O. MacCulloch, p. 71.
[4] *Custom and Myth*, A. Lang, p. 36.   [5] *Ibid*.

or "bullroarer." This present-day toy has been described by Professor Haddon as perhaps the most ancient, widely-spread, and sacred religious symbol in the world.[1] It consists of a slab of wood which, when tied to a piece of string and whirled rapidly round, emits a roaring, fluttering, and unearthly noise. The Australian natives, among whom the *turndum* or Bullroarer is still in use, claim that it enables their sorcerers to fly up to Heaven.[2] One woman believed that in the sound of a bullroarer she heard the Australian Great Spirit "descend in a mighty rushing noise."[3] The bullroarer, used always as a sacred instrument, is still employed in New Mexico, the Malay Peninsula, Ceylon, New Zealand, Africa, and Australia, and under the name of *Rhombus* it figured prominently in the Mysteries of Ancient Greece. Mr Andrew Lang describing an exhibition at the Royal Institution says that when first the bullroarer was whirled round it did nothing in particular, but that upon warming to its work it produced "what may best be described as a mighty rushing noise as if some supernatural being 'fluttered and buzzed its wings with fearful roar.'"[4]

Primitive races imagine that by mimicking any effect they desire to produce they actually produce it; that the making of a fire causes sunshine, the sprinkling of water brings rain, and so forth.[5] There is thus a great probability that the mysterious and hitherto perplexing bullroarer was used to call or evoke the Supreme Spirit. Ezekiel describes the voice of the Spirit as "a great rushing,"[6] and there is a similar reference in The Acts to "a sound from Heaven as of a rushing mighty wind."[7]

---

[1] *The Study of Man*, p. 327.   [2] *Custom and Myth*, p. 35.
[3] *Ibid.*, p. 35.   [4] *Ibid.*, p. 31.
[5] J. G. Frazer, *The Golden Bough*, iii. p. 121.   [6] iii. 12.
[7] ii. 2. Dionysos, who possessed several of the attributes subsequently

The objects represented in figs. 227 and 228, must, I think, be meant to represent Bullroarers. There are examples in the British Museum varying from this laurel-leaf form to that of a diamond lozenge. The Greek term RHOMBUS implies that ancient bullroarers were rhombus shaped.

A writer in *The Hibbert Journal*[1] points out that in Australia, as at the present day in Scotland, the bullroarer is regarded as a "thunder spell." Its roaring represents the muttering of thunder, and in the words of the

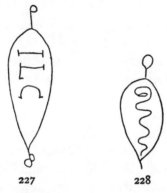

227   228

Australian native, "Thunder is the voice of Him (pointing upwards) calling on the rain to fall and make everything to grow up new." Whether this idea of "growing up new" applied simply to physical nature, or whether it was understood in a poetic and mystic sense, is difficult to determine; but the *leitmotiv* of "dying to live" runs right through the initiation ceremonies of Australia.[2] Among the European mystics of the Middle Ages the bullroarer

assigned to Jesus Christ, and at whose rites the Bullroarer was employed, was surnamed Bromius, *i.e.* the roarer, and he was sometimes referred to as Father Roarer: *cf. The Gnostics*, King, p. 126. The panther was sacred to Dionysos.

[1] Vol. viii. No. 2, pp. 406–410.
[2] *Mélanges d'Histoire des Religions*, H. Hubert et M. Mauss, Paris, 1909, p. 131.

was apparently considered to be an emblem of the regenerating power of the Holy Spirit. The regenerative number eight is apparent on fig. 227, and on fig. 228 there appears a roughly executed serpent, the symbol of regeneration. No beast of the field has had so many lessons exemplified by its attributes as the serpent. The sloughing of its worn-out skin led to its adoption as a symbol of the spiritual re-birth, but there was also seen to be a close analogy between the serpent's crawl in the dust and the earth-creeping attitude of materialism. Thus the same object served sometimes as the symbol of two diametrically opposed ideas, and in allegory one meets as constantly with the Evil as with the Good Serpent. It was the serpent of materialism—more subtle than any beast of the field—that seduced Eve in Eden. During the wanderings of the Israelites the dual symbolism of the Serpent is brought into juxtaposition in the story that the children of Israel were mortally bitten by serpents, and that those only who looked upon the Serpent uplifted by Moses were healed. There is a Maori legend that Heaven and Earth were once united, but subsequently were severed by a serpent.[1] It has been the mission of the mystics and the poets to attack materialism and remarry the sundered Earth and Heaven. The idea that the Serpent symbolised Materialism elucidates many traditional but fictitious enmities, such as that between the Stag and serpents and between the Roc and serpents.

Mysticism has always maintained that the concourse of whirling atoms termed "matter," but which science has been quite unable either to reduce to its ultimate or to define, is unsubstantial and unreal, and that the only *substance* in this universe is the invisible Force called Spirit, a Force which alone moulds and controls matter to its desire

[1] *Custom and Myth*, p. 46.

like clay in the hands of a potter. They preached in season and out of season, the dogma that spirit was permanent and matter mere appearance. Among other mystic flotsam from the past, Freemasonry has inherited and preserved the tradition of a "mystic tie," described as "that sacred and inviolable bond which unites men of the most discordant opinions into one bond of brothers, which gives but one language to men of all nations, and one altar to men of all religions."[1]

This mysterious bond of union cannot be anything else than SPIRIT, the Influence which links minds of similar tastes into kinship and hitches Earth to Heaven. Among

229   230   231   232   233

Mons. Briquet's emblems are some objects which he describes as "*crotchets*," but which in reality are *links* (see figs. 229 to 231). In fig. 232 the link is attached to the fourfold emblem of Divinity, an emblem which was also attached to the compasses in fig. 183 ; and in fig. 233 the interlocking of two links forms a mystic tie suggestive of the Regenerative *eight*. Some of these ties or knots are a combination of the "S" of *Spiritus* and of the figure eight. The extremities of the octagonal S in fig. 234 are two *esses*, standing for *Sanctus Spiritus*. From the S of fig. 221 (*ante*, p. 83), rises the quadrifoil, and the "finials" of fig. 239 are four trefoils. In fig. 244 the three circles of perfection have been introduced, and in fig. 240 the inference of the upward and downward four has been supplied by the cross.

[1] *A Lexicon of Freemasonry*, Mackey, p. 227.

In figs. 241 and 243 the all-pervading S is hallowed
with a cross, and in fig. 242 it is surrounded by the circle

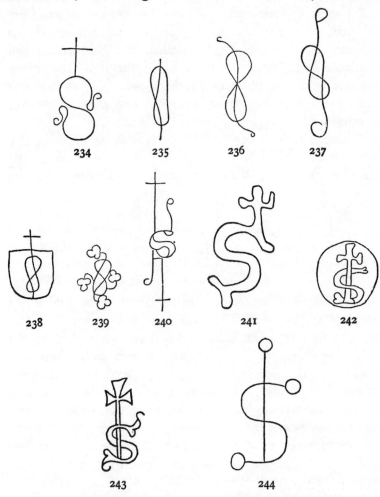

of eternal perfection. The mystics were links in a long
chain of spiritual tradition ; they were the units of a procession which it was believed started from the Golden Age
and from the land of Heaven. The tongues of mysticism

have most generally been the poets who have claimed
that—

> " From the Word, the Word is kindled,
> From a spark the world is lit :
> So by golden links extended,
> Verse by verse the Song is knit." [1]

In *The Advancement of Learning* Bacon refers to " that
excellent and Divine fable of the Golden Chain, namely,
that Men were not able to draw Jupiter down to the earth ;
but, contrariwise, Jupiter was able to draw them up to
Heaven."   In the *Essays* he writes : " A little or superficial
test of Philosophy may perchance incline the Mind of Man
to Atheisme ; but a full draught thereof brings the mind
back againe to Religion.   For in the entrance of Philosophy,
when the second causes, which are next unto the senses,
doe offer themselves to the mind of Man, and the mind
itselfe cleaves unto them and dwells there, an oblivion of
the Highest Cause may creep in ; but when a man passeth
on farther and beholds the dependency, continuation and
confederacy of causes, and the workes of Providence, then,
according to the allegory of the Poets, he will easily believe
that the highest linke of Nature's chains must needs be
tyed to the foot of Jupiter's chaire."

Tennyson expresses this idea in the couplet :—

> " The whole round earth is every way
> Bound by gold chains about the feet of God." [2]

and it is to this same chain that Blake refers in the familiar
lines :—

> " I give you the end of a golden string,
> Only wind it into a ball ;
> It will lead you in at Heaven's gate,
> Built in Jerusalem's wall."

[1] Cf. *The Popular Poetry of the Finns*, C. J. Billson, p. 7.
[2] *Passing of Arthur.*

At times the golden string was represented by eight-like knots as in figs. 246 and 247, but the more usual form

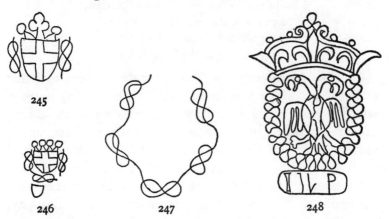

245

246   247   248

was a sequence of plain *esses* as in fig. 248, where the chain surrounds the Eagle of Omnipotence.

Into the inner chain of the Arms of Jerusalem have

COLLEGII
S 3. ROSARII.

250

COAT OF ARMS OF JERUSALEM
249

been woven the S of Spiritus, the R of Regeneratio, and the eight-like mystic tie. Among the chain-border orna-ments of the seventeenth-century book-plate, illustrated in fig. 250, will be noticed the initials S and SS.

Shakespeare describing the symbols of nobility carried

at the baptism of Queen Elizabeth details, " collars of SS."
These, like other paraphernalia of Heraldry, were once
symbolic, and the collar of SS represented the golden chain
of *Sanctus Spiritus*. A solitary S may almost invariably be
read as *Spiritus*, a double SS as *Sanctus Spiritus*, and a treble
SSS as the three acclamations, *Sanctus ! Sanctus ! Sanctus !*
Three eight-like *esses* making the number 888 bore the
additional signification " Jesus," the numerical value of the
letters J, E, S, U, S, amounting exactly to 888. By some
such similar method of computation the number 666 was
recognised as " the mark of the beast."

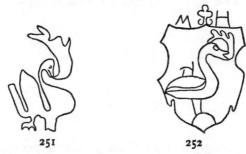

251   252

In *Fragments of a Faith Forgotten*, Mr Mead says that the
Generative Power was called not only wind but also a
serpent, " the latter because of the hissing sound it produces."[1]

The meaning of the geese emblems herewith puzzled
me for a long while until the idea struck me that the flame
emerging from the mouths was intended to represent the
goose's hiss.

There is little doubt that this was a fortunate guess ;
that the goose was assumed to be full of the Holy Spirit,
and that its sibilant hiss was understood to be the emission
of Spirit. The word *goose* is evidently allied to *goost*, the
ancient form of ghost, *i.e.* spirit. The Anglo-Saxon for
goose was *gōs*, which again brings us back to ghost or *ghoost*

[1] P. 15.

as it sometimes used to be spelt.[1] PLUTARCH says that "the Egyptians give the name of Jupiter to the *breath*" :[2] it was probably for this reason that the goose or breath-bird was sacred to Juno the female JUPITER. It is perhaps for the same reason that the Hindoos represent BRAHMA the Breath of Life as riding upon a goose, and that the Egyptians symbolised Seb the Father of Osiris as a goose which they termed "The Great Cackler."[3]

According to the Hindoo theory of creation, the Supreme Spirit laid a golden egg resplendent as the Sun, and from this golden egg was born BRAHMA, the progenitor of the Universe. The Egyptians had a similar story, and described

253   254   255

the sun as an egg laid by "the primeval goose," in later times said to be a God.[4] It is probable that our fairy tale of the goose that laid the golden eggs is a relic of this very ancient mythology. In fig. 254 the goose is seen sitting upon its nest, and in fig. 255 it is associated with its traditional egg.

The suggestion underlying the tale of the slain goose of the golden eggs would appear to be that Spirit or Inspiration is the magic provider of daily and perpetual treasures ; and that the fool who kills his goose is the un-

[1] Skeat, *Etymological Dictionary.*   [2] *Isis and Osiris.*
[3] Renouf, *Hibbert Lectures,* p. 111. The Egyptian name for a certain kind of goose was *Seb.*
[4] *Religion of Ancient Egypt,* W. M. Flinders Petrie, p. 68. According to Mr Baring-Gould, the Roc of the *Arabian Nights* "broods over its great luminous egg, the sun"; cf. *Curious Myths of the Middle Ages,* p. 411.

compromising Materialist who murders imagination. "The letter killeth, the Spirit giveth Life."

In fig. 252 the "blessed fowl" was standing on a mountain top ; in fig. 256 it symbolises a Way to regeneration ; over fig. 258 is the Morning Star, and over fig. 257 the Fleur de Lys of Light.

The mystics deemed themselves to be watchful and unslumbering geese, and the geese emblems, now under consideration, probably illustrate the prophecy of ISAIAH : " He will lift up an ensign to the nations from afar, and

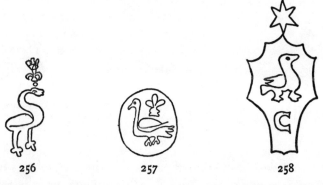

256   257   258

will hiss unto them from the ends of the earth : and behold they shall come with speed swiftly : none shall weary nor stumble among them ; none shall slumber nor sleep." [1] With this may also be compared the prophecy of Zechariah : " They went their way as a flock, they were troubled because there was no shepherd. *I will hiss for them, and gather them* ; for I have redeemed them : and they shall increase as they have increased. And I will sow them among the people : and they shall remember me in far countries ; and they shall live with their children, and turn again." [2]   Surmounting fig. 253 is the R of the regenerate or redeemed. The original sanctity of the goose may

[1] v. 26–27.   [2] Chap. x.

account for our expression, "silly goose," the word silly
being of pious derivation, and meaning originally blessed,
happy, innocent, and gentle.   At the time of Cæsar's invasion the goose was *tapu* to the Britons.[1]   There is no
ground for the popular idea that the goose is in any respect
a foolish fowl, but on the contrary it is described by those
who have studied its habits as "the wisest bird in Europe."[2]

A symbolic relative of the "silly" goose is the "silly"
sheep, which in figs. 259 to 261 is seen in the traditional
aspect of the Agnus Dei raising up the Ensign of Christ.

259   260   261

The Lamb with its fleece of snow was the symbol of meek-
ness, innocence, and purity.   Much pastoral poetry is repre-
sentive of something more than Arcadian philandering, and
the Shepherds and Shepherdesses of the poets are not infrequently allegoric.   With mystic intuition a modern poet has
well written :

"She walks, the lady of my delight,
   A shepherdess of sheep ;
Her flocks are thoughts.   She keeps them white,
   She guards them from the steep ;
She feeds them on the fragrant height
   And folds them in for sleep."[3]

[1] Rhys (Sir J.), *Hibbert Lectures*, p. 175.
[2] Cf. *Animals, Artisans, and Other Studies of Birds and Beasts*,
C. J. Cornish.   [3] Mrs Alice Meynell.

In allegory there are usually three meanings attributed to every symbol, thus—taking sheep as an instance—there are the three degrees : (1) the white and innocent thoughts of the mind ; (2) the man himself who has become lamb-like ; (3) the "Lamb of God" : similarly, there is : (1) he who rules and shepherds his own thoughts; (2) he who shepherds his fellow creatures ; and (3) the supreme Good Shepherd. It was to shepherds watching their flocks by night that the angel of the Lord is said to have announced the coming of the Christ. Just as, according to Isaiah, the watchful and unslumbering *geese* were collected and gathered together, so does Ezekiel assemble the *sheep* : "For thus saith the Lord God ; Behold, I, even I, will both search my sheep, and seek them out. As a shepherd seeketh out his flock in the day that he is among his sheep that are scattered ; so will I seek out my sheep, and will deliver them out of all places where they have been scattered in the cloudy and dark day. And I will bring them out from the people, and gather them from the countries, and will bring them to their own land, and feed them upon the mountains of Israel by the rivers, and in all the inhabited places of the country. I will feed them in a good pasture, and upon the high mountains of Israel shall their fold be : there shall they lie in a good fold, and in a fat pasture shall they feed upon the mountains of Israel. I will feed my flock, and I will cause them to lie down, saith the Lord God. I will seek that which was lost, and bring again that which was driven away, and will bind up that which was broken, and will strengthen that which was sick." "Thus," concludes Ezekiel, "shall they know that I the Lord their God am with them, and that they, even the house of Israel, are my people, saith the Lord God. And ye my flock, the flock of my pasture, are men, and I am your God, saith the Lord God." [1]

[1] xxxiv.

PETER exhorting the elders among his hearers to feed the flock of God until the Chief Shepherd shall appear,[1] observes : " Ye were as sheep going astray, but are now returned unto the Shepherd and Bishop of your souls."[2]

The pastoral staffs herewith are symbols of the Good Shepherd and the Bishop of All Souls'.   The Cross of Light surmounts fig. 263, and figs. 262 and 264 are distinguished by the Trefoil of the Deity.

The idea of a heavenly Shepherd or Feeder, the giver of Divine Nectar, is common to nearly all primitive beliefs.

262   263   264

In fact, after the eighth century, Christianity largely discontinued the use of the Good Shepherd emblem because it was so widely employed among Jews and Pagans.[3]   In the Hermetic literature of Egypt (300 B.C. ?) God is referred to as the Shepherd and King who leads with law and justice, and deputes his Logos (" the Word made flesh "), his firstborn Son, to take charge of the Sacred Flock.[4]

This holy flock numbered not only sheep but doubtless also geese and kine, and there are certain early Christian inscriptions wherein the neophytes are termed

[1] I, v.   [2] I, iii. 25.
[3] *The Romance of Symbolism*, S. Heath, p. 122.
[4] Cf. *The Hymns of Hermes*, G. R. S. Mead.   Also *Personal Religion in Egypt before Christianity*, W. M. Flinders Petrie, *passim*.

"suckling calves."[1] It is fabled that Apollo was the possessor of a herd of sacred cattle, and that as a punishment for violating them destruction fell upon certain unruly followers of Ulysses. The sacred herd of "curvehorned cattle, milk dispensers to the household" reappears in the traditional legends of Finland, which are pre-eminently interesting, as they preserve an exceptional percentage of Chaldean lore. The Finns, who still maintain an uncanny reputation for magic, are supposed to have originally migrated from Asia, and in their racial characteristics are distinct from any of their neighbours.

The writer of Ezekiel was a "priest, the son of Buzi, in the land of the Chaldeans by the river Chebar,"[2] and it is interesting to compare Ezekiel's assembling of the sheep with the *Kalevala's* mustering of the cattle :

> "Come ye home, ye curve-horned cattle,
> Milk dispensers to the household.
>
> .   .   .   .   .
>
> Let the cattle rest in quiet,
> Leave in peace the hoofed cattle,
> Let the herd securely wander,
> Let them march in perfect order,
> Through the swamps and through the open,
> Through the tangle of the forest ;
> Never do thou dare to touch them,
> Nor to wickedly molest them."[3]

The injunction against molesting the cattle of the Sun is paralleled in the *Kalevala* by the warning :

> "Never venture to approach thou
> Where the golden herd is living."[4]

Canaan, the Eldorado of the Hebrews, was fabled to

---

[1] Cf. *The Quest*, vol. i. p. 631.   [2] i. 3.
[3] Runo, xxxii. 371–378.   [4] *Ibid.*, 428–429.

be a land flowing with milk and honey, presumably the same honey that, according to the *Kalevala*,

> " Is fermenting and is working
> On the hills of golden colour ;
> And upon the plains of silver,
> There is food for those who hunger ;
> There is drink for all the thirsty,
> There is food to eat that fills not,
> There is drink that never lessens." [1]

The figure of Christ the Good Shepherd is frequently represented with a vessel hanging on his arm or *suspended on*

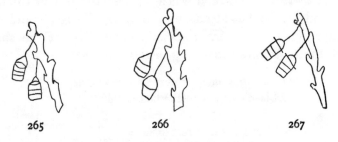

265   266   267

a tree. " This," says Mr Sydney Heath, " is the mulctra or milk-pail, and was considered symbolic of the spiritual nourishment derived from CHRIST." [2] Figs. 265 to 267 presumably represent mulctras suspended from a branch.

Among the ancients, milk was regarded as a Heavenly nourishment and the laver of regeneration, and it is still administered by Hindoos to dying persons. The modern descendants from Zoroastrianism use it sacramentally, and such is the belief in its cleansing efficacy that scrupulous Parsees still carry a small bottle in their pocket wherewith to purify themselves from any unhallowed contact.

By the primitive Christians, CHRIST the Good Shepherd was identified with ORPHEUS, and an early emblem in the

[1] xxxii. 407–418.   [2] *Romance of Symbolism,* p. 123.

Catacombs represents Him sitting ORPHEUS-like among the birds and beasts, charming them with the golden tones of His music. ORPHEUS, fabled to be the son of Apollo the protector of flocks and cattle, is said to have been the inventor of letters and of everything that contributed to civilisation,[1] and in later times there sprang up a mystic order which maintained an enthusiastic worship of his memory and doctrines. He was regarded as the first poet of the Heroic Age, anterior both to HOMER and HESIOD, and his characteristics reappear in the *Kalevala* in the person of WAINAMOINEN. This culture hero is recorded to have been the son of UKKO, "the lord of the vault of air," and to have been sent by his All-righteous Father to teach men music and the arts of agriculture. The *Kalevala* tells how WAINA-MOINEN seated himself "on a hill all silver shining" [Sir Walter Raleigh's *silver mountains* (?)], and how he lured the wolves out of their lairs, the fish out of the rivers, and the birds out of the branches. Finally :—

"The whole of Tapios people,
All the boys and all the maidens,
Climbed *upon a mountain summit*,
That they might enjoy the music." [2]

In Egypt the culture hero and world-harmoniser was OSIRIS the regenerator. OSIRIS is said to have invented agricultural instruments, to have taught men how to harness oxen to the plough, and how rightly to worship the Gods. After having bestowed these blessings upon his own country-men, he assembled a host with which he set forth to conquer the world, not with weapons, but with music and eloquence. The beneficent career of OSIRIS was, however, cut suddenly short by the murderous trickery of TYPHON, his envious

[1] Bacon expounds Orpheus as "Philosophy," an interpretation that is probably correct.
[2] Runo, xli. 60, 63.

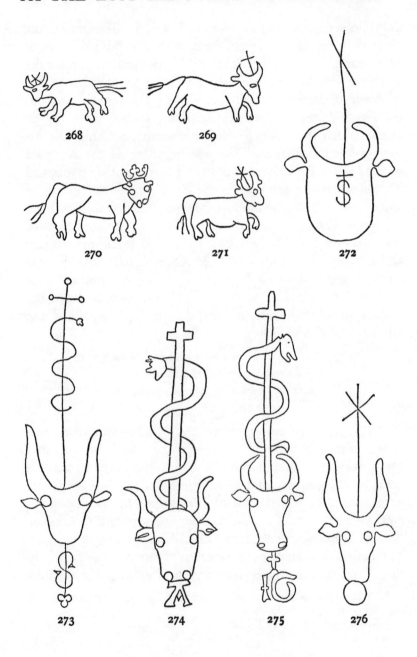

and malicious brother. Subsequently the soul of Osiris was supposed to inhabit the body of the sacred bull Apis, at whose death it transferred itself to a successor. The individual animal that was recognised to be Apis was selected by certain signs, a white *square* mark on the forehead, another in the form of an *eagle* on its back, and a lump under its tongue in the shape of a *scarabæus.*[1] When found the sacred animal was fed with *milk* for *four* months, and placed in a building facing the East. To the Egyptians, Apis, the sacred bull, was admittedly a faint shadow of the

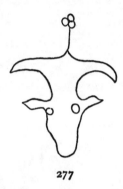

277

Creator, and the Babylonish Bulls undoubtedly had once a similar significance. The designs herewith are evidently symbols of the sacred Bull.

In Symbolism each detail has invariably some meaning. The heart of Love is woven on to the forehead of fig. 278, the features of fig. 279 are the octagonal SS of *Sanctus Spiritus*, the S of *Spiritus* is associated with figs. 272 and 273, and under fig. 280 is the Mystic Tie. The three circles of perfection appear as the nostrils of fig. 281, and the tails of figs. 268 to 271 are obviously *trinity in unity*. The circle under fig. 276 identifies The Perfect One, and the Aleph-Tau under fig. 274, the First and the Last. The

[1] *Age of Fable*, Peacock, p. 314.

rudely designed pastoral crook surmounting fig. 282 is an implication of the Good Shepherd, over fig. 283 is the Trefoil of the Trinity, and the I.C. under fig. 275 are the familiar initials of Jesus Christ.

Fig. 284 is a combination of crescent moon and Bull's head, and the horns of fig. 285 are again the crescent moon which is here associated with the symbol of the Creator

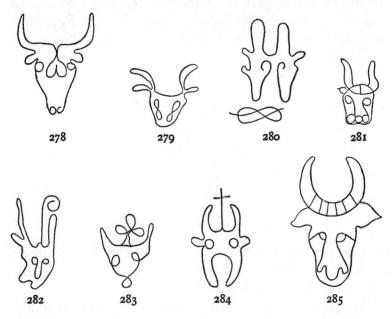

278   279   280   281

282   283   284   285

because the Moon was held to be a sign of the Heavenly host that was assembled by Osiris. The writer of Ecclesiasticus refers to her as " an instrument of the armies above, shining in the firmament of Heaven, the beauty of Heaven, the glory of the stars, an ornament giving light in the highest places of the Lord," and there was a Rabbinic legend that the Stars accompanied the Moon, waiting upon her as a reward for her giving light during the darkness of the long night. " At the commandment of the Holy One," says the writer of Ecclesiasticus, "they will stand in their order and never faint in their watches."[1] The emblems herewith depict this legend of the moon attended by the starry Hosts of Heaven. Fig. 286 has survived as the arms of Turkey, and fig. 287 as those of Egypt.

One must differentiate between the symbolism of the Bull, the Ox, and the Cow. The Bull represented the Deity in His male aspect of Creator, the Cow the productive milk-yielding qualities of the Magna Mater. For this reason the Cow was sacred to Isis, was worshipped among the Hindoos, and is still revered as a sacred symbol

286 287

of the Deity by the inhabitants of the Gold Coast. The strong, toiling, and patient Ox, dragging the plough over the hard-parched soil and compelling the earth to yield her increase, was the symbol of unremitting toil and self-sacrifice. It was among the oxen that Christ, not without reason, is recorded to have been born.

The oxen that labour and endure, the geese that neither slumber nor sleep, and the stars which at the commandment of the Holy One stand untiring in their watches, symbolically represent the units of the Heavenly Host marshalled by the God of Light.

[1] *Cf.* Ecclesiasticus xliii.

CHAPTER VI

THE HOSTS OF THE LORD

> " The healing of the world
> Is in its nameless saints.   Each separate star
> Seems nothing, but a myriad scattered stars
> Break up the night and make it beautiful."

THE Moon was regarded as the awakener and assembler of the Stars, the Stars were pictured as the glorified souls of saints and heroes, and the Night-sky spangled with the lights of Heaven was viewed as a symbol of the hosts of the Lord.   In the mythologies of both East and West Night, the Nursing-Mother of the Golden Stars, is addressed as an awe-inspiring, noble, and beneficent Being. To the Christian mystics Night similarly appealed as the period of Christ's progress, and

> " His knocking time ; the soul's dumb watch,
> When spirits their fair kindred catch." [1]

Upwards of four thousand years ago, one of the Vedic poets wrote : " Night approaches illumined with stars and planets, and, looking on all sides with numberless eyes, over-powers all meaner lights.   The immortal goddess pervades the firmament, covering the low valleys and shrubs, and the lofty mountains and trees ; but soon she disturbs the gloom with celestial effulgence.   Advancing with brightness at

[1] H. Vaughan.

length she recalls her sister morning ; and the nightly shade gradually melts away. May she at this time be propitious ! She in whose early watch we may calmly recline in our mansions, as birds repose on the trees. Mankind now sleep in their towns ; now herds and flocks peacefully slumber, winged creatures, even swift falcons and vultures. O night ! avert from us the she-wolf and the wolf ; and, oh ! suffer us to pass thee in soothing rest ! Oh, morn ! remove in due time this black, yet visible overwhelming darkness, which at present enfolds me. Daughter of heaven, I approach thee with praise, as the cow approaches her milker ; accept, O night ! not the hymn only, but the oblation of thy suppliant who prays that his foes may be subdued."

By the Egyptians the Moon was personified as masculine and was identified with Thoth, the pathfinder and the awakener of sleeping minds. It is presumably the face of Thoth—the man in the moon—that is seen in fig. 288. The use by the early Christians of the moon as a symbol of Heaven must be related to the ancient Indian belief that the path of those who did " pious works in the village " led finally to the moon, where, in the company of the Gods, their souls enjoyed a full recompense for their labours.[1]

In Plutarch's treatise *On the Face in the Moon* it is said that the Good remain in the Moon in the enjoyment of perfect tranquillity, busying themselves with the regulations of affairs on earth, furnishing oracles, and rendering various good services to mankind. But should anyone whose purification was incomplete try to force his way thither he was scared away by the apparition of a terrifying and appalling Face.[2] Seemingly this was a fable devised cunningly to deter premature and uninvited entrance into

[1] *Brahmin Knowledge*, L. D. Barnett, p. 53.
[2] *The Gnostics*, p. 347.

the next world by the unlawful method of suicide. Note how threatening and admonitory a frown is portrayed on the Faces of figs. 290 to 292.

In one of the Vedic hymns the supreme Spirit is introduced pronouncing some of his own attributes. "I pass like the breeze," He is made to say : "I support the Moon, destroyer of foes."[1] In the prayer previously quoted the Night was hailed as the disturber of the gloom which was melted by her Divine effulgence, and the five-

288   289   290   291   292

pointed zigzags surmounting figs. 293 to 296 were the symbol of this effulgence.

> "Ah! but I rejoice in Thee, O Thou my God ;
> Thou zigzagged effulgence of the burning stars.
> Thou wilderment of indigo lights ;
> Thou grey horn of immaculate fire."[2]

The ancients regarded the number five as sacred to the God of Light, and the attributes of Deity were held to consist of *five*, namely, Being, Sameness, Diversity, Motion, and Rest.[3] The horns of fig. 285 (*ante* p. 104) are doubtless for this reason marked with *five* divisions.

It was the ambition of the mystic to become the perfect centre of a five-fold Star. "Therefore, O my God, fashion me into a five-pointed star of Ruby burning beneath the

[1] *The Hindoos*, anon., p. 148.
[2] *Treasure House of Images.*
[3] Plutarch, *On the E at Delphi.*

foundations of Thy Unity that I may mount the Pillar of
Thy Glory and be lost in admiration of the triple unity of
Thy Godhead."[1]

This passage is an expression of the idea underlying the
Stars illustrated in figs. 297 to 303.

293

294

295

296

Reviewing the mystic armies of the sky, we find them
to have been composed of units typified while on earth by
oxen (the toiling and enduring), sheep (the innocent and
pure), and geese (those filled with the Holy Spirit). The

---

[1] Compare also: "My Oneness is My design and I have designed it for
thee; therefore clothe thy soul with it that thou mayst be the Dawning-star
of My Unity for ever."—From the Arabic *Supreme Pen* of Baha Ullah.

Starry Hosts—recruited from earth—were believed to fight
everlastingly in their courses against darkness and to be
perpetually dispelling and outmanœuvring the spirits of
Evil. Legends of this cyclopean contest are to be found in
the annals of all nations. In Babylon the leader of the
Hosts of Light was MERODACH, a name meaning "the

297   298   299   300

301   302   303

young steer of day." Another of this god's titles was
"36,000 wild bulls," and he was also known as "annihilator
of the enemy," "rooter out of all evil" and "troubler of
the evil ones." As "King of the Heavens" MERODACH
was identified with JUPITER as well as with other heavenly
bodies. Dr Pinches observes that "traversing the sky *in
great zigzags* JUPITER seemed to the Babylonians to super-
intend the stars and thus was regarded as emblematic of
MERODACH shepherding them—'pasturing the gods like

sheep' as the tablet has it."[1] MERODACH, it is further
stated, ranged the stars in their order and assigned to them
their respective duties. He made the new moon to shine
and appointed him "the ruler of the night." In his
character of "Illuminator of the Night," MERODACH was
identified with SIN, the moon god and "light producer."
SIN, from whom Mount Sinai derived its name, was
described as "the mighty Steer whose horns are strong,
whose limbs are perfect": He was also said to be filled
with splendour and beauty and to be the "lord of the
shining crown."[2]

In India the "Leader of the milch kine to the fold"
and the eternal battler with the fiends of drought and darkness was INDRA. INDRA, supposed to have been a personification of the visible heavens, is described as "the god with
10,000 eyes": in other words he was the Watcher and the
Lord of Stars. In the Vedas INDRA is described as "like
a bull, impetuous, strong."[3]

> "Light was prisoned in the gloom,
> Indra freed her from its womb.
> Rain was prisoned in the cloud,
> Indra smote the demon proud;
> Ope'd the caverns of the night,
> Gave us rain and generous light!

> Hosts advancing to the fray
> Cry to Him on battle's day:
> And the strong man shouts his fame,
> And the lowly lisps his name."[4]

The Persians regarded the Supreme Spirit ORMUZ as
incessantly at war with the spirits of darkness, and in this

---

[1] *The Religion of Babylonia and Assyria*, Theophilus G. Pinches, pp.
58–61, 40.   [2] *Ibid.*, pp. 82–83.
[3] Dutt, p. 4.   [4] *Ibid.*, pp. 6, 9.

everlasting encounter, man as a free agent played a part with his soul as a stake.[1]

It is unnecessary to consider in detail this world-wide belief in the existence of a Holy War. Among the Greeks and Romans it was typified by JUPITER warring against the Titans ; in Scandinavia by the encounters of THOR and the giants, and a dragon slayer or a giant killer seems to be part of the tradition of every European and Oriental race, civilised or savage. In the Babylonist epic of Creation, the Spirit of Evil is represented as bringing into existence

304   305

giant serpents, sharp of tooth, and strong, with poison filling their bodies like blood ; terrible dragons of alluring brilliance, raging dogs, fishmen, and other monstrous forms. MERODACH, the conqueror of these horrors, is represented as striding over the prostrate body of a serpent which turns its head to attack him whilst the God threatens it with a pointed weapon. The Greeks represented APOLLO, the God of Day, struggling with and strangling a Python. The Egyptians portrayed HORUS treading upon crocodiles and grasping noxious animals in his hands. CHRIST promised his disciples power to tread down serpents and scorpions, and in Isaiah it is prophesied, " In that day the Lord with his sore and great and strong sword shall punish leviathan

[1] S. A. Kapadia, *The Teaching of Zoroaster*, p. 26.

the piercing serpent, even leviathan that crooked serpent; and he shall slay the dragon that is in the sea." [1] In the illustrations on p. 112, the radiant Being is seen treading down snakes and dragons, and in fig. 305 He is carrying the five-pearled ensign of the promised Dawn.

In the Finnish version of this universal fable, the task of bridling the wolves and destroying the dragon is assigned to ILMARINEN, " the great primeval craftsman " ; but Finland being a land of lakes and marshes, local colour necessitated a fresh-water monster, and the devastating dragon thus figures as a cruel and devouring pike.   This terrible-fanged fish was seven boats' length in its back, and its extended gorge was three great rivers' width in breadth.   ILMARINEN, its conqueror, is instructed :—

> " Do not thou be so despondent,
> Forge thee now a fiery eagle ;
> Forge a bird of fire all flaming—
> This the mighty pike shall capture."

The legend continues :

> " Then the smith, e'en Ilmarinen,
> Deathless artist of the smithy,
> Forged himself a fiery eagle ;
> Forged a bird of fire all flaming.
>
> .   .   .   .   .
>
> Then the bird, that noble eagle,
> Took his flight, and upward soaring,
> Forth he flew, the pike to capture." [2]

After a terrible combat the demon fish is overcome and eventually borne off to the branches of an oak-tree.

The eagle has already been considered as the symbol of the Omnipotent Spirit.   In the designs herewith the head of an eagle is blended with five-rayed fiery flame, and lest

[1] Isaiah xxvii. 1.   [2] *Kalevala*, xix., Runo.

there should be any misunderstanding, the designers of figs. 306 and 307 have emphasised their meaning by the S of *Spiritus* and the Star-cross of Light. The eagle may here be regarded as that " Hawk of gold " which was the symbol of Horus, and which the sky is said mystically to mirror—

> " The stars seem comets, rushing down
> To gem Thy robes, bedew Thy crown,
> Like the moon-plumes of a strange bird,
> By a great wind sublimely stirred ;
> Thou drawest the light of all the skies
> Into Thy wake." [1]

The design herewith (fig. 311) is lettered Olmuz, perhaps one among the many variants of the great name Ormuz. Not

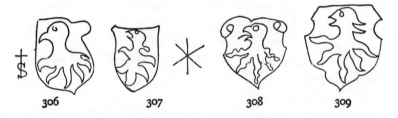

306   307   308   309

only do the letters SS support the crown, but the whole design is traced in quivering lines, representing the flickering fire of spirit.[2] The heart-shaped body of the bird implies the God of Love.

The Moon was, as has been seen, the awakener and the assembler of the stars. The Lord and Leader of the Hosts was the Sevenfold Spirit symbolised by the Eagle, but this sevenfold power was sometimes represented by the constellation known as the Great Bear, and in fig. 312 this Bear is represented on the Eagle's breast.

---

[1] *Aha!* A. Crowley ; *The Equinox*, p. 46, vol. 1, No. 3.
[2] Note the flaming necks of many other eagle emblems.

The Greeks relate in star stories that it is the "Great Bear" that "*keeps watch.*"[1] Red Indians have a myth that the Bear is immortal, and that though it apparently dies, it rises again in another body.[2] This seems at one time to have been a very extensive belief, and among the Ainos (a primitive people found in the Japanese Islands of Yesso and Saghalien) the bear still receives an idolatrous veneration. Although, as Professor Frazer points out, the animal cannot be described as sacred, and is certainly not a

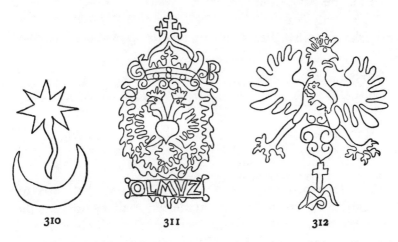

310   311   312

totem,[3] yet when the Ainos kill a bear they go through an apologetic and propitiatory ceremony, saying : "We kill you, O Bear ; come back soon into an Aino."[4]

The constellation of the Great Bear was believed never to set,[5] but to keep an everlasting watch and ward over the universe. The seven great stars that constitute the Great Bear have not the faintest resemblance to the form of a bear, yet they appear to be known almost universally by

[1] *Custom and Myth*, A. Lang, p. 128.   [2] *Ibid.*, p. 176.
[3] *The Golden Bough*, xi. 375–376.   [4] *Ibid.*, p. 379.
[5] *Age of Fable*, Peacock, p. 35.

this name, even among savages in whose country no great bears exist.[1] The origin of the name Great Bear is quite unknown, although Max Müller endeavoured to prove *more suo* that it arose from the corruption of a word meaning something originally different. This constellation was once known as the "Sheepfold";[2] and it would appear from the emblems herewith that the Great Bear was regarded as a symbol of the Great Spirit, the Triple Perfection (note the three circles on the collar of fig. 314), the Light of the World, the Alpha and Omega, or Jesus Christ.

The only reason I can surmise for this symbolism is the material fact that Bears hibernate during winter and sub-

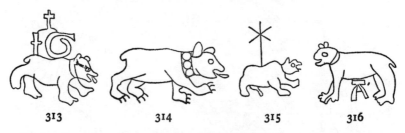

| 313 | 314 | 315 | 316 |

sist for long periods upon their own fat, and that thus by the simple system of analogy underlying all symbolism the Bear became elevated into an emblem of the Self-Existent, the Everlasting, the I AM. The foliage among which the Great Bear in the ornament herewith is seated is the mystic Amaranth, a fact confirmatory of this theory, for the Amaranth of the poets was a familar and well-recognised symbol of the everlasting and the incorruptible.[3]

---

[1] *Custom and Myth*, A. Lang, pp. 121–142.

[2] *The Perfect Way*, p. 331.

[3] *Amarantos* = the everlasting. Its blood-red flower never fades, but remains red to the last. *Cf.* Milton—

> "Immortal Amaranth, a flower which once
> In Paradise, fast by the Tree of Life,
> Begun to bloom; but soon for man's offence,
> To Heaven removed where first it grew."—*Paradise Lost.*

317

The constellation of the Great Bear consists of Seven Great Stars, two of which point to the Pole Star, the fixed hinge and pivot upon which turns the Universe. The reason why the ancients christened the constellation of the Great Bear by this apparently inappropriate name was in all probability its constitution of *Seven* Great Stars. The association of *Seven* with the Spirit of God has persisted to the present day, and Christians still speak of the *seven*fold gifts of the *Septi*form Spirit. ORMUZ, the supreme God of Light, was said to sit at the head of a Hierarchy of *Seven* Holy Immortals.[1] Of INDRA the Vedas state :

> " *Seven* bright rays bedeck his brow,
>   *Seven* great rivers from him flow." [2]

The Hindoos describe OM, the solar fire, as riding in a car drawn by *seven* green horses preceded by the Dawn, and followed by thousands of Genii worshipping him and modulating his praises.[3] The Egyptians expressed the name of the Supreme Being by a word of *seven* vowels,[4] and the association of seven with the Great Spirit was apparently universal.[5]

It is evident that the mystic has in all ages conceived himself as a miniature facsimile of the Spiritual Powers above him, and there is small doubt that the devisers of these Bear emblems, self-applying the words of Isaiah,[6]

[1] *The Rigveda*, E. V. Arnold, p. 19.
[2] Dutt, p. 10.
[3] *The Hindoos*, p. 155.
[4] *The Gnostics*, King, p. 319.
[5] Plutarch, discussing the symbolism of numbers, says : " And what need is there to talk about the others when the Seven, sacred to Apollo, will alone exhaust the whole day, should one attempt to enumerate all its properties? In the next place, we shall prove that the Wise Men quarrelled with common custom as well as with long tradition, when they pushed down the Seven from its place of honour and dedicated the Five unto the god as the more properly pertaining to him."—*On the E at Delphi.*
[6] lix. 9–11.

regarded themselves as little bears : " We wait for light,
but behold obscurity : for brightness, but we walk in
darkness.   We roar all like bears and mourn sore like
doves."   Wherefore, continues Isaiah, the Almighty
wondered that there was no intercession, and, cloaking
Himself with zeal, raised up a standard against His
enemies.   The call of the Spirit was symbolised by the
Horn associated with the designs herewith.

Observe how at the sound of this Horn the Great
Bear is awakened from the impassive pose of the preceding

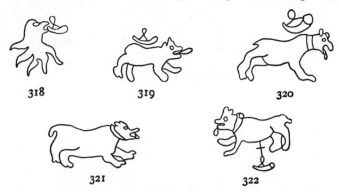

318   319   320

321   322

designs and transported into an attitude of fury.   " According to their deeds," says Isaiah, " accordingly He will repay
fury to His adversaries." [1]

That the Horn typified the Call of the Spirit is manifest
from the S of *Spiritus* in fig. 323, and by the SS of *Sanctus
Spiritus* introduced into figs. 326 and 325.   Note also the
Cross of Lux surmounting fig. 324.

There is a MS. in the British Museum (eleventh
century), wherein DAVID is represented receiving inspiration
from the Holy Spirit in the form of a Dove.   Overhead
the Divine Hand projects from a cloud and extends a Horn,
from which issue *five* flames or rays of light.[2]

[1] lix. 18.   [2] Cf. *Christian Symbolism*, Mrs Henry Jenner, p. 40.

The Three Rays striking down on to fig. 328 are the Three Light Rays that occur frequently in Egyptian hieroglyphics;[1] the more modern descendant of these three rays is the three-lobed Fleur de Lys, whence the heraldic three feathers of the Prince of Wales.

In Scandinavian mythology the Horn was fabled to be

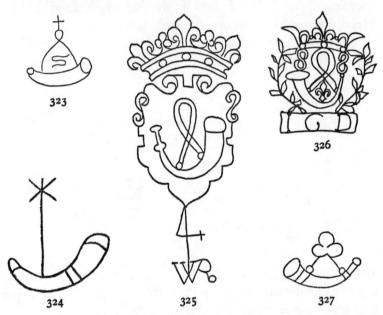

323

326

324   325   327

preserved under Yggdrasill, the sacred world-tree. According to the Finns, it was in "the midst of Heaven," and the *Kalevala* attributes to it the same magical properties of making the desert blossom like the rose, as were assigned to the Holy Grail—

> " Fetch the cow-horn from a distance,
> Fetch it from the midst of heaven ;
> Bring the mead-horn down from heaven,
> Let the honey-horn be sounded.

[1] *Signs and Symbols of Primordial Man*, A. W. Churchward, *passim*.

" Blow into the horn then strongly,
And repeat the tunes resounding ;
Blow then flowers upon the hummocks,
Blow then fair the heathland's borders :
Make the meadow's borders lovely,
And the forest borders charming,
Borders of the marshes fertile." [1]

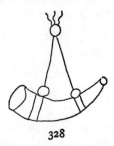

328

The ineffable music of this mystic horn is introduced by
Tennyson as a prelude to the vision of the Holy Grail—

" At dead of night I heard a sound
As of a silver horn from o'er the hills
Blown, and I thought, ' It is not Arthur's use
To hunt by moonlight ' ; and the slender sound,
As from a distance beyond distance grew,
Coming upon me—O never harp nor horn,
Nor aught we blow with breath, or touch with hand,
Was like that music as it came." [2]

Sometimes the Horn was dulcet in its call ; at other
times it was the thunderous trumpet rally of the gods, and
it figures significantly in our fairy-tale of Jack the Giant
Killer. Jack, having overcome certain notorious giants,
arrives at the enchanted castle of the infamous GALLIGANTUA.
Aided by a wicked conjurer, GALLIGANTUA has betrayed
many knights and ladies into his castle, and by black
magic has transformed them into disgraceful shapes. On

[1] Runo, xxxii.　　　　[2] *The Holy Grail.*

advancing to the attack of this castle of iniquity, the hero Jack finds hanging up on the outer door a golden horn strung on a silver chain, and underneath the horn are inscribed the lines :

> "Whoever shall this trumpet blow
> Shall soon the giant overthrow,
> And break the black enchantment straight ;
> So all shall be in happy state." [1]

Jack sounds a blast, whereupon the castle trembles to its vast foundations, and the giant and the conjuror, thrown into horrid confusion, tear their hair and bite their thumbs at the knowledge that their infamous reign is at an end. In due course Jack slays the giant, the transformed lords and ladies are set free and return to their proper shapes, and the enchanted castle crumbles away into the air like a wisp of smoke.[2] It is probable that this fairy-tale is a veiled allegory, that the enslaved and transformed lords and ladies typify the noble qualities and principles of the mind or City of the Soul, and that the wicked giant is the personification of Vice, Selfishness, or Mammon, just as the giants of mythology, which the Greeks portrayed with dragon-like tails, typified the lusts and passions of the soul. It was prettily feigned by the story-tellers that the giants devoured sheep and oxen, *i.e.* the innocent and industrious principles in the little world of Man.

In Northern mythology the Horn figures as the property of HEIMDAL, the watchman of the gods,[3] who was stationed by the Rainbow Bridge into Valhalla, where he maintained an unsleeping vigil against the attacks and machinations of the giants. "I am forced to the conclusion," says Professor

[1] *English Fairy Tales*, J. Jacobs, p. 111.

[2] The story of Jericho collapsing at the sound of the silver trumpets is probably a variant of this fable.

[3] "Heimdal was originally identical with Tyr, said to be the source of our word Tuesday."—*Northern Mythology*, F. Kaufmann, p. 69.

Rydberg, "that Heimdal . . . belongs to the ancient Aryan Age, and retained even to the decay of the Teutonic heathendom his ancient character as the personal representative of the sacred fire."[1] At the clarion call of HEIMDAL's horn, the gods and heroes mustered for the contest, it being said that there were five hundred and eighty doors in Valhalla, and that eight hundred[2] warriors poured out from each door when they heard the summons "to fight the wolf."[3] According to MILTON, "The towers of heaven are filled with armed watch," and on the attack of Satan :

> "Michael did sound
> The Archangel trumpet : through the vast of Heaven
> It sounded, and the faithful armies rang
> Hosanna to the Highest."[4]

In French Romance the far-famed Horn figures as the property of the legendary hero ROLAND, and the Horn of Roland is said to have been a widely understood symbol of heretical preaching.[5] According to the French legend, it had the terrific power of shattering the granite rocks, and of making itself heard full fifteen leagues away. So terrible was the endeavour with which ROLAND sounded his mystic horn that his temples cracked with the effort, and the blood streamed from his mouth. Yet, runs the story, his pains were not fruitless, for "now the Frenchmen listen." Fig. 329 may represent equally well either ROLAND careering on horseback and rallying the Frenchmen with his rousing call, or HEIMDAL, the Scandinavian hornblower, mounted upon his famous steed Goldtop,[6] and assembling the Heroes for the final fight.

---

[1] *Teutonic Myth*, p. 405.
[2] 800=the hundredfold regenerate (?).
[3] *The Edda*, p. 33.   [4] *Paradise Lost*, vi.
[5] *Dante*, Eugene Aroux.
[6] *Northern Mythology*, F. Kaufmann, p. 83.

It was an ancient custom in the Scottish Highlands to summon the clans for war by means of a fiery cross carried swiftly by fleet messengers from place to place. This mysteri-

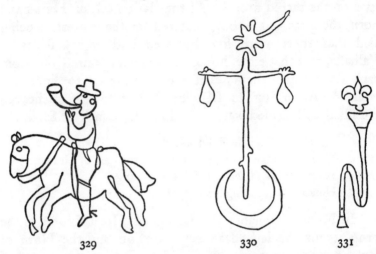

329   330   331

ous but never-failing call to arms consisted of a small cross of light wood dipped into the blood of a goat and set aflame at its extremities. Fig. 330 appears to illustrate this mystic summons. The cross is poised between the horns of the

332   333   334

awakening and rallying Moon ; its summit is being anointed with what a mystic would term " the inundating fire of the Void," and the objects hanging from the extended arms represent presumably either drops of blood or flecks of flame. Figs. 331 and 332 illustrate the inspiring call of the Prophet JOEL, " Blow ye the trumpet in Zion and sound an alarm in my Holy Mountain," and again, " Blow the trumpet in Zion, sanctify a fast, call a solemn assembly, gather the people, sanctify the congregations." This blowing of the trumpet was a prelude to the Millennium when "the Lord shall utter His voice before His army, for His camp is very great."[1]

"Mine eyes have seen the glory of the coming of the Lord ;
He has sounded forth the trumpet that shall never call retreat."

Over the Horn shown in fig. 333 is a hammer-head, expressive of the verse, " Is not my word like as a fire ? saith the Lord ; and *like a hammer* that breaketh the rock in pieces ?"[2] In conjunction with the Horn of fig. 334 is a flame in the form of a sword.

At times the symbolic Horn was associated with a Bell which, according to DURANDUS, typified "acute" and insistent preaching. The Bell formed an essential element in Oriental religious usage, and in Celtic Christianity it was regarded by new converts as the actual type of the Godhead.[3] Of the 258 Bell emblems illustrated by Mons. Briquet, 239 are decorated with *three*fold tops, the trefoil, the Fleur de Lys, or the three circles of Perfection—and all the designs herewith are associated by similar emblems of the Deity. Fig. 336 is distinguished by the initials of Jesus Redemptor, and there is little doubt that the symbolists regarded the Bell not only as the call of CHRIST, but as a sign of CHRIST Himself. It is related that whenever the faith or the right was in jeopardy, a Bell rang in the Temple of the Sangreal and that on the sounding of that Bell a Knight went forth sword in hand in its defence.

Bells were fabled to possess the power of dispelling plagues, storms, and unclean spirits, and ST ANTHONY, whose experience with evil spirits was proverbially ex-

[1] Joel ii. 11.
[2] Jeremiah xxiii. 29.
[3] *The Gnostics*, King, C. W., p. 72 (1st edition).

tensive, is said to have gone among the ruined temples of paganism routing out by means of his bell the devils that infested them. At the modern consecration of a bell, the Bishop says prayers over it which abound in mystic allusions ; amongst others, to the trumpet destroying the walls of Jericho and the thunder driving back the Philistines

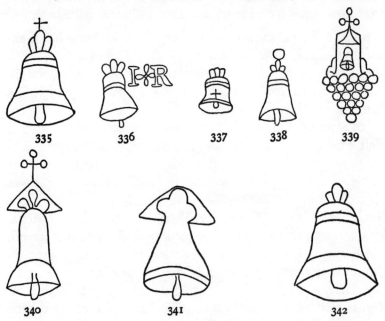

335   336   337   338   339

340   341   342

at Samuel's sacrifice.[1] The *Golden Legend* opens with Satan and the spirits of the air sweeping around the unsilenceable bells and striving in vain to dash down and destroy them.

The Bells of the Spirit—that octave of the Renaissance which the mystics kept pealing throughout the long vigil of the Dark Ages, are related to

"The cheerful cock, the sad night's comforter,
Waiting upon the rising of the sun." [2]

---

[1] *Curious Myths of the Middle Ages*, S. Baring-Gould, p. 609.
[2] *Cornelia*, T. Kyd, 1595.

Figs. 343 to 348 represent this "native bellman of the night" who

> "Rings his silver bell to each sleepy wight
> That should their minds up to devotion call." [1]

Although the cock was regarded with disfavour by the orthodox church as being somewhat of a devil's messenger

343   344

345   346   347

for having crowed at Peter's denial, among the poets it has universally been hailed as the Trumpeter of Day. "Methought I saw," writes one of the Elizabethans—

> "A royal glimmering light streaming aloft,
> As Titan mounted on the lion's back
> Had clothed himself in fiery pointed beams,
> To chase the night and entertain the morn,
> Yet scarce had Chanticler rung the midnight peal." [2]

---

[1] *Faerie Queene*, Spenser, Bk. 5, canto vi.
[2] *The Order of the Garter*, Geo. Peele, 1593.

The cock figures in Scandinavian mythology under the name of Gullinkambi (*i.e.* goldcomb), and his mission, like that of HEIMDAL, was to awaken and speed forth the Heroes.[1]

The origin of Chanticler's symbolism was probably twofold. He hailed the rising sun and he possessed a crimson comb, which one may surmise, was taken to represent the zigzagged effulgence of the day and the "fiery-pointed beams" of morning. Thus the Cock was doubly sacred to the Sun, and he was regarded as the Herald who announced the Coming of APOLLO.

> "Father of Lights! what sunny seed,
> What glance of day hast Thou confin'd
> Into this bird? To all the breed
> This busy ray Thou hast assign'd;
> Their magnetism works all night,
> And dreams of Paradise and light."[2]

It is a point of Chinese faith that their sun and Saviour ZAS enters the world at midnight of the 24th day of the 12th month. On that occasion a golden cock which is said to be seated on the topmost bough of the Tree of Life does not wait for the dawn, but in honour of the advent of the spiritual sun crows all night long. The character of this allegoric cock is pointed by the statement that when he begins to crow, "all the cocks in the world are thus stirred up and begin to crow." The Chinese believe that it is the cock's function to awaken the glorious sun which, in dispelling darkness, is held to disperse the evil spirits of night. These spirits, so the Chinese think, abhor the truth of the Sun's light and shrink back into the darkness of Hell.[3] That the cock was the special foe of demons

[1] *Northern Mythology*, Kaufmann, p. 96.   [2] H. Vaughan.

[3] Presumably this is the origin of the popular idea that ghosts necessarily slink home at cockcrow. Mr J. W. Johnston has several ancient lamps made in *cock* form.

and the power of darkness was similarly the belief of other nations, and, in the *Avesta*, ORMUZ Himself is made to translate the morning song of the cock into the words : "Rise ye men and praise the justice which is most perfect. Behold the demons are put to flight ! "[1] In the symbolic writing of the Chinese the Sun is still represented by a cock in a circle,[2] and a conscientious Parsee would suffer death rather than be guilty of the crime of killing one. In fig. 348 the Bird of Dawn is clapping his golden wings as the Sun rises behind him.

348

Just recently Chanticler has been rather prominently before the public owing to the genius of M. Rostand, the Provençal poet. The symbolism of M. Rostand's drama is described by M. Jean Delaire[3] as follows :—

"Chantecler is the type not only of *evolving*, but of *evolved* humanity. He is man as he may be, man as he will be when he has fully realised the divinity latent within him. He typifies the humanity of the future, as well as of the past and the present.

"At first we see Chantecler as man only ; at the close of

---

[1] *Teutonic Mythology*, Rydberg, p. 305.
[2] *Symbolic Language of Art and Mythology*, R. Payne-Knight, p. 70.
[3] In *The Occult Review*.

the sublime poem we see him as the God-in-man. We hail in him a humanity that has learned its supreme lesson, that has reached a point in its evolution when it not only perceives the Ideal, but is willing to die for it; when it is not only ready to die for it, but—infinitely more difficult task—to realise it in its daily life. Its ideal has become the ideal of *service for love's sake*, "The utmost for the Highest."

"His illusions shattered, his dream dispelled, his love alienated, his message ridiculed, Chantecler yet rises above despair; nay, in his hour of despair he is stronger than ever, more absolutely convinced of his mission, more completely faithful to his trust. He *will* believe in his heaven-appointed task, even though heaven itself seems against him, even though the sun has risen while he, Chantecler, listened, entranced, to the voice of the Nightingale. He *will* believe himself necessary to Nature's plan : For is not man himself one of the cosmic forces that shape the world ?

"Who knows, he asks with the sublime audacity of genius, who knows that if I sing daily my song of dawn, and after me, in other farms, other birds take up the refrain of my song, every morn, for a long, long while, who knows if some day—some day—there will be no more night ?

> '. . . Si je chante, exact, sonore, et si, sonore,
> Exact, bien après moi, pendant longtemps encore,
> Chaque ferme a son Coq qui chante dans sa cour,
> Je crois qu'il n'y aura plus de nuit !
> —Quand ?
> —Un jour ! '

"Was any system of idealistic philosophy ever more precise in its message and its promise ? *Think* the ideal, *live* the ideal, and it becomes the real, it weaves itself into our daily life, it becomes part of ourself, it becomes our truest, inmost self. Let all mankind cherish lofty ideals, love the light, desire the light, summon the light in its daily aspirations, and lo, the light is there, illumining the world—the inner world—for ever.

Chantecler does not know *when* this day will dawn, but — it will come — 'some day ' — and meanwhile — ' to work ! ' "

CHAPTER VII

KING SOLOMON

"Man is not dust, man is not dust, I say!
   A lightning substance through his being runs;
A flame he knows not of illumes his clay—
   The cosmic fire that feeds the swarming suns.
As giant worlds, sent spinning into space,
   Hold in their centre still the parent flame;
So man, within that undiscovered place—
   His centre—stores the light from which he came.

"Man is not flesh, man is not flesh, but fire!
   His senses cheat him and his vision lies.
Swifter and keener than his soul's desire,
   The flame that mothers him eludes his eyes.
Pulsing beneath all bodies, ere begun;
   Flashing and thrilling close behind the screen,
A sacred substance, blinding as the sun,
   Yearns for man's recognition in the seen."
                                      ANGELA MORGAN.

THE ancients supposed that the soul consisted of four elements, fire, air, earth, and water; and that these, when united, took the form of fire and became *flame*. This heavenly composition was scattered like seed among men and animals, where it became mingled in various proportions with earth, and its purity more or less alloyed and impaired. It was believed that after death the impurities of matter were purged away by immersing the soul in water, ventilating it in the currents of the wind, or refining it by fire. The Supreme Spirit was idealised as im-

maculate fire and symbolised as a pure and elemental flame
burning in infinitude.

Among the Chinese, this infinite One was regarded as
a fixed point of dazzling luminosity, around which circled

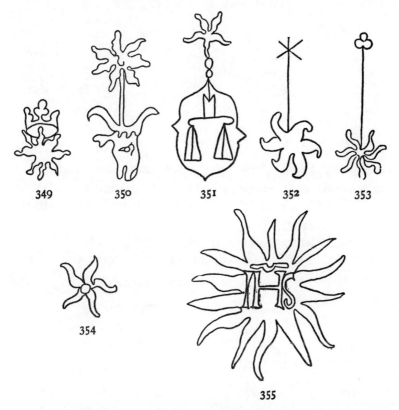

349   350   351   352   353

354

355

in the supremest glory of motion the souls of those who
had successfully passed through the ordeals of earth and
had adequately purified their corporeal grossness.[1]

In the preceding chapter an illustration was given of
the head of an Eagle associated with the cosmic Flame.
This spiritual Fire of the Universe is shown herewith as

[1] H. A. Giles, *Religions of Ancient China*, p. 48.

the goal of ascent, and in figs. 350–353 it appears as one of the Ways. The letters I H S forming the centre of fig. 355 prove Jesus Christ to have been identified with the Fire of Life, and the contraction mark surmounting the

356   357   358

monogram I H S shows that these letters were correctly understood and employed in their original meaning I H S O U S, not in their modern misinterpreted sense (*J*)*esus* (*S*)*alvator* *H*(*ominum*).

From Flame as the symbol of Spirit, to the Sun, the Centre and Sustainer of the material Universe, the Primal

359   360   361

Source and Origin in whose light and warmth creation lives and moves and has its being, is less than a step. In the Sun emblems here reproduced the solar features are not clumsily executed, but prove upon close scrutiny to be supplementary symbols.

Three small circles of perfection form the Face of fig. 359. The Heart of fig. 360 is the symbol of Love, and if

fig. 361 be turned upside down, there is revealed the sign
of the cross.

The S of *Spiritus* is attached to fig. 361 and this S also
appears in the centres of figs. 362, 364 and 365.   Into the
face of fig. 362 the deviser has ingeniously introduced the
crescent moon, and the alternating sharp and twisting rays
of fig. 366 probably denote respectively the piercing beams
of Light and the flaming fires of Love.

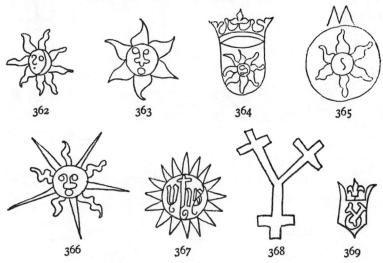

The centre of fig. 367 is not the conventional I H S, but
reads Y H S, Y being the initial of Yesha, an equivalent of
Jesous.   This letter Y is sometimes found in the form of
a separate symbol and is of vast antiquity.   It is reverenced
in China, where it is known as the Great Unit or the Great
Term, and its three limbs are said to denote Three-in-One
and One-in-Three.[1]   Fig. 368 is composed of three equal
crosses, fig. 369 is associated with the Circle of Perfection,
figs. 370 and 371 are hallowed by the cross, and the tail of
fig. 373 is woven into the S of *Spiritus*.

[1] H. A. Giles, *Religions of Ancient China.*

The Sun—a universal symbol of the Deity—was often represented as a wheel, and figs. 374–378 show this wheel emblem in the course of its evolution. The rays constituted

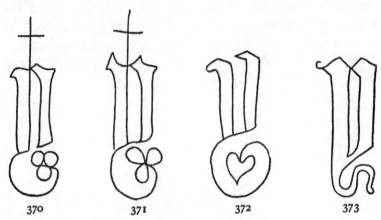

370   371   372   373

the spokes and the Perfect ONE was regarded as both centre and circumference.[1]

The simplest form of Sun Wheel or the Excellent Wheel of Good Law is a circle quartered into four seg-

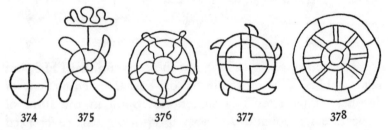

374   375   376   377   378

ments. In figs. 375 and 376 this idea is seen somewhat elaborated, and we shall meet later with other forms, some infinitely more complex.

Underneath fig. 379 is a capital B, and at times this sacred initial was, like Y, employed as a separate symbol. The letter B stood for Brahma, the Breath of all that

[1] *Sacred Mysteries among the Mayas*, Le Plongeon, p. 55.

moves and of everything that is fixed, the "Gem of the Sky," the "Saviour," and the "Lord of Stars."

According to the Vedas, "what the sun and light are to this visible world, that are the supreme good and truth to the intellectual and visible universe ; and as our corporeal

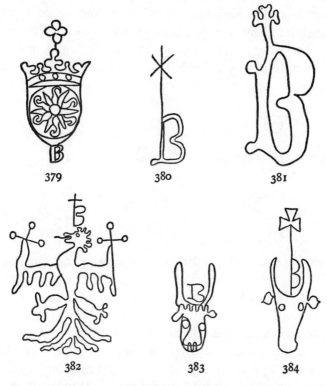

379   380   381

382   383   384

eyes have a distinct perception of objects enlightened by the sun, thus our souls acquire certain knowledge, by meditating on the light of truth which emanates from the Being of Beings : that is the light by which alone our minds can be directed in the path to beatitude."[1]

Brahma was the "Being of Beings," the "most excellent

[1] *The Hindoos*, p. 153

Ray," and the giver of effulgence. The letter B forms the centre of the Sun-wheel herewith, and forms an expressive hieroglyph of the belief that the universe "is created from and by Brahma *as the web from the spider* and as the sparks from fire." [1]

Not only was Brahma represented to be the Spinner of Creation, but, says Dr. Barnett, " He is sometimes typified macrocosmically by the purusha in the Sun." The word *purusha* literally means " man," and in figs. 386 and 387 this man within a solar wheel, or Figure in the Sun, is unmistakably depicted. In one hand He carries a palm

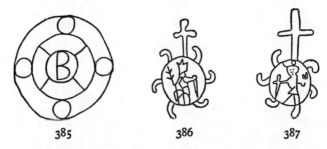

385   386   387

or olive branch, and in the other the sword of the Spirit ; in both cases He is portrayed crowned, and in fig. 386 is apparently throned. A Vedic *Te Deum* addressed to this Spiritual Lord of Light runs : " I know that Great Spirit, sun-hued, beyond the darkness. Knowing Him, man escapes Death ; there is no other way to walk. A Great Lord is the Spirit, mover of the understanding, ruler of this pure approach, Light unfading. The Spirit dwells ever as inward soul, an inch in stature, within men's hearts, conceived by the heart, the imagination, the thought ; deathless they become who know this. He knows what may be known, but there is none to know Him. Men call Him the Primal, the Great Spirit. Subtler than the

[1] *Brahma Knowledge*, L. D. Barnett, p. 21.

subtle is He, greater than the great, the soul lodged in covert in living things. I know Him the ageless, ancient, All-soul. That same is the Fire, that is the Sun, that the Wind, that the Moon ; that same is the Bright, that Brahma, that the Waters, that the Creator, that is the Un-fading, that is the lovely (Light) of Savita ; thence has streamed forth the ancient intelligence." [1]

The Egyptians defined "Spirit" as a subtle Fire,[2] and a similar opinion existed among the Hindoos, in whose conception this mystic element spread until it permeated the streams, quivered in the trees, and, in fact, pervaded the universe.

This Oriental theory of the Oversoul has been familiarised to English readers by Emerson, and it has also been condensed with felicity by Alexander Pope in the familiar lines :

> " All are but parts of one stupendous whole,
> Whose body nature is, and God the soul."[3]

The impersonal and abstract conception of the Vital Fire was known as Brahm, and Brahm the impersonal and invisible is not to be confounded with Brahma, the First Person in the Hindoo Trinity.

Of Brahm, the oversoul and origin of Fire, man was assumed to be a spark, and hence arose the apparent paradox :
" This my self within my heart is tinier than a rice-corn, or a barley-corn, or a mustard-seed, or a canary-seed, or the pulp of a canary-seed. This my self within my heart is greater than sky, greater than heaven, greater than these words. . . . This my self within my heart, this is Brahma, to Him shall I win on going hence."[4]

This goal of Ascent is represented in fig. 389 as a

---

[1] Condensed from pp. 98–101, *Brahma Knowledge*.
[2] *The Hindoos*, p. 144.
[3] *Essay on Man*, see Bk. i. 244–257,
[4] *Hinduism*, L. D. Barnett, p. 15.

flaming Sun, in fig. 388 as a solar wheel, in figs. 383 and 384 as the letter B, and in figs. 390, 391, and 392 as a seven-fold Fire or rose of flame. I am inclined to think that this flame, fire, rose, circular cloud, or whatever it may be (see centre of fig. 393), was deliberately represented as inchoate and incomprehensible.

In fig. 394 the relation of Brahm, the Mighty Breath, to

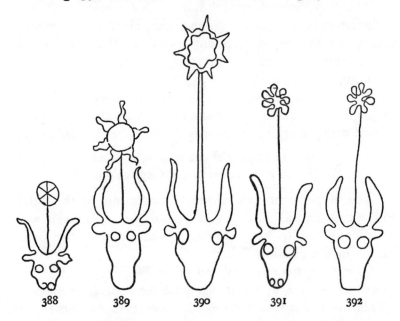

388   389   390   391   392

the mystic Hierarchy is diagrammatically expressed, Brahm, the Oversoul or "Cloud of Unknowing," surmounting the Trimurti or threefold manifestation of Himself.

Attached to the B of fig. 395 are the supplementary letters S and B, between which appears an index finger. As S almost invariably reads *Spiritus,* and the pointing hand presumably implies *nota bene,* this emblem may be deciphered as Spirit = Brahma. The S figures again in the Millenniary emblem below, and the B of fig. 397 is so ingeniously formed that its extremities read S S. In fig. 398 the summit of the B consists of the pastoral crook of the Good Shepherd.

Associated with the Suns on page 142 are the numerals 33, and in figs. 401 and 402 these numbers form the subject of separate emblems. The number 33 was reverenced in

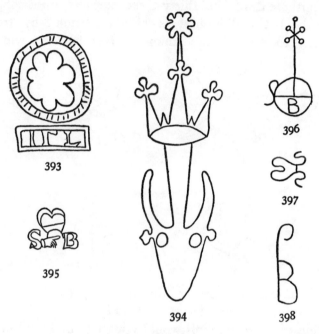

393

395

394

396

397

398

ancient Egypt, and is illustrated in *Signs and Symbols of Primordial Man*. There were reckoned to be 33 Mysteries, " the secrets of which," says Dr Churchward, " have up to the present time not been discovered." [1] The Mexicans portrayed 26 Lights, plus the seven stars of the Great Bear, *i.e.* a total of 33.[2] Centuries ago the world of Vedic religion " swarmed," we are told, " with gods " ; " yet," says Dr Barnett, " the number is usually given as *thirty-three*." [3]

[1] Pp. 117, 177.　　　[2] P. 272.　　　[3] *Hinduism*, p. 10.

The Christian Gnostics taught that the emanations from the Deity were "all summed up in one absolute Unity, 33 in all,"[1] and the age of Christ at the time of His Resurrection was computed as 33.[2] The authors of *The Perfect Way* state, "The age of full and final perfection for the man regenerate is the age of 33, mystically computed, thus implying his accomplishment of the thirty-three steps of initiation, of which the last and highest is his "ascension" by transmutation to final divine union.[3] Over fig. 401 will be

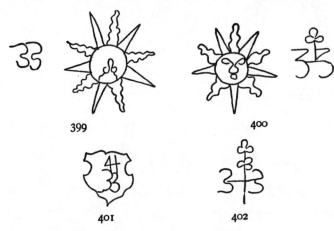

399   400

401   402

noticed a combination of the figure 4 (= the Divine Equilibrium) and the letter H (= Hierarch ?). The explanation of these symbols would appear to be found in the following passage from *The Perfect Way*: "In order to gain 'Power and the Resurrection,' a man must first of all be a *Hierarch*, that is to say he must have attained the magical age of 33 years. . . . He who shall attain to this perfection must be one who is without fear and without desire, save towards God. . . . Only when he has attained this equilibrium is he 'free.' Meanwhile, he

---

[1] *The Wedding Song of Wisdom*, G. R. S. Mead, p. 36.
[2] *Our Lady in Art*, Mrs H. Jenner, xxvii.   [3] P. 235.

makes Abstinence, Prayer, Meditation, Watchfulness, and Self-restraint to be the decades of his rosary. And knowing that nothing is gained without toil, or won without suffering, he acts ever on the principle that to labour is to pray, to ask is to receive, to knock is to have the door open, and so strives accordingly." [1]

I am told by a Freemason that there are 33 lights in a Masonic Lodge, 33 steps on entering the Lodge, and that the degrees in Freemasonry proceed from one upwards to ten or twelve, whence there is a sudden jump to the thirty-third and highest.

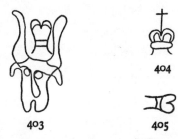

404

403   405

Among the numerous specimens of the letter B collected and classified by Mons. Briquet,[2] are some which are as much like M's as B's, and one of these combination M-B's surmounts fig. 403. The letter M when found in association with a Bull or a Sun emblem probably stood for MITHRA, the God of Sunlight. In Mithraism—the religion taught by ZOROASTER—MITHRA, the Sunlight, stands in the same relation to ORMUZ, the Supreme Sun, as in Christianity CHRIST, the Sun of Righteousness, stands to God the Father. In the circle of Perfection herewith are the letters M A surmounted by a mark of contraction, and these same letters reappear in fig. 407, where they are, in all probability, a contracted form of the word MITHRA.

The Persian MITHRA corresponds in many respects to

<hr />

[1] Pp. 222–223.   [2] *Les Filigranes.*

the Hindoo INDRA, and, Indra-like, MITHRA was the invincible leader of the celestial hosts, and the relentless enemy of suffering, sterility, vice, and impurity. With his " thousand ears and his ten thousand eyes," MITHRA was ever awake, and everlastingly on the watch to protect the world from the malignant hosts of Darkness. MITHRA as a warrior was not only the God of warriors and the Protector of all brave deeds and chivalrous adventures, but, like OSIRIS and other Culture Gods, he was the fecundator of all nature, the lord of wide pastures, and the giver of herds.

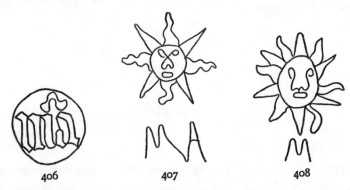

406   407   408

It was MITHRA who poured forth the waters and was the causer of growing plants. Not only was he the bestower of material benefits, but he was also likewise the giver of peace of heart and the maker of concord among all who worshipped him. Mr Mead states : " The secret of regeneration, of being born anew, or spiritually, or from above—in brief, the divinising of man—was the last word of the Mithra rites ; all else is introductory or ancillary." [1]

The worship of Mithra was at one time very widely extended, and is said to have been maintained in an unbroken tradition through the secret societies of the Middle Ages, until it came into the hands of the Rosicrucians, and

[1] *The Mysteries of Mithra*, p. 47.

thence by a faint reflex to the Freemasonry of our own times.[1]

MITHRA, as the mediator between Light and Darkness,[2] presented so many points of identity to Jesus Christ that the perplexed Fathers of Christianity were forced to the conclusion that paganism was aping their sacred rites. Tertullian complained that the devil by guile had perverted the truth and " emulously mimics even the precise particulars of the divine sacraments by the mysteries of idols. He, too, baptizes some—of course his own believers and faithful ; he promises the remission of sins by a bath. If I still remember rightly, Mithra there signs his soldiers on their foreheads, celebrates also the offering of bread, introduces an image of the resurrection, and purchases for himself a crown at the sword's point." [3]

It is well known that in the transition from paganry to Christianity the Christian clergy, finding it impossible to wean the populace from old customs or to eradicate primitive beliefs, discreetly met the situation by diverting pagan festivals to the honour of Christ. It is not so generally known that December 25th, the Christmas Day of Christendom, was necessarily thus fixed for the reason that this date was the birthday of MITHRA, and that the obdurate heathen flatly refused to relinquish their cherished festival. It was not until A.D. 400 that the Church Fathers accepted the inevitable and tactfully adopted the Birthday of MITHRA as the official Birthday of Christianity. At the beginning of the fifth century S. Chrysostom, referring to the festival of the pagan Sun god, wrote : " On this day also the birthday of Christ *was lately fixed* at Rome in order that, while the heathens were busy with their profane ceremonies, the

[1] *The Gnostics*, King, p. 117.
[2] *Fragments of a Faith Forgotten*, Mead, p. 56.
[3] *The Mysteries of Mithra*, Mead, pp. 56, 57.

Christians might perform their sacred rites undisturbed. They call this (25th December) the birthday of the Invincible One (Mithra) ; but who is so invincible as the Lord ? They call it the Birthday of the Solar Disc ; but Christ is the Sun of Righteousness."[1]

The twenty-fifth day of the twelfth month in the year was the birthday of ZAS, the Saviour Sun of ancient China, and it was also the birthday of the Egyptian gods OSIRIS and HORUS, of the Greek DIONYSOS, of the Hindoo VISHNU, and of the Syrian TAMMUZ.[2] The cock which

409

signalised the advent of Zas was also sacred to Mithra, Phœbus, and, in fact, to the Sun deities of practically all nations. When perched at the summit of a pillar, as in the figure herewith, the emblem was, I am told, known as the "Cock of Abraxas." The name ABRAXAS, which is at the root of the famous magic-word Abracadabra, was one of the numerous mystery words coined to express mathematically the unspeakable name of the Supreme Spirit. "Abraxas" was accepted as a mystic equivalent of "MITHRAS," because the numerical values of the two names both alike work out to the number 365. It was asserted that there were as many heavens as there were days in the year, and

[1] *Romance of Symbolism*, S. Heath, p. 37.
[2] *Aryan Sun Myths*, anon., pp. 62, 65, 71, 84.

the number 365 was a convenient expression for the Lord of these 365 spheres.[1] Among the Assyrians, MERODACH, the Sun god, was known by a different name during each month of the year,[2] and the twelve signs of the Zodiac were once seemingly twelve aspects of the One Great Spirit.

MERODACH was regarded as a solar deity, as the mediator between gods and men, and as the God who raised the dead to life.[3] He corresponds in his attributes and symbols to the Persian MITHRA, and MITHRA was identified with the Greek DIONYSOS.[4] DIONYSOS, like the Egyptian OSIRIS, was

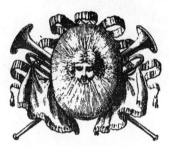

410

"the twice-born" god of regeneration. He is found portrayed as the Sun god seated on a star-spangled globe.[5] His beauty is compared to that of APOLLO, and, like him, he is represented as possessing eternal youth. He is fabled to have marched at the head of an army of men and women inspired by divine fury, and to have achieved his bloodless conquests by teaching mankind the use of the vine, the cultivation of the earth and the making of honey.

The Ox or Bull, which was the symbol of OSIRIS, of MERODACH, and of MITHRA, was also regarded as an

---

[1] *The Gnostics*, King, pp. 254, 259.
[2] *Babylonian and Assyrian Religion*, T. G. Pinches, p. 102.
[3] *Chambers's Encyclopædia*, i. 518.
[4] *The Gnostics*, King, p. 116.
[5] Lemprière, art. "Bacchus."

incarnation of the generative power of DIONYSOS, and the eating of an ox was part of the cult of Dionysos.

Dionysus (Bacchus). (From a Painting at Pompeii.;

411

In fig. 411 [1] this Solar hero is represented with his symbolic animal, the panther.

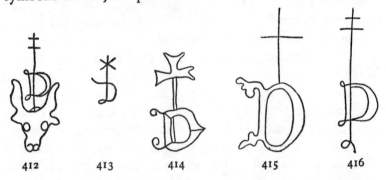

| 412 | 413 | 414 | 415 | 416 |

The letter D surmounting the Bull's Head in fig. 412 is the initial of Dionysos, and this character served also as

[1] Reproduced from Smith's *Classical Dictionary*, by permission of Mr J. Murray.

a separate symbol. In figs. 414–416 it is hallowed with a cross, and in fig. 413 is associated the Star of Light. Our English word "day" (Latin *dies*) is affiliated with the Sanscrit *dyaus*, which is also the root of DIONYSOS, DIANA, DIONE or JUNO, JUPITER, ZEUS, and (presumably) ZAS. Fig. 412 is thus capable of two readings : either as DIONYSOS, the god of day, or as the path of the enduring is as a shining light that shineth more and more unto the Perfect Day.

The name DIONYSOS has survived in the form DENNIS to the present day, and the time-honoured tenet that Man is a spark of the primeval Light is traceable in many other proper names, such as LLEW, LUKE, LUCIUS, LUCY, and similar variants of *Lux* ; in CLARENCE, CLARA, etc., meaning "I shine," in PHŒBE (*shining*), JERMYN (*bright or glittering*), ANNORA (*light*), TRYPHOSA (*very shining*), and BLENDA (*dazzling*).[1]

Etymology offers evidence in every direction, not only of primeval sun-worship, but also of the well-known fact that it was customary for both kings and commoners to style themselves "light of the Sun" or even the Sun itself. The modern name SAMPSON or SAMSON is defined as meaning "splendid sun,"[2] and within historic times the emperors of Peru were entitled "Children of the Sun." The Egyptian City of the Sun known to the Greeks as HELIOPOLIS was originally named ON, and ON is evidently one of the most ancient titles of the Sun. We meet with it in its radical simplicity in the name of the Swedish King ON or AUN, and again in the later forms HACON, HAKON, or HAAKON. I have already (pp. 13–15) given reasons for my

---

[1] These definitions are quoted from Mrs Helena Swan's *Christian Names*, from which I also extract the following : ESDRAS = rising of light ; MALALEEL = shining of God ; ABNER = father of light ; SINDBERT = sparkling bright ; SEABERT = conquering brightness ; NORBERT = brightness ; ETHELBERT = nobly bright.   [2] *Ibid.*

belief that Ac meant great, and it is reasonable to assume that the primary meaning of HACON was "great Sun." There was a town in Macedonia named ACONTISMA. The oldest capital city known to history is the Egyptian HIERACONPOLIS, and the name of this sun-worshipping city is seemingly divisible into *Hier* sacred, *ac* great, *on* sun, *polis* city. The name of the highest peak in the Andes, ACONCAGUA, suggests that this mountain, like many others, was dedicated to and named after the great Sun. We again meet *Akon* in ODAKON,[1] the Sun god of the Philistines, and probably again in the alternative name DAGON, although the *Dag* of this term may be the *Dag* of Day and akin to the proper name DAGOBERT, now said to mean " Daybright."[2]

Mrs Swan interprets the two names EZRA and ZERAH as " Rising of Light," the Ra in both these instances being no doubt cognate with the Egyptian Ra, which not only was the name of the Sun god, but was also the usual Egyptian word for the Sun.[3] The Sanscrit for a prince is *Rajah* and for a King *Rajan*. Lemprière mentions seven ancient cities named ACRA, and the present capital of ASHANTEE bears that name : I suggest that it originally meant "Great Ra."

The once kingly but now common Cornish name CYMBELINE is Celtic for " Lord of the Sun,"[4] and the *Bel* of CYMBELINE is identical with the *Bel* of BELENUS, the Celtic APOLLO ; with the *Bal* of BALDER, the Sun god of Scandinavia ; and with BAAL, the great Sun god of the Phœnicians. It would thus appear probable that BALAK, the King of Moab, styled himself or was thus styled after Great Baal, and that the places named BELLAC in France and BELLEEK in Ireland were originally—like the famous BAALBEC —shrines dedicated to Great Baal, *i.e.* the Sun.

Compare the ODAK of ODAKON with the ODACH of MERODACH.
[2] Mrs Swan.   [3] Renouf, *Hibbert Lectures*, p. 109.   [4] Mrs Swan.

An interesting example of solar nomenclature is found in the word SOLOMON, each syllable of which severally means Sun.[1] Plutarch mentions a people whom he calls "the Solymi,"[2] and Hiero Solyma is a familiar synonym for the New Jerusalem, the Holy City, the spiritual City of the Sun.

There is a vast mythology relating to King SOLOMON, and the splendour of the Wise Man is proverbial in EUROPE, PALESTINE, ABYSSINIA, INDIA, AFGHANISTAN, PERSIA, and ARABIA. It is probable that there really lived some time about 3000 years ago a great personality whose beneficent and prosperous career impressed itself permanently upon the memory of the world ; but it is quite certain that legend has since been busy with his reputation, and that the SOLOMON of literature and legend is, to a large extent, a mythical and ideal hero. Tradition has it that when the great King was summoned from his earthly career he was re-established in the Sun, whence he controlled a vast empire of Fairies, Peris, Jinns, and hosts of radiant guise, who were his obedient vassals and implicitly obeyed his fiat. Mysticism has assumed that the Bridegroom of *The Song of Solomon* is the spiritual Sun of Righteousness risen Christlike with healing in His wings, and there is little doubt that *The Song of Solomon* is indeed a mythical and dramatic love duet between the mystic Sun and Moon.

The belief that SOLOMON was an inveterate sensualist appears to have originated from the literalisation and misconception of the time-honoured poetic fancy that the Sun was the great fecundator and All-Lover whose eye shone impartially upon the just and unjust. The poets frequently describe the Sun as an "amorist," a "hot-eyed amorist," as being "free and general," as shining with "hot eye" upon even the basest weed that grows, and so forth ;

[1] *Sol* is Anglo-Saxon, Icelandic, and Latin, for Sun.
[2] *On the Cessation of Oracles.*

and the apparently contradictory terms applied by the Bride to Solomon are wholly inapprehensible unless understood as being addressed to the divine Sun of the Soul. The Bridegroom is described as coming out of the wilderness like pillars of smoke,[1] an expression suggestive of the pillar of smoke by which the Israelites were led during *daytime* through the wilderness. He is acclaimed as "a precious ointment," as being "comely as Jerusalem," yet "terrible as an army with banners."[2] He is also likened to "a company of horses," and in the question, "Tell me, O thou whom my soul loveth, where thou feedest, where thou makest thy flock to rest at noon,"[3] is probably an allusion to the sacred herds of the Sun. The "dove-eyed" Bridegroom is described as being "in the clefts of the rock and in the secret places of the stairs,"[4] an idea that is nonsense except it be understood as a reference to the all-pervasive character of the Oversoul. "He brought me," says the Bride, "to the banqueting-house, and his banner over me was love"; a phrase suggestive of "The King of Love my Shepherd is." The Bridegroom, speaking of his wine and milk, extends, like Christ, the invitation, "Eat, O friends; drink, yea, drink abundantly, O beloved,"[5] and again, knocking Christlike at the door, he exclaims, "Open to me, my sister, my love, my dove, my undefiled: for my head is filled with dew and my locks with the drops of the night."[6] This passage is obviously the inspiration of the lines :—

> "God's silent, searching flight;
> When my Lord's head is filled with dew, and all
> His locks are wet with the clear drops of night;
> His soft, soft call,
> His knocking time; the soul's dumb watch
> When spirits their fair kindred catch."[7]

---

[1] *Song of Solomon* iii. 6.   [2] vi. 4.   [3] i. 7.
[4] ii. 14.   [5] v. 1.   [6] v. 2.   [7] H. Vaughan.

But the dew-drenched locks of Apollo are a poetic common-place, and in *The Faerie Queene*, for instance, Spenser writes :

> " At last the golden Oriental gate
> Of greater Heaven 'gan to open fair,
> And Phœbus fresh as bridegroom to his mate
> Came dancing forth, *shaking his dewy hair*,
> And hurl'd his glistening beams through gloomy air." [1]

The opener of the Gates of Day was Janus = Dianus = Dionysos, and in fig. 417 the D of Dionysos is associated with the symbol of the mountains, whence, as a Psalmist

417

says, " cometh my relief." The exultation of the Bride at the speedy coming of her Sun-like Lord and champion is expressed in the ecstatic passage : " The voice of my beloved ! Behold, he cometh leaping *upon the mountains*, skipping upon the hills. My beloved is like a roe or a young hart. Behold he standeth behind our wall, he looketh forth at the windows, shewing himself through the lattice.[2] My beloved spake and said unto me, Rise up my love, my fair one, and come away. For, lo, the winter is past, the rain is over and gone ; the flowers appear on the earth, the time of the singing of birds is come, and the voice of the turtle[3] is heard in our land." [4]

[1] Bk. i., canto v., st. 2.
[2] Compare Shakespeare's " Revealing Day through every cranny peeps,'
Lucrece.   [3] The turtle dove = the Holy Spirit.   [4] ii. 8-12.

King Solomon was sometimes represented in the St George-like attitude of a Dragon-slayer, and the Arabians credit him with waging a perpetual warfare against wicked genii and giants.[1] This feature brings Solomon still further into line with ORMUZ, MITHRA, MERODACH, OSIRIS, INDRA, and other Solar Saviours.

By the ancients the Sun was generally depicted as a charioteer driving a team of four horses. This immortal chariot of the Sun is in all probability the subject of the passage : " King Solomon made himself a chariot of the wood of Lebanon. He made the pillars thereof of silver, the bottom thereof of gold, the covering of it of purple, the midst thereof being paved with love." [2] This verse, like the rest of the poem, is a tissue of symbolism. The wood of Lebanon was a simile for incorruptibility,[3] silver typified knowledge, gold was the symbol of wisdom, and purple—a combination of red and blue—presumably denoted a conjunction of the red of Love and the blue of Truth. The assertion that Solomon " *made himself*" a chariot, expresses the vital essence of mysticism, *i.e.*, that man is his own fate and the maker and controller of his own destiny. It was a cardinal doctrine that the humblest individual might in time develop his spark of Personality into a spiritual Sun, and by his own efforts, charioteer-like, drive his soul into the innermost Halls of Heaven. " The righteous," says the writer of Matthew, " shall shine forth as *the sun* in the kingdom of their Father." [4] Elisha is recorded to have had a vision of the mountain of the Lord filled with chariots and horses of fire. The writer of Psalm lviii. refers to the chariots of God being "twenty thousand, even thousands of angels," and the Indian mythologists conceived Indra

---

[1] *Century Cyclopædia of Names*, B. G. Smith, art. " Solomon."   [2] iii.
[3] *Flowers in Language : Association and Tales*, Pratt and Miller, p. 18.
[4] xiii. 43.

and the Immortals driving their cars of light and lustre, which "gemmed the sky like stars at night."[1]

In Bonaventura's *Life of St Francis*, there is narrated an incident which occurred, it is said, in Assisi. According to this account St Francis was sleeping one night in a hut, and was "absent in the body from his sons." Suddenly at about midnight, while some of the brethren were taking rest and others keeping watch, "a chariot of fire of marvellous brightness, entering by the door of the house, turned thrice hither and thither through the dwelling, and over the

418

chariot a shining ball of fire rested, in appearance like unto the Sun, making the night radiant."[2] This phenomenon— an experience to which other mystics have testified and which is illustrated in fig. 418—was known as the "Vision of Adonai."

It is to be inferred that the poet who was responsible for *The Song of Solomon* had personally experienced this coveted "Vision of Adonai," and that he alludes to it in the passage, "I went down into the garden of nuts to see the fruits of the valley and to see whether the vine flourished and the pomegranates budded. *Or ever I was aware my soul made me like the chariots of Amni-nadib.*"[3] The *Song*

---

[1] *Indian Poetry*, Dutt, p. 161.   [2] Ch. iv.

[3] vi. 12. Commentators have imagined this to mean that the heroine was suddenly and forcibly abducted by an admirer.

continues, "Return, return, O Shulamite, return, return that we may look upon thee. What will ye see in the Shulamite ?" The answer, " As it were the company of two armies," is extremely suggestive of the charioteer Host seen and recorded by Elisha : [1] "It came to pass as they still went on and talked that behold, there appeared a chariot of fire and horses of fire and parted them both asunder, and Elijah went up by a whirlwind into Heaven. And Elisha cried ' My father, my father, the chariots of Israel and the horsemen thereof ! And he saw him no more.' " [2]

In the printer's mark above illustrated the team are represented as stumbling at the dazzling radiance of their driver. The horse, as exemplified in subsequent chapters, was the emblem of the Intellect, and the reason for representation of *four* horses is because *four* is the number of equity, and four horses symbolise the discordant faculties of the Mind brought into control and trained to the equipoise of Perfection.

The Hindoos portray the chariot of OM the Sun as being drawn by seven green horses preceded by ARUNA the Dawn and followed by a countless host of good genii.

Among the titles of the Sun are *Dyumani*, "The Gem of the Sky," *Tarani*, "the Saviour," *Grahapati*, "the Lord of the Stars," and *Mitra*, "the Friend," generally understood to mean *friend of the water lily* which expands her petals at the rising of the sun and closes them on his setting.[3] In *The Song of Solomon* the bride is significantly termed "lily of the valley," and the description of her "altogether lovely" bridegroom concludes with the expression, "This is my beloved and this is *my friend*." [4]

In fig. 419 the gentle-eyed Dionysos is portrayed within a Temple, and this pavilion of the Day is curtained with

[1] 2 Kings vi. 17.
[2] 2 Kings lii. 11–12.
[3] *The Hindoos*, pp. 155–157.
[4] vi. 16.

drapery, probably representing "the curtains of Solomon."[1]
The attendant virgins may be equated with those who in
the *Song* applaud the precious name of Solomon. "Therefore do the virgins love thee : Draw me ; we will run after
thee. . . . We will be glad and rejoice in thee, we will
remember thy love more than wine. The upright love

Dionysus (Bacchus) enthroned. (Ponce, Bains de Titus, no. 12.)

419

thee."[2]   "Behold," sings the Bride, " thou art fair my love ;
thou hast doves' eyes. Behold thou art fair, my beloved,
yea, pleasant : also our bed is green. The beams of our
house are cedar, and our rafters of fir."[3]

This mysterious "green" bed has proved such a
stumbling-block to commentators that they have found it
necessary to postulate the existence of a shepherd lover, so
stricken with poverty that all he could bestow upon his
bride was a mean couch of grass. But the colour *Green*

[1] i. 5.   [2] i. 4.   [3] i. 15-17.

was at one time a widely understood emblem of evergreen or everlasting, and this explanation also rationalises the *green* horses of the Hindoo Sun god. The Egyptians placed *green*stone amulets in their tombs as representative of eternal youth and as a type of that which is everlasting, evergreen, fresh, young, and immortal. At the present day both Christians and Mohammedans in Palestine make vows to St George[1] in case of danger and distress, and address him as " the evergreen green one." The " green bed " of Solomon would thus seem to be a poetic allusion to the everlasting nuptials of the Sun, and it follows that the " beams of our house " which " are cedar and our rafters of fir," have reference to the City or Temple of the Sun. The lofty fir-tree was the symbol of elevation,"[2] and the House of Cedar, incorruptible and strong, may be compared to the Temple of Solomon, the symbolic Nova Solyma, the New Jerusalem, the City of the Sun, the spiritual city which lay *four*square and whose length was as large as its breadth.[3]

The tradition that the Temple of Solomon is the Kingdom of Heaven has been restrained—along with much other detritus from mythology and fable—by the Freemasons, whose vocation is avowed to be the rebuilding of the Temple or City of the Soul.

The mystics primary consideration was to transform the dark cave or stable of his individual mind into a miniature Temple of the Holy Spirit ;[4] his next to become a nail, stone, or pillar in the greater cosmic Temple of King Solomon. The covenant, " Him that overcometh will I

[1] *St George for England*, compiled by H. O. F., p. 13.
[2] *Flowers in Language, etc.*, p. 21.
[3] " The length and the breadth and the height of it are equal," Revelation xxi. 16.
[4] " Know ye not that ye are the Temple of God and that the Spirit of God dwelleth in you ? "—1 Corinthians iii. 16.

make a pillar in the Temple of my God "[1] is reflected and expressed in the Pillar designs here illustrated.

During the fifteenth century there seems to have existed in Europe a masonic grade known as the Golden Column.

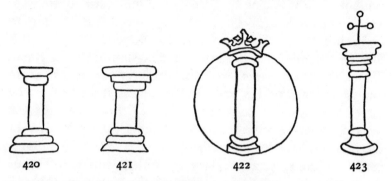

| 420 | 421 | 422 | 423 |

At this period there was published a work entitled *Le Songe de Poliphile*, containing in the form of an acrostic the concealed information that the author was a certain Brother Francis, a "Golden Column of the Templar Order."[2]

| 424 | 425 | 426 |

In the description of the Temple building given in the Book of Kings,[3] it is said that SOLOMON set up two pillars in the porch, naming that on the right-hand Jachin and that

[1] Revelation iii. 12.
[2] *Mystical Traditions*, Cooper Oakley, i. p. 114.
[3] I Kings vii. 21, 22.

on the left Boaz, "and upon the top of the pillars was lily-work; so was the work of the pillars finished." This Fleur de Lis or lily-work is duly apparent in the emblems herewith, and the Fleur de Lis, as we have seen, was a symbol of light. The Star cross of Light surmounting fig. 426 is therefore equivalent to "Lily-work." According to Dr Churchward's *Signs and Symbols of Primordial Man*, this Star-cross symbol was the Hieroglyphic sign of the Egyptian HORUS. HORUS, which was the earlier name of OSIRIS in one or another of his various forms, was described in the sacred writings as "Lord of the Pillars," "the Light of the World," the "Lord of Life and Light," the "Bruiser of the Serpent," the "Conqueror of the Dragon," the "Overcomer of the powers of Darkness and Drought." HORUS the "All-seeing one" was "Lord of the Northern Lights" and "God of the Pole Star," the "Diffuser of Light," the "Giver of rays," the "Teacher of the Way," and was regarded as symbolic of the Power which leads the soul from death, darkness, and ignorance to the mansions of the Blessed. He was the Divine Healer and the Good Physician, the Prince of Peace and Goodwill, the Manifestor of the Ever Hidden Father, and Builder of the Temple of Peace. HORUS "arose from the dead and established himself for ever." He was the representative of eternal youth, the green shoots of trees and of everything that is good. Among his titles was "Prince of the Emerald Stone," and his emblem was the eagle hawk. This evergreen Solar God was said to have rent the veil of the Tabernacle (of the flesh), and among the Druids he was known under the name Hesus.[1] It would seem that the Egyptian Horus and the Christian Jesus both to a large extent personified the same ideal and that there were excellent reasons for the statement

---

[1] *Signs and Symbols of Primordial Man*, pp. 51, 52, 63, 88, 93, 108, 111, 186, 234, 246, 271, 275, 278, 280, 281.

of the Hebrew prophet : " Out of Egypt have I called my son." [1] It is possible that the sacred H here illustrated stands for HORUS, and that the letter O stands for his later appellation OSIRIS. But the letter or word O is itself a hieroglyph for the round sun,[2] and the correctness of my surmise that the ON of SOLOMON and HACON meant sun is somewhat confirmed by the fact that we meet with variants of these names in the forms SALOMO and HACO. Other variations of SOLOMON are SULEIMAN and SOOLEMAUN, which

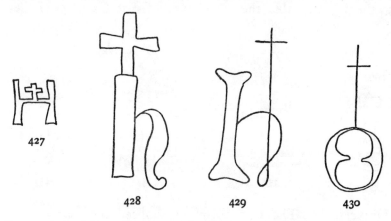

427

428   429   430

become significant in view of the fact that the city of ON is written in the Old Testament in two ways, AUN and AN, both of which are rendered into English by the word ON.[3] It thus becomes more than a coincidence that the King of Sweden was named ON or AUN, and there must be a radical relation between these terms and the OM or AUM of the Hindoos.

In Egypt the letter O originally represented " the emaning mouth of a fish which gives birth to water as the life of the world." It thus represented the water of life,

[1] Hosea xi. 1 ; Matthew ii. 15.
[2] *Anacalypsis*, Higgins, i. 109.
[3] *Origin and Language of Myths*, Kavanagh (Morgan), i. 32.

and was regarded as the symbol and sign of the sustainer of new life and new birth.[1] Within fig. 430 the designer has significantly introduced the regenerative number 8.

The three triangles or rays upon the summit of fig. 431 are a very ancient form of the threefold Light of the World. They represent "the name of the Great Giver of Light" and were used with this significance among the primordial Egyptians, Mexicans, and off-shoot races.[2] These ancient peoples also made wide use of this Dual Pillar symbol, and to them is traceable the expression, "Great Architect of the

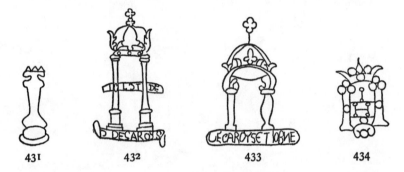

| 431 | 432 | 433 | 434 |

Universe."[3] The two pillars symbolised the gateway of eternity and were used as a type of eternal stability. The precise meaning of each particular pillar has varied slightly among different races and at different epochs, but the ideas underlying them are fundamentally uniform. *Jachin* and *Boaz*, the twin pillars in the porch of King Solomon's Temple, mean Strength and Beauty, and when *three* pillars are represented, as in figs. 442 and 443, they denote Wisdom, Strength, and Beauty.[4] This symbol of *three* pillars occurs among the Hindoos, and was also used by the Mayas of Mexico and the Incas of Peru. Among these it represented

---

[1] *Signs and Symbols of Primordial Man*, Dr Churchward, p. 346.
[2] *Ibid.*, pp. 35–188.   [3] *Ibid.*, p. 159.   [4] *Ibid.*, p. 38.

their Triune God or Trinity. The Egyptians also depicted
their Trinity in the form of three pillars known respectively

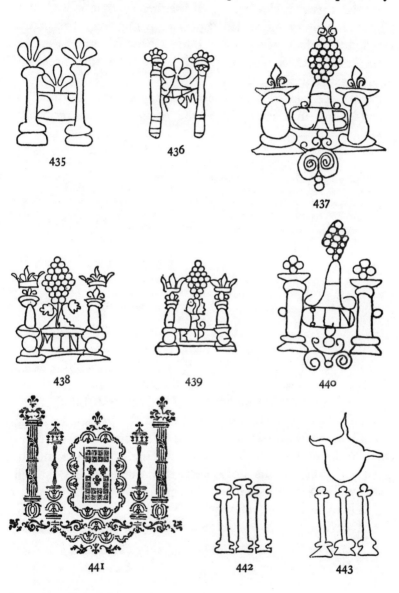

435

436

437

438

439

440

441

442

443

as "Wisdom," "Power," and "Goodness."[1] Judging from the evidence of emblems it may be safely assumed that the three circles which subsequently symbolised the Christian Trinity and which appear above fig. 423, originally typified "Perfect Wisdom," "Perfect Power," and "Perfect Goodness." Over fig. 443 will be noticed the threefold flame of the Perpetual Fire.

Figs. 444 to 446 are described by Mons. Briquet as "nails," and in the minds of the designers these probably

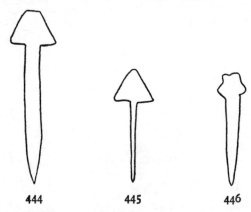

444 445 446

symbolised the promise of Isaiah, "I will fasten him as a nail in a sure place ; and he shall be for a glorious throne to his father's house. And they shall hang upon him all the glory of his father's house."[2] It is also probable that this symbol of the nail had some relation to the passage in Ezra, "And now for a little space grace hath been shewed from the Lord our God, to leave us a remnant to escape, and to give us a nail in his holy place, that our God may lighten our eyes and give us a little reviving in our bondage."[3]

There is further reference to a nail in Zechariah, "The Lord of hosts hath visited his flock, the house of Judah,

[1] *Signs and Symbols of Primordial Man*, Dr Churchward, p. 44.
[2] xxii. 23, 24. [3] ix. 8.

and hath made them as his goodly horse in the battle. Out of Him came forth the corner, out of Him the nail." [1] The expression " corner " here presumably means " corner-stone."

The " corner-stone " here illustrated is presumably

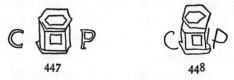

447 448

Christ, " In whom all the building fitly framed together groweth unto an holy temple in the Lord : In whom ye also are builded together for an habitation of God through the Spirit." [2]

Dr Moncure D. Conway [3] has closely identified the character and sayings of Jesus Christ with those of Solomon.

449 450 451

The study of emblems proves that the mystics of the Middle Ages entertained similar notions of this identity, and that in their eyes the glorious Solomon, leaping over the mountains of Bether, was none other than Jesus Christ. The figures herewith may represent the Ruler of Nova Solyma and the Prince of Peace, or it is possible that fig. 449 may be intended for MITHRA, who was generally repre-

[1] x. 3-4. [2] Ephesians ii. 21-22.
[3] Cf. *Solomon and Solomonic Literature.*

sented as a young man with his head covered by a turban, after the manner of the Persians ;[1] but the question need not be debated, for apparently SOLOMON and MITHRA were simply two among many other names for the same personification. The Mexicans portrayed HORUS with an open mouth and pointing finger, representing him as preaching or as a " Sayer of Sayings in the Temple."[2] It will be noticed (see *ante*, p. 27) that the effigies of Jesus Christ are all open-mouthed, and that the portraits of King Solomon herewith similarly depict him as the utterer of wise words. " Because the preacher was wise, he still taught the people knowledge ; yea, he gave good heed, and sought out, and set in order many proverbs. The words of the wise are as goads, and as nails fastened by the masters of assemblies, which are given from one shepherd."[3]

[1] Lemprière.
[2] *Signs and Symbols of Primordial Man*, p. 281.
[3] Ecclesiastes xii. 9, 11.

CHAPTER VIII

THE FAIR SHULAMITE

"Who is she that looketh forth as the morning, fair as the moon, clear as the sun, and terrible as an army with banners?"—SONG OF SOLOMON.

THE qualities attributed to the heroine of *The Song of Solomon* are so numerous, contradictory, and conflicting, that criticism, unable to reconcile them, assumes that the poem does not refer to a single personality, but is an anthology of secular songs used at Semitic marriage festivals, revised and loosely connected by an editor without regard to temporal sequence.[1]

But if, as I have shown reason to suppose, the Bridegroom is King Solomon himself, it naturally follows that the fair Shulamite is she of whom he wrote : " I loved her and sought her out from my youth : I desired to make her my spouse, and I was a lover of her beauty." [2] These words are addressed to the personification of "Wisdom," a word that has nowadays lost its true meaning, and unfortunately fails to convey its original significance. Among the ancients " Wisdom " implied Love and Knowledge blended in perfect and equal proportions. Our English word "Truth " personifies what is perhaps the nearest approach to the original conception ; but " Wisdom " meant more than

[1] *Encyclopædia Biblica*, art. "Canticles," Cheyne.
[2] Wisdom of Solomon viii. 1.

Truth. It was used to personify the Celestial Influence which at a later period was described as the "Holy Spirit." "Wisdom, which is the worker of all good things," says Solomon, "taught me: for in her is an understanding spirit, holy, one only, manifold, subtil, lively, clear, undefiled, plain, not subject to hurt, loving the thing that is good, quick, which cannot be letted, ready to do good. Kind to man, steadfast, sure, free from care, having all power, overseeing all things, and going through all understanding, pure, and most subtil spirits. For wisdom is more moving than any motion : she passeth and goeth through all things by reason of her pureness. For she is the breath of the power of God, and a pure influence flowing from the glory of the Almighty : therefore can no defiled thing fall into her. For she is the brightness of the everlasting light, the unspotted mirror of the power of God, and the image of His goodness. And being but one, she can do all things : and remaining in herself, she maketh all things new : and in all ages entering into holy souls, she maketh them friends of God, and prophets. For God loveth none but him that dwelleth with wisdom. For she is more beautiful than the sun, and above all the orders of stars : being compared with the light, she is found before it. For after this cometh night : but vice shall not prevail against wisdom."[1] "Whoso findeth me," says Wisdom of herself, "findeth life, but he that sinneth against me wrongeth his own soul ; All they that hate me love death."[2]

In Egypt Wisdom was personified by Isis,[3] a manifold goddess of whom it was inscribed : "I am that which is, has been, and shall be, and no man has lifted my veil." Similarly of "Wisdom" the Hebrews wrote : "The first

[1] Wisdom of Solomon vii.   [2] Proverbs viii.
[3] Isis was worshipped under different names in different provinces. At Thebes she was *Mut*, at Bubastes *Sekhet*, and at Dendera *Hathor*.

man knew her not perfectly, no more shall the last find her out. For her thoughts are more than the sea and her counsels profounder than the Great Deep." It is noteworthy that the writer of *The Song of Solomon* is himself perplexed at the complex character of his own heroine. Like Pilate who asked : " What is Truth ? " he leaves unanswered his own query, " Who is she that looketh forth as the morning, fair as the moon, clear as the sun, and terrible as an army with banners ? " [1]

It was customary in the Temples of Isis for certain chants or Hymns of Invocation to be sung by the priests and priestesses. These functions were accompanied by spectacular and dramatic effects—the forerunners of the classic Mysteries and the comparatively modern Miracle Plays. In the worship of Isis it was customary for a priestess to impersonate the Moon-goddess and for a priest to play the part of Osiris, her Sun-god Bridegroom. The ceremony thus assumed the form of a dramatic dialogue— and occasional chorus—between Isis and Osiris. It is probable that pageants of this mystic marriage between the Sun and Moon were once a widespread custom ; they were certainly customary in Crete, where periodically the King and Queen, wearing the masks of a bull and cow respectively, acted the solemn rite.[2] The manuscripts of some of the Egyptian invocations have survived the ages, and four of them have recently been published under the title of *The Burden of Isis*. A comparison with *The Song of Solomon* makes it appear probable that the latter is not an anthology of Jewish Wedding Songs, but the libretto, almost unedited, of a Sun and Moon Mystery Play. For comparison a few passages are here cited side by side :

[1] *Song of Solomon* vi. 10.
[2] *The Dying God*, J. G. Frazer, p. 69.

FROM THE
SONG OF SOLOMON.

FROM AN
INVOCATION TO OSIRIS.
(*The Burden of Isis.*)

Because of the savour of thy good ointments, thy name is as ointment poured forth; therefore do the virgins love thee, i. 3.

Hail, thou sweet-scented one! There is unguent for the hair at thy coming. Sweet-scented odours are upon thy hair, with unguents that proceed from himself, p. 47.

I am sick of love, ii. 5.
Draw me, we will *run* after thee, i. 4.

I am inflamed with loving thee! Hail! Approach! Behold, I weep for thee alone; come to me who *runneth* because of my desire to behold thee, p. 44.

Behold, thou art fair, my love; behold, thou art fair; thou hast doves' eyes, i. 15.

Behold! the beautiful face of the beloved Lord turned towards us, p. 31.

Come thou in peace, O our Lord whom we behold; our prince, p. 31.

How fair is thy love, my *sister*,[1] my spouse, iv. 10.

Come to the one who loveth thee, O thou who art beautiful. Come to thy *sister*; come to thy wife, p. 21.

The voice of my beloved! *behold, he cometh* leaping upon the mountains! ii. 8.

Behold! he cometh! p. 49.

Until the day break, and the shadows flee away, ii. 17.

Thou illuminest at the daybreak and thou restest at evening; this being thy daily work. He bringeth thee to the mountains, p. 41.

---

[1] One of the titles of Isis was "the royal wife and *sister*."

Come to me, thou uniter of Heaven to Earth, who causeth his shadow daily in the land, messenger of Heaven to Earth! p. 43.

I sought him, but I found him not. *I will* rise now, and *go about the city* in the streets, iii. 1–2.

I am seeking after love ; *behold me existing in the city!* great are its walls. I grieve for thy love towards me—thou hast departed, p. 36.

My beloved had withdrawn himself, and was gone : my soul failed when he spake : I sought him, but I could not find him ; I called him, but he gave me no answer, v. 6.

Behold thou my heart which grieveth for thee. Behold me seeking for thee ; I am searching for thee to behold thee ! Lo ! I am prevented from beholding thee ; I am prevented from beholding thee, O An ! (An = the Sungod), p. 21.

The smell of thy garments is like the smell of Lebanon, iv. 11.

The odour of thy limbs is like odours of Punt, p. 46.

Awake, O north wind ; and come thou south ; blow upon my garden, that the spices thereof may flow out, iv. 16.

Breezes blow for thee with perfume, O husband, elder, lord, beloved ! p. 38.

Thou art *terrible* as an army with banners, vi. 4.

Hail, thou Great and *terrible* one ! p. 5.

The rain is over and gone ; the flowers appear on the earth, ii. 11–12.

Remove thou storms of rain, and give thou sunshine to the land with fecundity, p. 48.

His head is as the most fine gold. His legs are as pillars of marble set upon sockets of fine gold. Thy teeth are as a flock of sheep which go up from the washing, v. 11, 15 ; vi. 6.

Thy hair is like turquoise over his body. Lo ! the lapis lazuli is above thy hair : thy skin and thy flesh are like iron of the south ; thy bones are formed of silver. Thy teeth are to thee as fine lapis lazuli, p. 47.

These general similarities of style and subject-matter are striking, but there are also many further remarkable points of contact. The name OSIRIS is derived, according to Le Plongeon, from a Maya verb meaning *to desire vehemently*, and the word has thus sometimes been interpreted as "He who was very much desired and dearly beloved."[1]

The period when the invocations to Osiris were first written is not known. As their latest editor suggests, it is probable that in the earliest times they were committed to memory and handed down by means of oral tradition from generation to generation. Sanctified by age and doubly sanctified by sacred associations, it seems probable that an Osirian temple-chant fell into the hands of some Syrian scribe, by whom it was religiously edited, christened *The Song of Solomon*, and as such preserved. The reference to "Pharaoh's chariots"[2] may not impossibly be a passage that escaped the editorial eye of the Jewish adapter.

Although the *dramatis personæ* of *The Song of Solomon* consists simply of the Bride, the Bridegroom, and a chorus of priestesses, there is, it will be noticed, a sort of epilogue relating to a mysterious "little sister."[3] This little sister is perhaps NEPHTHYS, who, according to Professor Petrie, was "a shadowy double of Isis, reputedly her sister and always associated with her : she seems to have no other function."[4] Or not improbably the "little sister" may be Isis herself, the name Isis being derived by Le Plongeon from the Maya word *icin*, meaning "little sister."[5] In this case *The Song of Solomon* must be raised to a generation higher and understood as a dialogue between the parents of

---

[1] *Sacred Mythology among the Mayas*, p. 87.   [2] i. 9.
[3] "We have a little sister and she hath no breasts. What shall we do for our sister on the day that she shall be spoken for?"—*Song of Solomon* viii.
[4] *Religion of Ancient Egypt*, p. 44.   [5] *Queen Moo*, p. 154.

Isis and Osiris, *i.e.* Knepth and Nut. The Egyptian, like all ancient mystics, conceived his deities not as solitary, but as having each his or her dual, affinity, and counterpart. In Hindoo story the divine Cow exclaims to her consort the divine Bull : " For what am I but a double and a copy and an echo of a Being which is Thou ? " [1]

If, as is almost invariably the case in mythology, the Mother is but the counterpart of the Father, the Child constituting the Triad must naturally have been the counterpart of its parents. Osiris the son is therefore essentially identical with Knepth, and Isis the daughter or little sister is the duality of the Great Mother Nut. The apparent paradox, " Ra is the soul of Osiris, and Osiris the soul of Ra," may be the better understood in comparison with the Christian tenet that Christ is not only " the Son," but is also the likeness of the Father, and a Personality in whom " dwells all the fulness of the Godhead bodily." [2]

It is significant that in *The Song of Solomon* not only is the Bride the sister of the Bridegroom, but she is also his living counterpart, double, image, and echo. She is a shepherdess ; he a shepherd. He is terrible as an army with banners ; she looketh forth terrible as an army with banners. She is black ; his locks are black as the raven. He feedeth among lilies ; she is a lily among thorns. He is fair ; she all fair, and the fairest among women. Both have a garden, both are most exquisitely perfumed, and both are associated with a chariot.

Those features of " the Shulamite," which apparently conflict with one another, may be summed up as follows : She is smitten, wounded, and despised, yet the daughter of a prince, and beautifully shod. She is the keeper of a vineyard, the awakener of those who sleep, a spring, a fountain,

---

[1] *The Heifer of the Dawn*, A. W. Bain, p. 72.
[2] Colossians ii. 9.

a well, and the giver of peace. Behind her veil lurk the eyes of a dove. She describes herself as "black," yet is likened to a lily, to a rose, to the morning, to the moon, to the sun, to an impregnable fortress, and to an army terrible with banners.

In the Wisdom of Solomon, Wisdom is described as "one only," yet "manifold," and this manifoldness was equally a characteristic of Isis, whose attributes and epithets were so numerous that in the hieroglyphics she is called the "many-named," the "thousand-named," and in Greek inscriptions the "myriad-named."

In the Apocryphal "Acts of Thomas" there is a short poem which Mr G. R. S. Mead has edited under the title *The Wedding Song of Wisdom*. It is believed to have been originally composed in Syriac, but there is more probability that like the so-called *Song of Solomon* it reached Syria by means of oral tradition and referred in the first instance to Isis. Whether or not this is so, from internal evidence it is indubitable that "the maiden" of *The Wedding Song of Wisdom* is identical with King Solomon's bride. Her Wedding Song runs as follows :—

> "The Maiden is Light's Daughter ;
> On her the King's Radiance resteth.
>
> Stately her Look and delightsome,
> With radiant beauty forth-shining.
>
> Like unto spring-flowers are her Garments,
> From them streameth scent of sweet odour.
>
> On the Crown of her Head the King throneth.
> (With Living Food) feeding those 'neath Him.
>
> Truth on her Head doth repose,
> She sendeth forth Joy from her Feet." [1]

---

[1] *The Wedding Song of Wisdom*, G. R. S. Mead

The suggestion that this mystic poem refers to the same personality as the Bride of King Solomon is strengthened by the curious lines :

> " Her fingers are secretly setting
> The Gates of the City ajar."

Compare this reference to the City of the Soul with the lines in *The Song of Solomon* : " My beloved put in his hand by the hole of the door. I rose up to open to my beloved. I opened to my beloved."[1] Note also that " her brides-maids too are *Seven* who lead the dance before her,"[2] and compare with " Wisdom hath builded her house. She hath hewed out her *Seven* pillars, she hath sent forth her maidens."[3]

Among the Gnostics, Wisdom was known as SOPHIA, the Virgin of Light. This heavenly Maiden was said to have been co-existent with God, and as His Master-Workwoman to have descended to earth glorying in the work of creation. But by some dolorous mischance the maiden Sophia became entangled in the very matter she had helped to bring into being. Finding herself unable to regain her heavenly estate, and having no rest either above or below the earth, she cried out in lamentation to her Great Mother, who, pitying her daughter's distress, invoked the aid of the Creator. Whereupon Eusoph, the Great Light, sent Christ his Son who " emanated and descended to His own sister."[4] Here we again meet with the conjunction of a brother and sister, which is one of the conspicuous elements of the ISIS and OSIRIS myth, and likewise of *The Song of Solomon*.

The conception of SOPHIA falling away from her heavenly estate is some explanation of the Shulamite's self-reproach,

---

[1] v. 4, 6.　　　[2] *The Wedding Song of Wisdom.*
[3] Proverbs ix. 1.
[4] *The Wedding Song of Wisdom.*

" Mine own vineyard have I not kept ";[1] and this lament is still further elucidated by a reference to the legend of a descent into the under-world by ISHTAR—the Assyrian equivalent of ISIS. It is related that ISHTAR, the daughter of SIN, the God of Light, stooped from her heavenly estate and descended into the land of darkness where " they behold not the light, but dust is their bread and mud their food."[2] On drawing nigh the gates of this dismal land, ISHTAR spake : " Ho, porter ! Open thy gate ! Open thy gate that I may enter in ! " The porter reports her presence to ALLATU, the Queen of the under-world, who, though raging with hatred at her unwelcome visitor, grants her entry on the condition that at each of the seven gateways to the infernal kingdom ISHTAR shall relinquish some portion of her queenly apparel. At each gate she is accordingly stripped of a garment, and in due course is ushered into the presence of Allatu nude and without power. Whereupon the raging ALLATU struck ISHTAR with all manner of blights and diseases ; " but," continues the legend, " ISHTAR was not left for ever in the clutches of ALLATU." The news of her distressful condition was conveyed to her parents SIN and EA, who thereupon created a rescuer named UDDUSHU-NAMIR, a word signifying " his light shines."[3] ISHTAR is revivified by being sprinkled with the Waters of Life, and on being escorted back to the upper-world has, at each of the seven gates, restored to her the various pieces of apparel of which previously she had been deprived.

The heroine of *The Song of Solomon* is mentioned as the opener of the door and the crier about the city : Wisdom is described as " secretly setting the gates of the City ajar " : and it is said, " She crieth at the gates, at the entry of the

[1] *Song of Solomon* i. 6.
[2] *Babylonian Religion*, L. W. King, p. 179.
[3] *The Religion of Babylonia and Assyria*, M. Jastrow, jr., p. 142.

city, at the coming in at the doors. Unto you, O men, I call ; and my voice is to the sons of man."[1] One of the titles of Isis was "The Opener of the Ways." ISHTAR was the knocker at the door, and threatened the porter of the under-world : "I will smite the door, I will shatter the bolt, I will smite the threshold and tear down the doors, I will raise up the dead."[2]

> "Ishtar, the Goddess of Morning, am I ;
> Ishtar, the Goddess of Evening, am I ;
> (I am) Ishtar, *to open the lock of heaven belongs to my supremacy.*"[3]

But to appreciate *The Song of Solomon* in the fulness of its symbolism one must consult not only mythology and philology, but also fairy-tales, which, in many cases, are mythology still living.

Like most ancient literature, *The Song of Solomon* and many other books now contained within our Bible circulated originally by word of mouth. The sacred *Popul Vuh* of the Mayas, the *Rig-Veda* of the Hindoos, the *Zenda-Vesta* of the Persians, and the popular *Kalevala* of the Finns, are collections of legends and traditions, most of which were handed down from mouth to mouth, circulating thus for untold centuries before they were formalised and committed to writing. It is startling to find that some of the classic myths that one associates with Greece and Rome have their counterparts—modified merely to the difference of custom and environment—among savage and undeveloped races such as the Maoris and Zulus, peoples who, so far as is known, have never possessed any system of writing. Little or no distinction can be drawn between classic Myth and popular Fairy-tale : myth was obviously once Fairy-tale,

---

[1] Proverbs viii. 3, 4.

[2] *Babylonian Religion*, C. W. King, p. 180.

[3] From a hymn to Ishtar quoted in *The Religion of Babylonia and Assyria*, M. Jastrow, jr., p. 311.

and what is often supposed to be mere Fairy-tale proves in many instances to be unsuspected Theology.

There is an Indian story known as *The Descent of the Sun*, which, as its title shows, is a Solar myth. Literally translated, it should be called *The Glory of the Going Down of the Sun*, but this, says its translator,[1] is only the exoteric physical envelope of an inner mystical meaning, which is *The Divine Lustre of the Descent (Incarnation) of Him who took Three Steps*, *i.e.* VISHNU or the Sun, the later KRISHNA or Hindoo APOLLO. These Three Steps of the Sun indicate not his Rise, Zenith, and Setting, but a somewhat inverted cycle, *i.e.* His Going Down, His Period of Darkness, and His Rising Again. To primitive man these mystical three steps summarised and symbolised the mystery of birth and death, *lux ex tenebris*, a dazzling light in most profound darkness, a heavenly body doomed to put on mortality and suffer for a period in this lower world of darkness, birth, and death. Mr Bain preludes his translation (?) with a quotation from Sanscrit : " And in a dream I saw a lotus fallen from Heaven," and the name of his heroine, the Goddess SHRI, means not only " Sacred Lotus," but also " Lustre." The descent of ISHTAR is a version of that fallen Lotus, and the Song of Solomon is a love duet between a lily among thorns and SOLOMON the Sun. The Hero of *The Descent of the Sun* is named KAMALAMITRA, which means the Lover of the Lotus, *i.e.* the Sun ; MITRA is MITHRA, and means Sunlight. The story runs that once upon a time on the slopes of Himalaya there lived a young King of the Spirits of the Air named KAMALAMITRA, " for he was a portion of the Sun." [2] The Lord of Creatures bestowed upon KAMALAMITRA a wife of beauty so surpassing that KAMALAMITRA grew boastful, whereupon the two lovers

---

[1] *The Descent of the Sun : A Cycle of Birth translated from the Original MS.*, by F. W. Bain.   [2] P. 3.

were separated by the Gods and doomed to a period of
pilgrimage over the terrifying sea of mortality. The tale
then unfolds their misadventures, concluding with a final
reunion and apotheosis.

There is a Babylonic legend that King SARGON the
First was set adrift on the EUPHRATES in a rush basket.
He was rescued by a gardener, who brought him up as
his own son, and while still a gardener the Goddess ISHTAR
fell in love with him, and eventually made him ruler of
the Kingdom.[1]

There is a Talmudic legend that King SOLOMON was
once robbed of his magic ring, whereupon he assumed the
humble rôle of a scullion in the kitchen of the King of the
Ammonites, and eventually became the lover of the King's
daughter.[2] Variants of these Solar stories—of which the
last is taken from Miss Miriam Roalfe Cox's collection of
CINDERELLA variants—form the foundation of nearly half
the world's fairy-tales ; the other half may be said to consist
of their counterpart, *i.e.* the adventures of the little girl who
is temporarily abused and ill-treated, but eventually marries
the prince. *The Song of Solomon* is not only a bridge link-
ing theology to folk-lore, but it contains several finger-posts
pointing definitely to the story known nowadays as CINDER-
ELLA. The elements of this prehistoric and universal fairy-
tale are present in the legend of ISHTAR's descent into the
under-world. ISHTAR, deprived of her beautiful robes, plays
the rôle of CINDERELLA ; ALLATU is the cruel stepmother, and
UDDUSHU-NAMIR plays the prince. In Egypt Isis, burdened,
long-suffering, and lamenting, played CINDERELLA, and
OSIRIS was "the beautiful prince of godlike face."[3] In the
Greek story of CUPID and PSYCHE, VENUS, jealous and

---

[1] *Babylonian Religion*, King, p. 199.
[2] *Cinderella*, M. R. Cox, p. 521.
[3] *Burden of Isis*, p. 48.

vindictive, plays the stepmother ; CUPID, with his "hairs of gold that yielded out a sweet savour, his neck more white than milk, his hair hanging comely behind and before, the brightness whereof did darken the light of the lamp,"[1] plays the prince ; and PSYCHE—of such passing beauty and maidenly majesty that no earthly creature could by any means sufficiently express—is CINDERELLA. The task of separating grain imposed upon PSYCHE and performed for her by ants is *identically* the task imposed, according to one version, upon CENDRILLOT.[2] PSYCHE's two envious and spiteful sisters—"naughty hags armed with wicked minds"—are the two proud sisters of the fairy-tale. CUPID, sun-like and SOLOMON-like, "slips through the smallest crack of the window," and awakens PSYCHE with the light touch of a golden arrow."[3]

The principal point of contact between the heroine of *The Song of Solomon* and the heroine of our nursery story is the crystal slipper,—"How beautiful are thy feet with shoes, O prince's daughter ! "[4] Yet this same glorious princess is described by the poet as smitten, wounded, and despised. Her "mother's children" (the proud sisters) were angry with her, compelling her to perform unworthy tasks, yet eventually her beloved prince brings her to "the banqueting-house" (the ball), and the banner of Love waves over her.

No one knows where or when the story of Cinderella originated. It is a household tale in Europe, Asia, Africa, and America, and is as familiar to uncivilised as to civilised nations. Under the auspices of the Folk-Lore Society, 345 variants collected from all parts of the world have been published in book form, the editor remarking that the number might have been indefinitely increased had not the

---

[1] Adlington's translation from Apuleius.
[2] *Cinderella*, p. 455.
[3] *Age of Fable*, Bulfinch.   [4] vii. 1.

Society concluded that it was necessary to make an arbitrary stop to the apparently unending labour of collecting.[1]

The framework of the tale is that CINDERELLA, the daughter of a star-crowned king or queen, flees from her princely home in order to escape a distasteful marriage. She takes service as a goose-girl, a scullion, or in some other equally mean capacity, and bewilders the neighbours by appearing at church, or at the famous ball, in a succession of wonder-awaking dresses. The extraordinary character of CINDERELLA's changing robes furnishes not only the clue to the allegoric significance of CINDERELLA herself, but also throws unexpected light upon *The Song of Solomon*.

The varied garments assumed *seriatim* by the elusive CINDERELLA are described in explicit detail. One is said to have been " woven of the stars of heaven " ; another of moonbeams ; another of sunbeams ; another was " a pearl dress without slit or seam " ; another was " like the sea with fishes swimming in it " ; another was " made of all the flowers of the world " ; another was " covered with little golden bells and chains of gold " ; another was jet black ; another was " like the light." Sometimes these astonishing vestments are hidden one under the other beneath CINDER-ELLA's assumed cloak of ass-skin, cat-skin, mouse-skin, or louse-skin, and occasionally the little scullion emerges as " a beautiful girl, naked and shining like the Sun."

In several parts of Europe the story of Cinderella is known as " The Brother and Sister," and the heroine's adventures arise from her refusal to entertain her brother's proposals. She flies, exclaiming :

> " Open earth ! Open wide !
> For to be a brother's bride
> Is an awful sin." [2]

---

[1] Our English nursery version is a version imported from France towards the end of the seventeenth century; the less known but more primitive English story is known as " Cap o' Rushes."   [2] *Cinderella*, p. 428.

Isis was the sister of Osiris ; the Shulmanite was the sister of Solomon ; and in Proverbs it reads, " Say unto Wisdom, thou art my sister." [1]

From time immemorial and by general convention, Truth has been represented as a naked girl. In the printer's mark herewith Time is seen helping Truth out of a cave, the motto reading : " Truth brings hidden things to light." The Scandinavian version of Cinderella, known as " The Princess

452

in the Cave," [2] relates that war having broken out, the King secreted his daughter in a cavern. With her were buried *seven* maidens and sufficient provisions for seven years. The princess works within the cave at golden embroidery, and waits in patient expectation of release. At the end of seven years she scrapes a hole with her knife in the cavern roof, and after working for three days, succeeds in effecting her escape.

Next to a cave the second most conventional location for Truth is the bottom of a well, and in the Portuguese and Sicilian versions of CINDERELLA the heroine is there placed.

---

[1] vii. 4.   [2] *Cinderella*, pp. 173, 377, 407.

A Fish at the bottom of the well conducts her to a palace of gold and precious stones, where she dons her golden shoes.[1]   As told in SICILY, she notices at the bottom of a well a hole whence light shines, and on raising the corner stone is admitted into a garden beautiful with flowers and fruit.   While hiding in her well, she is perceived by a prince, who falls sick of love, and whose case becomes so desperate that physicians cannot cure him,[2] and all hopes of recovery are given up.   This parlous condition of the lover is an essential element of the CINDERELLA cycle.   It is paralleled in the Song of Solomon by the passage : " Stay me with flagons, comfort me with apples, for *I am sick of love.*" [3]

In Denmark CINDERELLA is entitled *The King's Daughter in the Mound,* and in Jutland *The Princess in the Mound.*[4] The earliest " Mistress of the Mountain," the divine " Lady of the Mound," [5] was NUT, the mother of ISIS, the Cow or Mother of heaven, the Giver of liquid life.

In Jutland CINDERELLA is known as *The Princess on the Island,* and for *seven* years she lives on a distant Island accompanied by *seven* maids.   This is doubtless that Fortunate Isle, the Island of Eternal Life, which lies in the very midst of the ocean and figures prominently in all my theologies.   It is the same mystic island where " Reason rules, not Fantasy " ; Reason answering to Wisdom and Fantasy to her antithesis, Dame Folly :

> " This Island hath the name of Fortunate,
> And as they tell is governed by a Queen,
> Well-spoken and discreet and therewithal
> So beautiful that with one single beam
> Of her great beauty all the country round
> Is rendered shining." [6]

---

[1] *Cinderella*, p. 341.   [2] *Ibid.*, p. 348.
[3] xi. 5.   [4] *Cinderella*, pp. 267, 288.
[5] *Signs and Symbols of Primordial Man*, p. 123.
[6] Cf. *A New Light on the Renaissance*, Bayley, p. 161.

In a Slav version of Cinderella she "shines like the sun, so that near her one can see by night as well as by daylight" ;[1] and in a Scandinavian variant CINDERELLA is described as "something like the long beam of a shooting star through dense mist."[2]

The heroine, as a personification of Truth, is even more unmistakable in the male counterpart to the Cinderella stories, *i.e.* the cycle of tales where the rôles are reversed and the all-glorious princess is wooed and won by a little kitchen-boy or herd-boy. Several of these masculine variants of Cinderella are included in Miss Cox's collection, and according to one of them the King deposits his precious princess on the summit of a crystal mountain proclaiming that whoever succeeds in scaling its slippery sides shall have her in marriage. The Hero, "as black as a sweep and always by the stove,"[3] wins her by riding up the steep sides on a little ox.[4] This magic ox figures in fairy-tale very frequently and is often apparently the symbol of toil and labour : "Much increase is by the strength of the ox."[5]

There is a tale told among SLAV herdsmen and peasants of *A Maid with Hair of Gold*. This Princess is the daughter of a King whose crystal palace is built upon an island. She sits accompanied by twelve maidens at a round table—a table which may be equated with the Round Table of King Arthur and his twelve Knights. The golden light from the princess's hair is reflected on the sea and sky every morning as she combs it. The hero's name is GEORGE, and this GEORGE is evidently a relation of the St George of Christianity. On the accomplishment of his imposed tasks —one of which is the collection of the scattered and lost pearls of the princess's broken necklace, and another the

---

[1] *Cinderella*, p. 333.   [2] *Ibid.*, p. 228.   [3] *Ibid.*, p. 452.
[4] *Ibid.*, p. 447.   [5] Proverbs xiv. 4.

recovering of her lost ring from the bottom of the sea—
GEORGE comes face to face with the maiden. Whereupon
she arose from her seat and loosening her head-dress
exposed to full view the splendour of her wonderful hair,
which had the appearance of a waterfall of golden rays and
covered her from head to foot. The glorious light that
glittered from it dazzled the hero's eyes and he immediately
fell in love with her. The allegorical character of this story
is rendered evident by its conclusion. GEORGE is unhappily

453

slain, but is restored again to life by the princess, who
pours upon him the Water of Life. " Ah me," said
GEORGE rubbing his eyes, " how well I have slept ! "
" Yes," answered the princess smiling, " no one could
have slept better, but without me you would have slept
through eternity." [1]

In the Temple of LUXOR the Creator is depicted as
modelling two figures—a body and a soul : ISIS is animating them with life.[2] " I," says ISIS, " inflame the hearts of
hundreds of thousands." [3] In *The Song of Solomon* the

[1] *Fairy Tales of the Slav Peasants and Herdsmen*, Emily J. Harding, p. 87.
[2] *A Guide to the Antiquities of Upper Egypt*, A. E. P. Weigall, p. 75.
[3] *Burden of Isis*, p. 37.

heroine causes "the lips of those that are *asleep* to speak."[1] Similarly Cinderella *awakens* the household by her singing. The servants complain of being kept awake, but the young master throws away "his *habitual sleeping draught*," hastens to CINDERELLA and exclaims, "I hear you, I hear you!"[2] One may also compare the invitation of Wisdom, "Come, eat of my bread and drink of the wine that I have mingled, forsake the foolish and live."[3]

"All night long," exhorts ZOROASTER, "address the heavenly Wisdom : all night long call for the Wisdom that will keep thee awake."[4]

There is a SLAV fairy-tale entitled *The Spirit of the Steppes*.[5] It relates to a princess whose brow was calm and pure as the Moon, whose lips were red as a rosebud and whose voice was so eloquent that it sounded like a shower of pearls. But wonderful beyond compare was the expressive beauty of her eyes. If she looked at you kindly you seemed to float in a sea of joy ; if angrily, it made you numb with fear and you were instantly transformed into a block of ice. This princess, whose name was SUDOLISA, was waited upon by *twelve* companions who were almost as charming as their mistress. Many a prince came from afar and entered the lists as a suitor, but none was successful in winning her love. It happened that the eye of KOSTEY, an infamous ogre who lived underground, fell upon the beautiful Island of SUDOLISA where, bright as so many stars, stood the twelve maidens, and amidst them, sleeping upon a couch of swansdown lay SUDOLISA herself, lovely as the dawn of Day. KOSTEY, the ogre, cast longing eyes at the princess, whereupon she, summoning her army, put herself at its head and led her soldiers against him. But KOSTEY

---

[1] viii. 9.   [2] *Cinderella*, p. 358.   [3] Proverbs ix. 56.
[4] *Solomon and Solomonic Literature*, Moncure Conway, p. 65.
[5] *Slav Tales*, pp. 187–206.

breathed upon the soldiers and they fell down in an overpowering sleep. Then he stretched out a bony hand to seize the princess, but she froze him into impotence by a glance. Then she retired into her palace and shut herself in. When the princess had departed, KOSTEY came to life again and at once recommenced his pursuit. On reaching the town where she dwelt, he put all the inhabitants into a charmed sleep, and laid the same spell upon the twelve maids of honour. Fearing the power of SUDOLISA's eyes, he dared not openly attack her, but surrounding her palace with an iron wall, left her in charge of a monstrous twelve-headed dragon. Then he waited in hopes that the princess would give in. Days passed, weeks grew into months, and still the kingdom of SUDOLISA looked like one large bedchamber. The people snored in the streets ; the brave army lying in the fields slept soundly, hidden in the long grass under the shadow of nettle, wormwood, and thistle—rust and dust marring the brightness of their arms. Amid this silent reign of sleep the princess, sad but expectant, alone kept watch. Fixing her eyes on that portion of the sky where the Sun first appears chasing away darkness like a flight of birds, she said :

> " Soul of the world, thou deep fountain of life,
>> Eye of all-powerful God,
> Visit my prison, dark scene of sad strife,
>> Raise up my soul from the sod ;
> With hope that my friend whom I pine for and love,
> May come to my rescue : say, where does he rove ? "

In response, the sun shone upon a distant land where Prince JUNAK, mounted upon a powerful steed and clad in armour of gold, gathered his forces against the giant KOSTEY. Thrice he had dreamt of the lovely princess imprisoned within her sleeping palace, and he was in love with her even without having seen her. The conclusion of the tale may be taken from another Slav story, which records that on the arrival of the Prince Redeemer, he was filled with bewilderment, for instead of one princess, he perceived twelve all equally beautiful, but understood on looking closer that eleven of them were merely the mirrored reflections of one sole princess. "I have come," said the Prince, "of my own free will to rescue you and restore you to your parents. If I should not succeed in saving you, sweet princess, life will no longer be dear to me, but I am full of hope, and I beg you first to give me a draught of the Strength-Giving Water from the Heroic Well." Events end happily, but before bestowing her hand upon her lover, the Princess asks him six riddles, of which the fifth is : "I existed before the creation of ADAM. I am always changing in succession the two colours of my dress. Thousands of years have gone by, but I have remained unaltered both in colour and form." With this claim compare that put forward by "Wisdom" in the Book of Proverbs, "I was set up from everlasting, from the beginning, or ever the earth was. When there were no depths, I was brought forth ; when there were no fountains abounding with water. Before the mountains were settled, before the hills was I brought forth."[1]

It is proverbial that the Spirit of man is a candle of the Lord,[2] and it is claimed for Wisdom that the Light which cometh from her shall never go out. In some versions of Cinderella, the heroine is concealed for the sake of her safety in a large silver candlestick. This candlestick is bought by a prince, who is astonished to find that it opens and contains a lovely girl.[3] In the accompanying design the figure of this Virgin of Light constitutes the candlestick.

[1] viii. 23–25. [2] Proverbs xx. [3] *Cinderella*, pp. 198, 210.

Another version of Cinderella represents her as being hidden for the sake of safety within a golden chest. Servants spying through the keyhole see the incomparable maiden, and, determining to sell her, they hawk the case and its contents throughout the world. Many are ready to buy the attractive box, but none is willing to make an offer for the girl, and the servants, therefore, throw her into a briar-bush.[1]

modio, fed vt in candelabro

454

" Wisdom," says Solomon, " is glorious and never fadeth away. Yea, she is easily seen of them that love her and found of such as seek her. She preventeth them that desire her in making herself first known unto them. Whoso seeketh her early shall have no great travail, for he shall find her sitting at his doors."[2] A Corsican version of CINDERELLA represents the heroine as being *no larger than one's little finger* and so tiny as hardly to be perceptible. A passing prince hearing the sound of her exquisite singing vows he will marry the unknown singer, but, Whence comes the voice? The answer is, " She is not distant,

---

[1] *Cinderella*, p. 314.   [2] Wisdom of Solomon vi.

the beautiful maiden, she is here at thy feet."[1] Compare this diminutive Cinderella with the passage from a Vedic *Te Deum* quoted on page 138, " The Spirit dwells ever as inward soul, *an inch in stature* within men's hearts."

The fairy-tales thus far quoted are not professedly allegories, nor are they the productions of literary artifice ; they are but wayside stories familiar to uneducated people. The allegorical theory of mythology and fairy-tale has, it is considered, been finally demolished by the discovery made by the Brothers GRIMM that fairy-tales have not descended from the educated to the uneducated classes, but *vice versa* have emanated, as it were, from the soil, ascending from the cottage to the castle, finally being collected from oral traditions and crystallised by littérateurs into book form. Mr Andrew Lang was of the opinion that fairy-stories are largely relics of savagery and barbarism, and that they bear self-evident traces of their bestial origin. The existence of barbaric elements need not be contested, but side by side with these there are unquestionably traces of a pure and primitive mythology which must have come down to us by word of mouth unedited, untampered with, and unsuspected.

In many cases the names of the *dramatis personæ* significantly reveal the meanings of the myths. The fact that these names vary in different localities seems to me entirely to discredit Mr Lang's theory that myth was probably carried from country to country by female captives. It will also still further discredit Max Müller's " disease of language" theory, for, as will be seen, the changed names of the characters are frequently of vital significance and reveal exactly the underlying meaning of the fable.

---

[1] *Cinderella*, p. 338. Compare Wordsworth :
"Wisdom is ofttimes nearer when we stoop
Than when we soar."

In BRAZIL the story of Cinderella is known as "Dona Labismina." According to this version "Labismina" is the name of a snake which was coiled round the neck of the heroine when she was born, but subsequently lives in the sea and plays the part of fairy godmother. It is obvious that the name is a form of the term *L'Abysme*, The Great Abyss, the Mother Serpent of unrevealed Wisdom, who dwelt in the primeval and unfathomable ocean. "The Goddess HATHOR"—sometimes regarded as identical with ISIS and at other times as her mother— "appears," says Mr Weigall, "sometimes as a serpent and sometimes she is the fairy godmother."[1] Very frequently CINDERELLA herself is named MARY, MARA, MARIETTA, or MARIUCELLA. The name MARY is by some writers identified with MIRIAM, meaning the sad and unfortunate one, the star of the sea, a drop of the sea;[2] others derive it from MARA the Nereid, "whose name may express the phosphoric flashing of the surface of the sea just as the name MAIRA expresses the sparklings of the dog-star SIRIUS."[3] Among the Serbs CINDERELLA's name is not CINDERELLA, but MARA.[4] In CORSICA CINDERELLA is named MARIUCELLA,[5] and her mother—as did HATHOR—takes the form of a cow. "Take comfort, MARIUCELLA," says the cow, "I am your mother." In SARDINIA CINDERELLA's name is BARBARELLA, manifestly a derivative from BARBERO and BARBELO, both of which were Gnostic names for WISDOM.[6] "Their derivation," says Mr Mead, "is very uncertain," but BARBARA means a foreigner, one from another country, and the meaning becomes clear on reference to the *Descent of the Sun*, wherein the glittering and

[1] *A Guide to the Antiquities of Upper Egypt*, p. 32.
[2] *Prænomia*, R. S. Charnock.
[3] *Girls' Christian Names*, Helena Swan.
[4] *Cinderella*, p. 271.   [5] *Ibid.*, p. 336.
[6] *Wedding Song of Wisdom*.

lustrous SHRI says : "I am a King's daughter from a far country."[1] The same idea is likewise emphasised in a Syrian version of this solar myth, wherein the Child of the Sun says : "I had clothed me as they were, that they might not guess I had come from afar, but from some occasion or other they learned *I was not of their country*."[2]

The syllables ELLA occurring in MARIUCELLA, BARBAR-ELLA, and CINDERELLA, are the Greek *Ele*, which means shiner or giver of light. ELE is the root of ELELEUS, one of the surnames of APOLLO and DIONYSOS.[3] It is also found in ELEUTHER the Son of APOLLO, in HELIOS the Sun, and in SELENE the Moon. The name of JUNO LUCINA—*i.e.*, JUNO in her aspect of Light-Giver — was ELEUTHO. The HELLESPONT takes its name from HELLE, a maiden who fled from her father's house to escape the oppression of her mother-in-law, but fell from a cloud into the sea and was drowned.[4] This HELLE must be a relative of HELIOS the Sun, and her drowning is probably a poetic account of the sun sinking into the sea.

In Finland CINDERELLA is known as "Beautiful CLARA."[5] CLARA is derived from *clareo*, I shine, and means bright, shining, clear, brilliant to the sight. In BOLOGNA the Candlestick-CINDERELLA is named ZIZOLA ;[6] evidently a derivation from ZIZA, which was one of the appellations of ISIS.[7]

According to a Jewish variant, CINDERELLA's name is CABHA, a word that means Aurora.[8] Aurora, derived from *aurum*, means the golden beauty of the morning, the rosy-fingered Dawn.

[1] *Descent of the Sun*, p. 87.
[2] *Hymn of the Robe of Glory*, G. R. S. Mead, pp. 18–19.
[3] Lemprière. [4] *Ibid.*
[5] *Cinderella*, p. 533. [6] *Ibid.*, p. 198.
[7] *Curious Myths of the Middle Ages*, S. Baring-Gould, p. 332.
[8] *Cinderella*, p. 354.

In Jutland CINDERELLA is named LUCY, from *lux*, light, or *luceo*, I give light. LUCY, derived from the same radical as LUNA the Moon, and LUCIFER the Light-Bringer, means "a shining child born at sunrise or daybreak."

It is thus seen that the popular names of CINDERELLA are as recondite and significant as the classic word PSYCHE of Greek myth. PSYCHE, who has much in common with CINDERELLA, means Breath or Soul, and by almost general consent PSYCHE is regarded as symbolic of the soul spark prisoned within the material body.

To arrive at the full meaning of the name Cinderella, one may refer to a Hindoo story entitled by its English translator (?), *A Heifer of the Dawn*.[1] A heifer figures frequently as the fairy godmother to CINDERELLA, and sometimes the little animal has golden horns. "All sweetness," says the *Rig-Veda*, "is collected in the Heifer," the Red One of the Dawn, and the word Heifer is still used in the Orient to signify a wife or Queen. The Heifer with golden horns is HATHOR, the giver of liquid life, and the golden horns are the golden horns of the new moon. DIANA appears repeatedly with the crescent so posed as to appear like the horns of a cow, and the same arrangement may be seen in fig. 285 (*ante*, p. 104). The story called *A Heifer of the Dawn* relates to a Princess who veils her identity under the disguise of a handmaid and appears day after day to a heartbroken and woman-hating King. This "Heifer of the Dawn" possesses the protean, elusive, and contradictory characteristics of Cinderella and of the fair Shulamite. First she appears clothed in dark blue like an incarnation of the night of new moon ; next she resembles the sky before the dawn touched with the first streak of red, and remarks : "O King, I am young, yet am I older than thou art." Next she resembles an incarnation of the sap of

[1] F. W. Bain.

the tree of youth and remarks that her name is MADHUPA-
MANJARI, *i.e.*, "a cluster of blossoms for the honey drinkers."
Next she seems in the King's eyes like an incarnation of the
dew of the morning and like an emblem of the love that
was *rising from its ashes in his own heart* embodied in a
feminine form ; next, as an essence incarnated by the will
of the Creator in a wholly different yet equally delicious
form and like the embodied peace of the King's own mind.
Next she seems in the King's eyes like the nectar of
reconciliation in feminine form and on her lips there was a
smile that sat like sunlight.   Finally, she seems like a
draught of the nectar of love longing incarnate in a feminine
form.   The bewildered and enraptured King grown " sick
of love " exclaims that he needed but the touch of her hand
to burst into a flame.   Then she looked at him with mock
gravity and said : " These are symptoms very dangerous and
alarming to the physician.   Thy case is parlous."   The
King says : " Thou mayst liken me *to a fire which was all but
extinguished* and could not be rekindled.   And then it blazed
up from its ashes with a pure flame such as it had never
put forth before."   Half frightened and half laughing, the
Heifer of the Dawn exclaims : " Aryuputra, let me go.   Hast
thou not guessed that I am the Queen ? "   Subsequently
the King remarks : " Said I not well that I was fire and she
the fuel ?   Or is it not rather I that am the fuel and *she*
that is *the fire*, for certainly she burns me like a flame."

In CATALONIA CINDERELLA is known as " The Fire
Blower "[1] on account of her occupation, and in JUTLAND
she is called " Whipper of the Ashes," to whip meaning to
stir up or poke.   It would thus seem that CINDERELLA, the
bright and shining one, who sits among the cinders and
keeps the fire alight, is a personification of the Holy Spirit
dwelling unhonoured amid. the smouldering ashes of the

[1] *Cinderella*, p. 311.

Soul's latent, never totally extinct, Divinity, and, by patient tending, fanning them into flame.

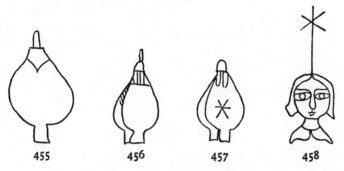

455   456   457   458

The above bellows no doubt represent those of the heavenly Fire Blower. Fig. 457 is distinguished by the cross of Lux, and this sign marks fig. 458 as a presentment of the Maiden herself. In Finland Cinderella is named TUNA, which is a diminutive of KRISTUNA or CHRISTINA, *i.e.* Christ personified as a little girl.

CHAPTER IX

CINDERELLA

" Beauty, Truth, and Rarity,
Grace in all simplicity,
Here enclosed in cinders lie."

SHAKESPEARE.

HAVING established the probability that CINDERELLA contains many traces of original allegory, it is permissible to consider this theory in closer detail, and to inquire into the meaning underlying CINDERELLA's protean changes of raiment. Her supernatural and mystical dresses seem unquestionably to symbolise the awakening, growth, and final apotheosis of Wisdom within the mind.

The Ancients conceived a primeval and self-existent Mother of all Wisdom, who figures in Mythology as the *Magna Mater*, the *Bona Dea*, the All-Mother of the Gods ; and in Romance this primal Mother appears as the fairy Queen or fairy Godmother.

The mother of King SOLOMON is mentioned in the Canticles as having crowned him on the day of his espousals.[1] In SLAV legend this Mother of the Sun is described sometimes as the Sea, into whose arms the Sun sinks wearily on the close of day ; at other times as sitting Fate-like in a golden castle, built seemingly of fire.

[1] *Song of Solomon* iii. 11.

196

It is almost a universal feature of the Cinderella tales that the heroine is the living image of her lovely Mother ; and thus a study of the Mother simultaneously reveals the character of the Daughter. In a Sanscrit legend, the Father, who was " of the race of the Sun," had a child exactly resembling him in every particular except age, and the Father observes, " He is not another, but my very self." [1] When SHRI, the heroine of the *Descent of the Sun*, is doomed to wander cheerlessly on earth, the Lord of Creatures says, " I must not leave her lovely body to the play of chance, for it has in it something of my own Divinity."

The relation, then, of Cinderella to her Star-crowned Mother—and of many other famous Mother-and-Daughters of Mythology—is that of the streamlet to the ocean, the spark to the fire, the *ego* to the Oversoul.

CINDERELLA'S fairy godmother or real mother [2] is variously described as an aged woman, a beautiful queen with a star upon her brow, a cow with golden horns, a water nymph, a mermaid living in a grotto of pearl and coral, and as a sea-serpent named LABISMINA.

The conception of the Sea as the Great Mother of all Creation is common to ancient cosmogonies. Whether this universal belief arose because physical life was known to have originated in water, or whether the sea was symbolically employed because of the innumerable analogies between Water and Wisdom, is a point that it would be futile to discuss : it cannot, however, be questioned that from the remotest ages the Spirit of Truth or Wisdom has been typified by Water and the Sea.

In Babylonian cosmogony the Deep or Depth was regarded as a symbol of Unfathomable Wisdom.[3] Wisdom,

---

[1] *An Essence of the Dusk*, F. W. Bain, p. 4.
[2] Not to be confused with the cruel stepmother.
[3] *Wedding Song of Wisdom*, Mead, p. 52.

the Spouse of the Supreme Creator, was said to dwell in the depths of the illimitable ocean, and was termed " the Lady of the Abyss " and the " Voice of the Abyss."[1] An ancient Irish Goddess—probably the most ancient—was named Domnu, and Sir John Rhys believes this word to have signified the Abyss or Deep Sea.[2] Three thousand years before Christ, a Chinese Emperor is said to have "instituted the music of the Great Abyss " in order to bring spirits and men into harmony ;[3] and from prehistoric times the term "Abyss" seems to have been extensively used to denote the Unknown, the Mysterious, and the Unfathomable. Labismina, the Sea-serpent godmother of Cinderella, is evidently a corruption from L'Abysme, the old French superlative of Abyss. It means the profoundest depth, the primal chaos, the unfathomable and unsearchable deep, and, according to Dr Murray, "a subterraneous reservoir of waters."[4]

Among the names of the Great Mother-Goddess Cybele were Ma and Maia, terms which in all probability were related to Maya, the name of the great empire that once flourished in South America. Traces of this empire exist in the ruined cities of Mexico, and there are some who maintain that it was the fertile parent from which sprang the civilisations of Egypt and Assyria. The meaning of the name Maya has been assumed to be the " Mother of the Waters" or the " Teats of the Waters Ma-y-a "— she of the four hundred breasts, as they were wont to express the Ephesian Goddess.[5] The reason given by

---

[1] " Why she was called ' The Lady of the Abyss,' and elsewhere ' the Voice of the Abyss,' is not known."—*Babylonian and Assyrian Religion*, T. G. Pinches, p. 62.

[2] *Hibbert Lectures*, 1886, Lecture VI.

[3] *Religion of Ancient China*, H. A. Giles, p. 8.

[4] *New Eng. Dict.*

[5] *Queen Moo and the Egyptian Sphinx*, A. Le Plongeon, p. xxxix.

BRASSEUR for this derivation is the fact that the soil of the MAYA country is honeycombed, and that just below the surface there exist innumerable and immense caves. " In these caves are deposits of cool, limpid waters, extensive lakes fed by subterraneous streams."[1] It thus seems probable that the term L'ABYSME, "a subterraneous reservoir of waters," is, like much other symbolism, traceable to the extinct civilisation of MEXICO, and that in LABISMINA the fairy godmother of CINDERELLA we have a relic of the un- fathomable MAYAN water-lakes.

In EGYPT the name for the *Waters* was *Mem*, a root from which have in all probability sprung the Irish *Mam* and the Welsh *Mam*—both words meaning *Mother*. In Chaldea MUMMU TIAWATH, the Sea, was she who brought forth everything existing, and MAMA meant the " Lady of the Gods."[2]

Among the Peruvians *Mama* meant *Mother*,[3] and the old SLAV word for *Mother* is also *Mama*.[4] King, after mentioning a local term for "the stream of the Great Ocean which flows out from the middle of the Perfect Man," continues : " This same Deity was called by the PHRYGIANS *Papa*,[5] because he appeased the confusion and chaotic tumult which prevailed before his coming."[6] Thus the first words that an infant learns to lisp relate in all prob- ability to its primeval Mother, the Sea.

The Mayan and Egyptian hieroglyph for water was a zigzag or wavy line representing the ripples of the stream or the waves of the sea, and water or spirit has ever since

---

[1] *Queen Moo and the Egyptian Sphinx*, A. Le Plongeon, p. xxxix.
[2] *Babylonian and Assyrian Religion*, T. G. Pinches, pp. 31, 94.
[3] Prescott, *Conquest of Peru*, bk. i. ch. i.
[4] *N. E. D.*
[5] Among the Mexicans *Papa* denoted a priest of high rank. This is of course the Christian Papa or Pope.
[6] *The Gnostics and their Remains*, C. W. King, 2nd ed., p. 90.

been generally represented by this prehistoric and almost universal sign. LE PLONGEON states that among the Mayas the wavy-line hieroglyph for water terminated with the head of a snake, because they compared the waves of the ocean to the undulations of a moving serpent. For this reason they named the Sea *Canah*, the Great and Power-ful *Serpent*.[1] *Anaconda*, the name of the giant serpent of South America, would thus seem to be resolvable into *anak* the giant, *onda* waves. This connection of the serpent with the sea is probably the true origin of the universal use of the serpent as a symbol of Celestial Wisdom, a symbolism for

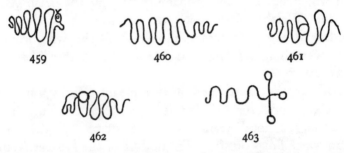

459 460 461

462 463

the reason of which a number of recondite and ingenious speculations have from time to time been put forward. From the above designs it is evident that the mediæval symbolists used the serpent with a knowledge of its primary and elemental meaning of sea waves, and this original connection between the serpent and water was no doubt an additional reason for the serpent's significance as an emblem of Regeneration.

It will be noticed that the head of fig. 463 has been sacrificed in order to introduce the three circles of Perfect Love, Perfect Wisdom, and Perfect Power, and several of the designs below have been crowned with this triple perfec-tion. The heart of Love is emerging from the mouth of

---

[1] *Sacred Mysteries among the Mayas and Quiches*, p. 114.

fig. 464, and from figs. 465 and 466 Light is being born
in the form of a *fleur-de-lys* and the cross of *Lux*. The

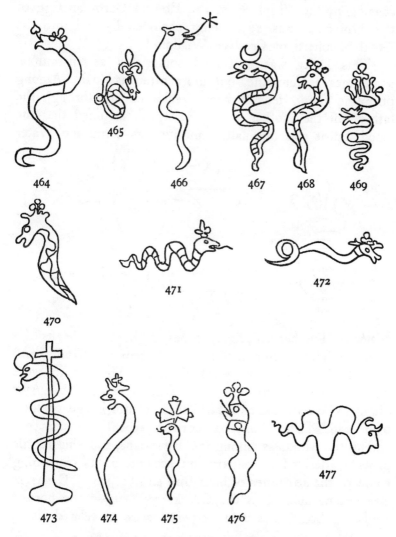

crescent moon was a symbol and attribute of Sɪɴ, the God of
Light, the Father of Iꜱʜᴛᴀʀ and the Creator of Light.

Several of these Serpent emblems are significantly en-folding an egg within their coils. According to ancient cosmogony the Virgin Egg, the Eternal Germ or Egg of the Universe, was ever being encircled by and into the Good Shepherd of Creative Wisdom.[1]

This Deity was conceived sometimes as masculine, sometimes as feminine, but more often as dual. Among primitive men, descent being reckoned not through the father but the mother, it may safely be assumed that the Good Spirit was originally conceived as being the Water

478   479

Mother. The Serpent, fig. 477, has the head and horns of a Bull, implying a combination of WISDOM the Mother and APIS the Creator and First Cause. Those who were initiated into the mysteries of OSIRIS were told that APIS ought to be regarded as a fair and beautiful image of their own soul.[2] The *cerastes* or horned serpent was as sacred among the Mayas as among the Egyptians, and this reptile probably derived its sanctity on account of its combining some of the attributes of both Bull and Serpent. CERASTES was a name applied by the Greeks to ZEUS—" the horned Zeus."[3] Sometimes two serpents were correlated, as in

[1] *The Chaldean Oracles,* G. R. S. Mead, i. 60.
[2] *Sacred Mysteries among the Mayas,* Le Plongeon, p. 98.
[3] Payne-Knight, *Symbol. Lang. of Ancient Art,* p. 138.

fig. 478, where one has two horns and the other but one, denoting, presumably, male and female. In Egypt, says Professor PETRIE, two serpents were usually represented together—one often with the head of ISIS, the other of SER APIS[1] (=OSIRIS), so, therefore, male and female.

The letter G surmounted with a crown is the initial of *Gnosis*, the Sacred and Celestial Knowledge, *i.e.* WISDOM. The V formed by fig. 479 is the initial of VISHNU, the Hindoo APOLLO, and will be considered in a subsequent chapter.

480   481   482   483   484

Over figs. 480 to 482 appear the initial M, standing presumably for MAAT, the Goddess of Truth. MAAT, the personification of original and celestial Reason,[2] was regarded as the Great Mother, and her name was spelled MAAT, MAUT, and MAHT. The lettering around the watermarked designs herewith reads MAHT or THAM according to the point from which one commences, or according to the side that one holds the transparency to the light. One of the designations of the Babylonish Great Mother was THAM. The serpents or wavy lines on fig. 483 certainly denote water, and it is probable that MAHT and THAM both originally meant Waters. It is possible that MATH and

---

[1] *Religion of Ancient Egypt*, Flinders Petrie, p. 26.
[2] *Perfect Way*, Kingsford and Maitland, p. 155.

THAM are simply permutations of the same four letters, each of which stands for an attribute of the fourfold Deity. It is claimed by mystics that the sacrosanct AUM of the Hindoos is a combination of similar initials, A standing for the foundative power of the Creator, U for the generative power of the Mother, and M for their engenderings or the Son. Thus the mystery name AUM is capable of permutations which in the Maya language read : [1]

U-A-M=I am the male Creator.

M-U-A=the Maker of these waters.

A-U-M=thy Mother's Son.

The Trinity A.U.M. in the alternative form "OM" is hailed as "He who resteth upon the face of the Milky Ocean, who art celebrated by a thousand names and under various forms." [2]

In India the syllable AUM is pronounced like a drawling Amen, and there must be a close connection between the AUM of India, the AMUN-RA and AMUN-KNEPTH of Egypt, and the JUPITER-AMMON of Greece. AMUN-KNEPTH was the Egyptian JUPITER, and this good genius was represented as a Serpent, which, according to HORAPOLLO, was "the emblem of the Spirit which pervades the universe." [3] It would thus appear that the Sea was from the first a symbol of unfathomable Truth or Wisdom, and that the Good Serpent was invariably identified as an alternative sign for the same idea. There was a tradition that the Garden of the Hesperides was guarded by three Nymphs and an ever-watchful Serpent named LADON. In Bohemia Cinderella is known as The Princess with the Gold Star on her brow, and her name is LADA. [4] It is probable that this is

---

[1] Queen Moo and the Egyptian Sphinx, Le Plongeon, p. 23.

[2] The Gnostics and their Remains, King, p. 27.

[3] Queen Moo, p. 49.

[4] Cinderella, p. 418; see also Frazer, The Dying God, pp. 261, 262.

either the feminine or diminutive form of LADON the Good
Serpent, and that the root of both words is to be found in
LA, a syllable which in the Maya language means "that
which has existed for ever ; the Eternal Truth." [1]

The Indian gods are said to upchurn the nectar of the
delectable Butter of the Brine, and the Hindoos affirm that
the three mystic letters AUM were "milked out" by the
Creator. According to an Indian version of CINDERELLA,
the heroine is the seventh of seven daughters, all of whom
wed the Prince. CINDERELLA having unjustly fallen under
a cloud of suspicion, the children say to their father : "Let
your seventh wife who is in the dungeon come forth.
Place seven curtains between her and us and watch what
happens." Cinderella is brought out and seven curtains
are placed between her and the children. Three streams
of milk spring from her breasts, and, penetrating the seven
curtains, run into the children's mouths.[2] It is not an
uncommon incident in fairy-tales for wine, honey, and
jewels to rain from the heroine's mouth ; but three milky
streams through seven veils is an idea so peculiarly bizarre
that, as Bacon says of certain fables, it proclaims a parable
afar off. Roman Catholics are taught that ST GERTRUDE
was divinely instructed, and that, as often as the Angelic
Salutation is devoutly recited by the faithful on earth,
three efficacious streamlets proceed from the Father, the
Son, and the Holy Ghost, most sweetly penetrating the
Virgin's heart.[3]

The Seven veils through which CINDERELLA's three
streamlets penetrate may be compared with the Seven gates
of the under-world through which ISHTAR passed, and the
Seven planetary spheres through which SOPHIA, the Virgin

---

[1] Sacred Mysteries among the Mayas, Le Plongeon, p. 54.
[2] Cinderella, p. 263.
[3] All for Jesus, Faber, p. 104.

of Light, arose. These seven spheres, whose movement
made the fabled music of the spheres, were supposed to be
imposed one upon another like a nest of inverted crystalline
bowls. PLATO conceived a heavenly Mermaid to be seated
singing upon each sphere, and these Seven Syrens of the
Spheres may be compared with the Seven Maidens of
CINDERELLA, the Seven Maidens of SOPHIA, the Seven
HATHORS or Fates, and the Seven Spirits which stand before
the Throne of God.[1]

According to Genesis, " In the beginning the earth was
without form, and void ; and darkness was upon the face of
the deep : and the Spirit of God moved upon the face of
the waters. And God said, Let there be light : and there
was light." According to Mexican traditions as stated in
the sacred *Popul Vuh*, " Everything was without life, calm
and silent ; all was motionless and quiet. Void was the
immensity of the heavens, the face of the earth did not
manifest itself yet : only the tranquil sea was and the space
of the heavens. All was immobility and silence in the
darkness in the night ; only the Creator, the Maker, the
Dominator, the Serpent covered with feathers, they who
engender, they who create, were on the waters as an ever-
increasing light. They are surrounded by green and blue."[2]

The Virgin of Light was widely regarded as the first-
born of the Supreme Spirit. " I," says WISDOM of herself,
" was set up from everlasting, from the beginning, or ever
the earth was. When there were no depths, I was brought
forth ; when there were no fountains abounding with water.
Before the mountains were settled ; before the hills was
I brought forth : while as yet he had not made the earth,
nor the fields, nor the highest part of the dust of the world.
When he prepared the heavens, I was there : when he

[1] Revelation i. 4.
[2] Quoted in *Sacred Mythology among the Mayas*, p. 111.

set a compass upon the face of the depth : when he established the clouds above : when he strengthened the fountains of the deep : when he gave to the sea his decree, that the waters should not pass his commandment : when he appointed the foundations of the earth : then I was by him, as one brought up with him : and I was daily his delight, rejoicing always before him." [1]

Hindoos believe that when the Creator dispelled darkness and produced the Waters, there floated upon them NARAYANA, the Divine Spirit. Among Christians this spirit of Wisdom is generally pictured in the form of a dove, and Milton thus invokes it :—

> " Instruct me, for thou knowest ; thou from the first
> Wast present, and with mighty wings outspread
> Dove-like sat'st brooding on the vast Abyss,
> And mad'st it pregnant : what in me is dark
> Illumine, what is low raise and support ;
> That to the height of this great argument
> I may assert Eternal Providence
> And justify the ways of God to men." [2]

In the *Kalevala* — which, be it remembered, is not nominally philosophy but merely the popular tradition of a rural people that has only of recent years been taken down from the mouths of the peasantry—ILMATAR the Creatrix of the Universe, the Virgin Daughter of the Air, is described as descending from her aerial Home and sinking quietly down on to the wide expanse of elemental waters. ILMATAR, described sometimes as the *Creatrix* and at others as the fairest " *daughter of* Creation," floats for *seven* long centuries upon the ocean's surface. Then—

> " The wind that blew around her,
> And the sea woke life within her." [3]

---

[1] Proverbs viii. 23–30.   [2] *Paradise Lost.*
[3] Runo, i. 136, 137.

A duck hovers over the waters, but is unable to find any footing until the Mother of the Waters uplifts her knee and shoulders from the waves, thus affording to the bird a nesting-place.   Seven eggs—six of gold and one of iron—are laid, and the duck broods over them for three days. Then the Mother of the Waters rolls the eggs into the ocean, where they are shattered into pieces.   From the yolk of one of them grew our Sun ; from the white, our Moon ; from the upper fragment of a shell rose the vault of heaven ; and from the lower half sprang the solid earth.   "Now," continues the *Kalevala*,

> " the time passed quickly over,
> And the years rolled quickly onward ;
> In the new Sun's shining lustre,
> In the new Moon's softer beaming,
> Still the Water-Mother floated,
> Water-Mother, maid aerial,
> Ever on the peaceful waters,
> On the billows' foamy surface,
> With the moving waves before her
> And the heaven serene behind her.
>   When the ninth year had passed over
> And the summer tenth was passing,
> From the sea her head she lifted,
> And her forehead she uplifted,
> And she then began creation,
> And she brought the world to order
> On the open ocean's surface,
> On the far-extending waters." [1]

In the emblems below are representations not only of the Water-Mother herself, but also of a duck floating on the far-extending waters.   The fact that Isis is referred to as a duck leads one to conjecture that there existed in Egypt a legend similar to that of FINLAND :—

[1] Runo, i. 245, 261.

" Come thou in peace to thy seat, O Lord Conqueror
Show us the Great Bull, the lovable Lord as he shall become
Thy duck, thy Sister Isis, produceth the sweet odours belonging
to thee and with thee." [1]

In many of these Water-Mother and Princess emblems
the hairs are carefully arranged as *Six*—just as in the JESUS
emblems (*ante*, p. 27) the hairs were represented as *three*.
In ancient MEXICO the hair of the Great Mother was

[1] *The Burden of Isis*, p. 34.

carefully arranged on her forehead in curls and crosses, the curls being made to form the crosses.[1] In the first edition of King's *Gnostics*[2] a facsimile of SOPHIA is re-reproduced with her locks carefully arranged three on either side of her head ; but in the second and revised edition of this work, SOPHIA's six hairs have been ignorantly embellished by the artist reviser into an indeterminate and meaningless number. It will be noticed that fig. 479 (*ante*, p. 202) is six-tongued, six denoting the attributes of the Deity, *i.e.* Power, Majesty, Wisdom, Love, Mercy, and Justice.[3] These or similar six powers were said to be the six roots or radicals of the Parent Flame, the Boundless Power which stood, standeth, and shall stand, and these six aspects of the Flame probably account for the six vestal virgins whose duty it was to keep alight the sacred Fire. Six perfections are attached to the Solar Wheel fig. 493, and in the six letters of the name J E S O U S the mystics saw an identity between Jesus and SOPHIA, the Daughter of Light.[4]

The natives of the SANDWICH ISLANDS have a tradition that in the beginning there was nothing but water, until the Deity in the form of a big bird descended from on high and laid an egg in the sea. That egg burst, and from it came forth HAWAI.[5] According to Greek Mythology, Love issued from the egg of Night floating in chaos.[6] The Hindoos teach that the Supreme Spirit by union with the Goddess Maya produced the waters, and in them deposited a productive seed. This germ became an egg, brilliant as gold, resplendent as a star, and from it was reproduced the

[1] *Signs and Symbols of Primordial Man*, A. W. Churchward, p. 369.
[2] 1864, plate v. fig. 1.
[3] *The Gnostics*, King, p. 61.
[4] *Fragments of a Faith Forgotten*, G. R. S. Mead, p. 369.
[5] *Polynesian Researches*, Ellis.
[6] Lemprière, Nox.

Supreme Being under the form of BRAHMA, the ancestor of all beings.[1]

Doubtless this sunlike egg is to be identified with the golden egg laid by the primeval Goose or Bird of the Spirit; it is also noteworthy that the claim is put forward by ISIS: "The fruit which I have brought forth is the Sun." The Egyptians affirmed that PTAH, the "Lord of Truth," emerged from an egg that came out from the mouth of AMUN-KNEPTH, the True and Perfect Serpent. The initial P associated with fig. 482 (*ante*, p. 203) possibly refers to Ptah; and the letters M T under figs. 486, 487, and 488 may be a contraction for MAHT, the Mother of Truth.

According both to the Mayas and Egyptians, the Great Serpent was "of a blue colour with *yellow* scales."[2] Yellow, or gold the colour of the Sun, is still recognised as the symbol of "Love, constancy, dignity, and wisdom,"[3] and yellow is to-day the royal colour in China, "the Celestial Empire." Yellow is likewise the priestly colour of Buddhism.

Among the Egyptians, and also according to SWEDENBORG, Blue, which is not now a canonical colour, was the symbol of Truth.[4] One of the bards of the *Kalevala* invokes ILMATAR (obviously *El Mater* or *God-Mother*) in the words:

> "Ancient Daughter of Creation,
> Come in all thy *golden* beauty;
> Thou the oldest of all women,
> Thou the first of all the Mothers.
>
> .   .   .   .
>
> Rise thou up, O Water-Mother,
> Raise thy *blue cap*[5] from the billows."[6]

---

[1] *Queen Moo*, p. 70.
[2] *Sacred Mysteries among the Mayas*, p. 109.
[3] *Christian Symbolism*, F. E. Hulme, p. 24.
[4] *Doctrine of Correspondences*, E. Madeley, p. 363.
[5] Notice the cap on figs. 486 and 488.
[6] Runo, xvii. 280, 294.

Among the Mayas Blue, being the colour of the vault of heaven, was symbolic of holiness, sanctity, chastity, hence of happiness.[1] In MEXICO, EGYPT, and CHALDEA, blue was worn during mourning as a token of the felicity which the soul, freed from the trammels of matter, was enjoying in the celestial regions. Egyptian mummies are frequently found shrouded in a network of blue beads. In order to signify their exalted and heavenly character the Gods were frequently painted blue. The term "blue-blooded" may have originated from this cause, and up to the time of the Spanish conquest of Mexico, those natives who offered themselves as propitiatory sacrifices to their Deity smeared their bodies with blue paint.[2]

Two shades of Blue have always been recognised by Mysticism and Poetry ; the fair Turquoise of a cloudless sky and the transcendental "Ultramarine"[3] of Lapis Lazuli. In INDIA the pure, unsullied, elemental blue is still the unearthly colour, the colour of the mystic lotus and the languorous, long-eyed Gods.

One version of Cinderella describes her distinctive dress as "blue like the sky" ; another as "of the colour of noontide sky" ; another as "sea-coloured" ; another as "dark blue covered with golden embroidery" ; another as "like the waves of the sea" ; another as "like the sea with fishes swimming in it" ; and another as "colour of sea covered with golden fishes."[4]

The Goddess Isis is denominated not only "Lady of the Beginning" and "Lady of the Emerald,"[5] but also "Lady of the Turquoise," and she invokes Osiris as the God of Turquoise and Lapis Lazuli. "With Turquoise

---

[1] *Queen Moo*, p. 90.
[2] *Ibid.*
[3] Ultramarine = "beyond the sea."
[4] *Cinderella*, pp. 130, 159, 181, 250.
[5] Evergreen immortality.

is thy hair twined and with Lapis Lazuli, the finest of Lapis Lazuli. Lo ! the Lapis Lazuli is above thy hair ! "[1]

In the symbolic mosaic with which the fair Shulamite hails King Solomon, he is described as "bright ivory overlaid with sapphires,"[2] the blue of the sapphire having doubtless the same signification as the deep blue of Lapis Lazuli.

A traditional epithet for MINERVA, the Greek Goddess of Wisdom, was "the blue-eyed maid," and in the story of the descent of the Sun, KAMALAMITRA works out his fate, spurred forward by the irresistible "*blue* light in the eyes of Shri." When Shri meets her lover in this under-world, she bathes him in a flood of *blue* colour from her wondrous eyes, and looking towards her, KAMALAMITRA finds the whole world vanish in a mist of *blue*. When next he met her, it is related that the blue colour of SHRI's wondrous eyes shot from them, and streaming about the room illuminated it with the glory of the setting sun.

The beauty of CINDERELLA "lights up the whole room," and, SHRI-like, CINDERELLA "shines like the Sun."[3] It is, too, almost a tradition that the Princess of Fairyland shall have blue eyes and hair like a waterfall of golden Light.

Black, the hue of another of Cinderella's robes, is now the symbol of evil, but evidently it had originally a good signification. Isis was at times represented as black, and DIANA, the Goddess of Light, was represented indifferently as white and black. Dr INMAN, whose eyes were fascinated by phallicism, attributes what was obviously a sacred blackness to an indecent, and, on his part, imaginary origin : " I have," he says, " sought in vain for even a plausible reason for the blackness of sacred virgins and children in certain

---

[1] *Burden of Isis*, p. 55.
[2] *Song of Solomon* v. 14.
[3] *Cinderella*, pp. 242, 333.

Papal Shrines, which is compatible with decency and Christianity. It is clear that, the matter will not bear the light."[1]

But there is no indecency about blackness, and its meaning is easily accessible. It was a symbol of "the Divine Dark" of Inscrutability, of Silence, and of Eternity. It was essentially one of the hues of Wisdom and was thus understood by Milton, who, referring to Cassiopeia, writes :

> " Goddess, sage and holy,
> Whose saintly visage is too bright
> To hit the sense of human sight ;
> And therefore to our weaker view
> O'erlaid with black, *staid Wisdom's hue.*"[2]

Many of the gods and goddesses of the past have been portrayed as dual-hued—*White* to signify Time and *Black* to denote Eternity, White for Day and Black for Night. Night, the Mother of all things, was portrayed in a starry veil, holding in her arms two children, one white, the other black. The Egyptians worshipped the Great Spirit as " Endless Time and Eternity." The colour of KRISHNA was blue, and his name means " Blue-black." OSIRIS, like HORUS, was sometimes black and sometimes white.[3] APIS, the sacred ox, was black with a whitish spot resembling a moon.[4] AMUN-KNEPTH, the unmanifest Divine Wisdom, was described as " a thrice unknown darkness transcending all intellectual perception,"[5] and the ancient Hindoo *Stanzas of Dzyan* speak of the White Brilliant Son of the Dark Hidden Father.[6] The Greek word for *darkness* is *kneph-*

---

[1] *Pagan Symbolism*, A. W. Inman, p. 80.
[2] *Il Penseroso.*
[3] *Signs and Symbols of Primordial Man*, A. W. Churchward, pp. 27, 78, 242.
[4] Lemprière.
[5] *Sacred Mysteries among the Mayas*, Le Plongeon, p. 53.
[6] *The Stanzas of Dzyan*, p. 30.

aios, which must be allied to KNEPH, the primeval Darkness that was on the face of the Deep. " There is in God," says Vaughan, the English mystic, "a deep and dazzling darkness," and it is undoubtedly with this Divine Black that the gods and goddesses of antiquity were frequently overlaid. " I," says the fair Bride of the Song of Solomon, "am black,"[1] but comely as the *tents* of Kedar and as the *curtains* of Solomon—a passage that may be compared with Isaiah's reference to the Deity "that stretcheth out the heavens like a *curtain,* and spreadeth them out as a *tent* to dwell in."[2]

Not only was CINDERELLA robed sometimes from head to foot in black, but it is an almost universal feature of the story that she sits by the stove and blackens her face with soot or ashes.[3] Similarly in masculine versions, Cendrillot is described as " black as a sweep and always by the stove." Cinderella's nickname is sometimes " sooty face," and one version relates how the Prince tears off her disguise and discovers beneath the soot a heavenly face.[4]

" No man," says Isis " has lifted my veil," and, Isis-like, CINDERELLA is not infrequently enveiled in mist. When hard pressed she flees exclaiming : " The mist is behind me, the mist is before me, God's sun is above me." At another time it is : " Mist behind, nobody sees whence I come," and all that the Prince sees when pursuing her is " something like the long beam of a shooting star through dense mist." Sometimes she exclaims :

> " Light before, behind me dark,
> Whither I ride no man shall mark."

---

[1] i. 5.   [2] Isaiah xl. 22.

[3] The smearing with ashes is probably symbolic of something—I know not what. The Hindoos invoke Shiwa, "actually smeared with ashes," as "that triumphant Lord who stands in mysterious meditation ashy pale, appearing to the left as a woman and to the right as a man."—*An Essence of the Dusk,* F. W. Bain, p. 3.   [4] *Cinderella,* pp. 224, 285, 452.

At others she cries out pleadingly :

> " Darkness behind me, light on my way,
> Carry me, carry me, home to-day."

When pursued by undesirables she flings over her shoulder a white veil woven of mist, rendering herself invisible, and occasionally she thwarts her pursuers by throwing balls or bags of mist and by scattering handfuls of pearls and jewels.[1]

Of the riddles put to the prince by the Slav Maid with the golden hair, one is : " Fire cannot light me, brush cannot sweep me, no painter can paint me, no hiding-place secure me." The lover correctly answers, " Sunshine." The maid then puts him another riddle : " I existed before the creation of ADAM. I am always changing in succession the two colours of my dress. Thousands of years have gone by, but I have remained unaltered both in colour and form." " Why," says the Prince, " you must be ' Time, including day and night.' "[2] This is admittedly the correct answer, and, among the ancients, Time was an attribute and aspect of the Deity. The Persians called Him " Time without bounds," or " Boundless Time," and the Egyptians spoke of Him as " The Great Green One, Endless Time, and Eternity." The two alternative colours of the Maiden's dress areas the prince guessed, the garb of Time including day and night, day being white and night being black, Wisdom alternately veiled and unveiled, manifest and inscrutable.

In fig. 485 (*ante*, p. 209) Isis the Duck is seen floating on the primeval waters, and surrounding her is a clock dial, the Face of Time. In the beginning, say the *Stanzas of Dzyan*, " The Eternal Parent wrapped in her Ever-Invisible Robes had slumbered once again for *Seven* Centuries. Time was

---

[1] *Cinderella*, pp. 323, 325, 331, 418. One variant of this couplet reads, " *White* before and *black* behind ; Nobody shall see where I go."—*Cinderella*, p. 476.

[2] *Slav Tales*, pp. 228, 229.

not, for it lay asleep in the Infinite Bosom of Duration."[1]   It
will be noticed that the characters on this clock Face consist
of the Cross of Light and the figure I, readable as either Isis
or Jesus.   In fig. 494 the clock hand consists of the *Fleur de
Lys* of Light and the heart of Love, and in the centre of
fig. 495 there appears in lieu of hands a *seven*fold flame or
cloud.   One of the first experiences of Komensky's Pilgrim
upon quitting the labyrinth of this world and beholding
things through the spectacles of the Holy Spirit is the
vision of a clock.   A strange light pervades everything, and
what previously had appeared to be but CHAOS, falls into a

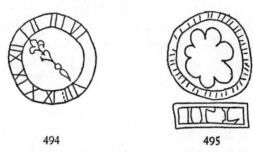

494   495

rhythmic, well-ordered system.   The seemingly meaningless and scattered wheels of life unite into the form of an
instrument similar to a clock, which shows the course of the
world and its divine guidance.   " I beheld," says Komensky,
" the world before me as a vast clock work, fashioned out of
divers visible and invisible materials ; and it was wholly
glassy, transparent, and fragile.   It had thousands, nay,
thousands of thousands, of larger and smaller columns, wheels,
hooks, teeth, dents, and all these moved and worked together,
some silently, some with much rustling and rattling of divers
fashions.   In the middle of all stood the largest, principal,
yet invisible wheel ; from it the various motions of the others
proceeded in some unfathomable manner.   For the power

[1] *Stanzas of Dzyan*, p. 18.

of the wheel penetrated through all things, and directed everything. How this was done I was not, indeed, able fully to fathom; but that it was truly done, I saw very clearly and evidently. Now, this appeared to me both wondrous and most delightful: though all these wheels shook continually, and sometimes vanished for a time—for the teeth and dents, and even the wheels and little columns, were sometimes displaced and fell to pieces—yet the general movement never stopped; for by some wondrous contrivance of this secret direction all that was wanting was ever replaced, filled up, renewed.

"I will speak more clearly: I saw the glory of God, and how heaven and earth, and the abyss, and all that can be imagined beyond the world as far as the endless limits of eternity, were full of His power and divinity. I saw how His omnipotence penetrated everything, and was the foundation of all things; that all that befell in the whole wide world was according to His will, the smallest things and the greatest; that also I saw."

Time or the Ancient of Days in the Semitic is RA, a word identified by Le Plongeon with the Mayan LA, meaning "that which has existed for ever: The Eternal Truth."[1] RA, says Dr Churchward, is called "the aged one of the confines of the Mount of Glory."[2] Isis was the "Mistress of the Mountain," the divine "Lady of the Mound."[3] In fairy-tale the Maid with the Golden Hair and the wonderful eyes of blue is placed not infrequently on the summit of a crystal mountain.[4] There is a Hindoo legend that the Lord of Time dwells on a transcendent mountain whose summit glows like a tongue of flame at sunset, and towards

[1] *Sacred Mysteries among the Mayas*, p. 54.
[2] *Signs and Symbols of Primordial Man*, p. 347.
[3] *Ibid.*, p. 123.
[4] *Cinderella*, pp. 447, 452.

which the Seven Stars of the Great Bear turn their eyes. The Slav peasants, who have a fairy-tale about this crystal mountain, say that a fire burns without ceasing upon its summit. Around this fire sit twelve Great Beings—the twelve months—and in the centre of the flame is an aged man with long white beard and bald head. " Man," said the Ancient of Days, addressing an inquisitive human visitor, " waste not thy life here ; return to thy cottage ; work, and live honestly. Take as many embers as thou wilt ; we have more than we need." Then having said this he disappeared, and the twelve Beings filled a large sack with embers, which they put upon the poor man's shoulders and advised him to hasten home.[1]

To appreciate the significance of Cinderella's supernatural garments one may refer with advantage to a Gnostic poem included among the apocryphal *Acts of Thomas the Apostle*. These verses, known generally as *The Hymn of the Soul* or *The Hymn of the Robe of Glory*, have, however, nothing to do with the original Greek text of the Acts of Thomas (A.D. 936), and their style and contents are quite foreign to the context. Mr G. R. S. MEAD, their most recent editor, describes them as manifestly an independent document incorporated by the Syrian redactor in the naïve fashion usual with such compilations.[2]

The Hymn of the Robe of Glory, in many respects a Syrian version of the *Descent of the Sun*, consists of 105 couplets, and is a masculine variant of Ishtar's descent into the under-world. The Heavenly Parents decide to despatch their son on an arduous quest for a certain Pearl which, lying in the sea, is guarded by a loud-breathing serpent. For this purpose the Boy is deprived of his kingly apparel, and is promised that on his return with the pearl his

---

[1] *Slav Tales*, 7.
[2] *The Hymn of the Robe of Glory*, G. R. S. Mead, p. 10.

magnificent garments shall be restored to him. He descends
to the land of BABEL—a word which LE PLONGEON derives
from Maya words meaning custom, way of our ancestors,[1]
i.e. convention — takes lodgings near the loud-breathing
serpent and awaits an opportunity to win the pearl.

> "Lone was I there, yea, all lonely,
> To my fellow-lodgers a stranger."

But gradually the natives of Babel lure the boy into
forgetfulness of his high origin and of his mission, and from
the weight of their victuals he sank into a profound sleep.
Meantime, the Parents perceiving all that was happening,
grew anxious and addressed a letter to their Son. "Up and
arise from thy sleep, remember that thou art a King's Son,
see whom thou hast served in thy slavedom, bethink thyself
of the pearl, remember thy glorious robe, thy Splendid
Mantle remember!" Whereupon, continues the story,

> "I snatched up the Pearl
> And turned to the House of my Father;
> Their filthy and unclean garments
> I stripped off and left in their country.
> To the way that I came I betook me,
> To the light of our Home to the Dawnland."

His wonderful robe is returned to him and he and his Pearl
are received with rejoicing at the court of his Royal Father.

Wisdom is proverbially not only an excellent jewel, but
the Pearl of Great Price. The monuments of Egypt call
precious stones "hard stones of Truth,"[2] and the pearl has
always been a symbolic *ne plus ultra*, doubtless by reason of
the numerous analogies existing between it and Truth. It
was once supposed that oysters came to the surface during
night-time and opened their shells, into which fell dewdrops

---

[1] *Queen Moo*, p. 34.
[2] *The Science of Correspondence*, E. Madeley, p. 363.

that turned into pearls. The Pearl was certainly regarded
as a symbol of the Soul or Spirit lying encased within the
human body. "There was a time," says Plato, "when we
were not yet sunk into this 'tomb,' which now we bear
about with us and call it ' body,' bound fast (to it) like
oyster (to its shell)."[1] There is, as Browning says, an "inmost
centre in us all where Truth abides in fullness," and the
pearl being spherical—a " very perfect orb of supreme loveliness "—it was for this additional reason doubtless adopted
as a symbol of Perfection. It is proverbial that not only are
the lips of knowledge a precious jewel, but that Wisdom is
herself Perfection and leads her followers to Perfection. The
number seven, so constantly associated with Wisdom, was by
old writers called the number of Perfection.[2] Christ likened
Heaven to a Pearl of Great Price, and the twelve gates of
the New Jerusalem were said to be twelve pearls ; "every
several gate was of one pearl."[3] "Blessed is the man,"
says Wisdom, " that heareth me, watching daily at my gates,
waiting at the posts of my doors. For whoso findeth me
findeth life."[4] Wisdom is indeed always connected with
the Perfect Pearl, and she is equally associated with the
Gateways of Heaven.

Sometimes Cinderella is called PRECIOSA ;[5] and fairies
lead her to a " golden portal," where a gold star lights upon

[1] *Phædrus* (250 c.). Compare also—
> " Living friends, be wise, and dry
> Straightway every weeping eye.
> What ye lift upon the bier
> Is not worth a single tear.
> 'Tis an empty sea-shell, one
> Out of which the pearl is gone ;
> The shell is broken, it lies there ;
> The pearl, the all, the soul, is here."—ANON.

[2] *Christian Symbolism*, Hulme, p. 11.

[3] Revelation xxi. 21.   [4] Proverbs viii. 34–35.

[5] *Cinderella*, pp. 162, 163, 216, 247, 348, 349.

her brow. She asks from her Father "a pearl dress without slit or seam " : She lets down her hair and shakes out showers of pearls : She is clothed from head to foot with necklaces of brilliants and precious stones, and gems fall from her lips when she speaks. At times she wears "a diamond dress," or a gold dress trimmed with diamonds, or a robe of silk thread thick with diamonds and pearls. According to *The Hymn of the Robe of Glory*, the vestment of the King's Son was "of gold tissue with jewels encrusted," and its seams were fastened with "adamantine jewels"[1] (*i.e.* diamonds), a description inviting comparison with Cinderella's dress of silk thread thick with diamonds and pearls.

The Robe of Glory is further specified as "all bespangled with sparkling splendour of colours" and as wrought "in a motley of colour."[2] Similarly, CINDERELLA has a dress "of all colours," specified sometimes as "a wonderful scintillating dress," "of splendour passing description." Another version graphically records the glitter of her robe as "like the curling of a stream in the sun."[3]

But perhaps the most striking of these coincidences is the musical properties of the Robe of Glory. The 90th couplet of *The Hymn* reads :

> "I heard the sound of its music
> Which it whispered as it descended."

Similarly, Cinderella has a dress that "rings like a bell as she comes downstairs." This remarkable garment is described as covered with little bells and chains of gold. At times it is a dress "of chimes" and at others "a robe of golden bells."[4] These golden chimes immediately suggest the

---

[1] *The Robe of Glory*, 26, 70.
[2] *Ibid.*, 26.
[3] *Cinderella*, pp. 272, 313, 396, 401.
[4] *Ibid.*, pp. 135, 136, 194, 195, 258, 321.

sistrum of the Goddess Isis. The sistrum, an instrument of little golden bells, which, when shaken, made music at her Festivals, was a symbol of the Awakener. "The sistrum," says Plutarch, "shows that the things that *are* must be *shaken* and never *cease from motion*, but be as it were stirred up when they slumber and are slothful."[1] The penetrating sound of Roland's Horn was audible "full fifteen leagues away"; the sound of Cinderella's golden bells could be heard "two hundred leagues all round," and their ceasing to ring was a sign of misfortune.[2]

According to a Breton version of CINDERELLA, narrated by a cabin boy thirteen years of age, CINDERELLA's father offered her a dress "like the Stars, like the Sun, *like the Light*,"[3] a description that may be compared with SWEDENBORG's account of the raiment of the angels. "Angels," he says, "are men, and live together in society like men on earth; they have garments, houses, and other such things, differing only from earthly things in that, being in a more perfect state, they exist in greater perfection. The garments with which angels are clothed, like all other things about them, correspond to what is in their minds; and therefore they really exist. Their garments correspond to their intelligence, and so all in the heavens are seen clothed according to their intelligence; and because some excel others in intelligence, therefore they are more beautifully clad. The garments of the most intelligent glow *like a flame* or glisten like the light."[4]

To draw the similarity still closer, one may note that Cinderella's robe is described sometimes as "a magnificent dress *of flame*," at other times like the Sun, the glitter of which people cannot at first face," "like the Moon," "like the Dawn," as "wrought of all the stars of Heaven," "the

---

[1] *Isis and Osiris.*
[2] *Cinderella*, p. 201.
[3] *Ibid.*, p. 376.
[4] *Heaven and Hell*, § 177, 178.

wonder of wonders," "woven of moonbeams," and "woven of sunbeams," and occasionally as so dazzling that it has to be carried "by relays of pages."[1]

In the apotheosis of the Sun, he is usually pictured as driving his four-steeded chariot. Similarly, Cinderella is equipped with a "golden chariot" or a "splendid chariot."[2] But, as is more usual and appropriate, her traditional cortege is a crystal coach and four white horses.

Cinderella, robed Apollo-like with the Sunlight, occasionally dons a mantle made of the skins of field mice, under which she cloaks her magnificent robes, and making herself of no reputation sets herself to the accomplishment of mean and everyday tasks. In the Temples of APOLLO it was usual to maintain white mice, which were regarded as sacred to the Sungod, and *Smintheus* the Mouse was one of the appellations of Apollo. The Greeks themselves were ignorant of the origin of this association of APOLLO and a mouse, and modern savants are equally at a loss to explain it. Numerous instances might be adduced in which a Hero or Heroine stoops to a term of servitude before fulfilling an exalted destiny. APOLLO tended the flocks of ADMETUS and served LAOMEDON for a wage; HERCULES was for twelve years in the service of EURYSTHEUS, after which he became immortal; SARGON was a gardener's boy, and SOLOMON a scullion. The mouse being the meanest and smallest of the animal world, it may have served as a symbol of the humble position which APOLLO had once filled, and to which he was conceived as being willing to again descend. If this were so, it was simply a prototype of the splendour of the immortal Light incarnating in a stable at Bethlehem. As the Dean of Ely recently observed, there is no danger of lowering God. "Even before the Incarnation men could

---

[1] *Cinderella*, pp. 80, 167, 190, 212, 274, 353, 368, 376, 396, 413.
[2] *Ibid.*, pp. 285, 406.

realise the incomparable exaltedness and incomparable condescension which meet in God."

The ancients conceived their divinities not as super-mundane beings of a different calibre from mankind, but as stooping sympathetically and not infrequently to don the mouseskin of humanity. "Come, my beloved," says SOLOMON to his Bride, "let us go forth into the field ; *let us lodge in the villages.*" [1]

In Indian mythology GANESA, the God of Wisdom, is represented as elephant-headed, and with his foot upon a mouse ; here, again, the idea intended probably being that he embraces the whole gamut of creation from the greatest to the least. In EGYPT the mouse was sacred to HORUS, the saviour God of Light.[2]

Not only does CINDERELLA cloak herself under a mantle of mouseskin, but among her disguises is the hide of an ass. The Ass upon which Christ rode into Jerusalem is pro-verbially the emblem of Humility ; and the Ass-skin mantle may be identified as the cloak of humility.

Sometimes the story of CINDERELLA is known as "The Hearth Cat," [3] and the heroine robes herself in a mantle made from the skins of cats. The Egyptians figured a cat with a human face on the arch of the *sistrum*, and used the same word MAU to denote both *cat* and *light*.[4] In her aspect of the Hearth Cat CINDERELLA evidently corresponds with the Roman conception of VESTA, the Goddess of Hearth [5] and Home. Vesta was represented as veiled, and her Temple was built in the form of the Round of Perfection. That CINDERELLA was identified with the Hearth Goddess

---

[1] *Song of Solomon* vii. 11.
[2] *Custom and Myth*, A. Lang, pp. 113, 116.
[3] *Cinderella*, p. 341.
[4] Renouf, *Hibbert Lectures*, p. 237.
[5] The word *hearth*, according to Payne-Knight, is from HERTHA, the German name for the Goddess VESTA.

is to be inferred from the lines which are put into her mouth :
"Mist before me, mist behind me, God Almighty above
me ! Little angels, guardian angels, protect the house
whilst I'm away." [1] The ancients conceived the *Magna
Mater* as the great Workwoman, and it was said of Wisdom,
"sweetly doth she order all things." [2] CINDERELLA's name
"LUCREZIA" further identifies her as the Goddess of Home
Life. Not only was LUCREZIA, the Roman matron, proverbially a pattern of immaculate chastity, but she was
also the ideal housekeeper, and when summoned by her
husband's messenger — unlike her neighbours—was discovered "at home employed in the midst of her female
servants and *easing their labour by sharing it herself.*" [3]

The words italicised are a clue to the meaning of
CINDERELLA's shoes, which are sometimes described as of
"*blue* glass," sometimes as of gold, sometimes as "Sun"
shoes, sometimes as pearl-embroidered or spangled with
jewels, and sometimes as "matchless." [4]

The meaning of these miraculous shoes, which are
graphically described as bounding towards Cinderella's foot
"like iron to a magnet," [5] may perhaps be elicited from
the *Concordance* to the writings of Emanuel Swedenborg. [6]
"Shoes," says Swedenborg, correspond to "the lowest
natural things," and "the soles beautifully shod" are
emblematic of the love of making oneself useful. The
desire of being helpful is the keynote of CINDERELLA's
character and the fountain of all her good fortune. The
tale generally opens by CINDERELLA and her two step-
sisters meeting an animal, a fairy, or an old man, who
implores them for some mean service. The proud sisters,
Pride and Selfishness, haughtily decline, but CINDERELLA,

---

[1] *Cinderella*, p. 421.
[2] Wisdom of Solomon viii. 1.
[3] Lemprière.
[4] *Cinderella*, p. 516.
[5] *Ibid.*, p. 161.
[6] Art. "Shoe."

the Celestial Spirit, consents, and is rewarded by subsequent good fortune. It is a cardinal feature of the story that CINDERELLA gives her services for nothing and volunteers to perform all the dirty work. The labour imposed upon her, and which she always performs with alacrity, is essentially the meanest of the mean. Often it is disgusting, and, according to quite twenty-five per cent. of the stories, consists of cleansing an unclean head. An old man or a fairy—or, according to one version, the Virgin MARY—meets Cinderella and her sisters and says with a simple and unaffected directness : " Louse my head." The proud sisters, with a volley of abuse, decline, but CINDERELLA accepts the undesirable task and combs out lice and nits, which *turn into pearls and jewels* as they fall. It is clear that the intention of the allegory, like that of Christ washing the disciples' feet, is that the meaner the service the greater its beauty. It is probable that the reason why the shoe was adopted as the symbol of the spirit of "let-me-do-it-for-you" was because the shoe protects its wearer and shields from dirt *by taking it upon itself.*

The symbolic vestures of humility under which Cinderella is occasionally draped are dresses of ass-skin, mouse-skin, cat-skin, and louse-skin, the lousing of a head being the emblem of as mean and revolting a service as one individual can perform for another. Yet, while in this lowest servitude, Cinderella has a vision of the glory that is essentially her own. In a Hanoverian version the little heroine peeps into a room where hangs a mirror in a golden frame. This mirror reflects a lovely girl radiant in royal robes, and with a crown of gold upon her head ; yet " she does not know it is herself." In due course she meets the prince and dons a dress " the like of which has never been seen." After having become a Queen, she looks again into the same mirror and recognises that it was she herself that long ago

she saw there reflected.[1] Compare with this incident the
76th couplet of *The Hymn of the Robe of Glory*, where the
hero exclaims of his robe :

> " At once as soon as I saw it,
> The glory *looked like my own self.*"

This couplet has been alternatively translated as " Myself
I saw as in a glass before my face." [2]

In a large and widely extended circle of CINDERELLA tales
the heroine is one of three daughters who, KING LEAR-
like, are asked to express the depth of their filial affection.
Cinderella, like Cordelia, makes no extravagant protestations,
but in every version replies that she loves her father " like
salt." She is accordingly turned out of doors, and is not
recalled until her misguided father has discovered by sad
experience the value of salt. In these stories it is invariably Salt with which Cinderella is identified, and Salt was
the symbol of Wisdom. Wisdom was frequently personified holding a salt-cellar,[3] and the bestowal of *Sal Sapientiæ*,
the Salt of Wisdom, is still a formality in the Latin Church.[4]
The heavenly SOPHIA appears in mystical Science as *sodium*
or salt, and her colour is yellow.[5] In the *Descent of the Sun*
SHRI is said to be the very salt of the sea of beauty, inspiring
in all who drank of it an insatiable thirst and an intolerable
craving for the water of the blue lakes of her eyes.[6] Christ
described His followers as the salt of the earth, and it was salt
that was employed by Elisha to sweeten the water of Jericho,
" And he went forth unto the spring of the waters, and cast

---

[1] *Cinderella*, pp. 191, 192.
[2] *The Hymn of the Robe of Glory*, G. R. S. Mead, p. 93.
[3] *New Atlantis* : a continuation of, by R. H., London, 1660, p. 23.
[4] *Christian Symbolism*, Mrs H. Jenner, p. 3.
[5] *The Perfect Way*, p. 56.
[6] Compare *Song of Solomon* ii. 4 : " Thine eyes like the fishpools in
Heshbon."

the salt in there, and said, Thus saith the Lord, I have healed these waters ; there shall not be from thence any more death or barren land. So the waters were healed unto this day, according to the saying of Elisha which he spake." [1]

There is a similar parable told of how MOSES sweetened the bitter waters of MARA, but instead of *salt* Moses threw in *wood*. It is curious to find that in a great many localities CINDERELLA is known as *Maria Wood*, varied sometimes into *Maria Wainscot* and *Princess Woodencloak*. According to these variants, a wooden sheath is fitted around Cinderella's body, or an oak-tree log is hollowed out so as to form a petticoat, and Cinderella gets in and out of her wooden sheathing at will. On one occasion she is observed emerging from her wainscot by a prince, who marries her.[2] There is a curious passage in *The Song of Solomon* relating to the mysterious "little sister." It reads : "What shall we do for our sister in the day when she shall be spoken for ? If she be a wall, we will build upon her a palace of silver ; and if she be a door, *we will inclose her with boards of cedar.*" [3]

According to SWEDENBORG, wood is the symbol of celestial goodness in its lowest corporeal plane. It is specially the type of goodwill to one's neighbour — a symbolism derived from the utility of wood for fire-making and house-building purposes. There must, I think, be some connection between CINDERELLA's wooden sheathing and SWEDENBORG's statement, " The quality of the innocence of little children has been represented to me by a something wooden, almost devoid of life." [4]

It is singular that Cinderella, if not a maid-of-all-work, is generally a goose-girl, or tender of geese. If a shepherdess

---

[1] 2 Kings ii. 21, 22.
[2] *Cinderella*, pp. 101, 105, 110, 303, 333, 410.
[3] viii. 8, 9.
[4] A *Concordance* to the writings of Swedenborg. Art. " Wood."

of sheep is she who tends her innocent ideas, a gooseherd is logically she who cherishes her spirituality. The geese that are guarded by Cinderella, having the wit to recognise the beauty of their incomparable mistress, sing in chorus :

> " Hiss, Hiss, Hiss !
> What a beautiful lady is this ;
> Just like the Moon and the Sun is she,
> Some nobleman's daughter she seems to me." [1]

Every Sunday Cinderella removes her wooden disguise and combs her hair, from which fall golden pips, and these pips are picked up by the goslings.[2]

There is a further very common and clearly symbolic feature in the story of Cinderella. When ill-treated by her stepmother, some friendly and sympathetic animal, such as a Blue Cow or a White Lamb, serves her as a confidante and good genius. The cruel Stepmother, who may safely be identified with Giant Circumstance, orders her stepdaughter to slaughter this very thing in the world she most loves. Grievingly Cinderella does so, and from the blood of her sacrifice there springs her beautiful dresses and her future happiness. It has been said, I believe by Fenelon, that " God alone knows how to crucify."

In some versions the task imposed upon Cinderella is grain-sorting, similar to that imposed upon Psyche. The meaning of this imposition is so suggestive that Dr Frazer has entitled one of his works *Psyche's Task*, and has dedicated it " to all who are engaged in Psyche's task of sorting out the seeds of good from the seeds of evil."

In his introduction to Miss Cox's collection of *Cinderella* tales, Mr Andrew Lang describes them as of immense antiquity, and as dating " from a period of wild fancy like that in which the more backward races are still or were

---

[1] *Cinderella*, p. 212.   [2] *Ibid.*, p. 334.

yesterday." [1] The evidence now brought together—and there is yet much more to be adduced—may, I am in hopes, do something to dispel this corroding theory of "wild fancy," and to support the contention of Bacon that "under some of the ancient fictions lay couched certain mysteries." Of the heroine of *The Faerie Queene*, whom Spenser identifies with Diana, the Goddess of Light, the poet writes : "In that Fairy Queen I conceive the most excellent and glorious person of our Sovereign the Queen and her Kingdom in Fairyland." *The Faerie Queene* is, as Spenser himself describes it, "a continual allegory or dark conceit," and the same may, I think, be said of Cinderella. The progression of Cinderella from fire-tender to King's daughter seems to me a dramatic representation of the mystic tenet, "Man does not perceive the truth, but God perceives the truth in man. The inner light is the natural ascent of the spirit within us which at last illuminates and transfigures those who tend it." [2] Of *The Song of Solomon* St Bernard asks : "Who is the Bride ?" and he answers, I think, correctly, "It is the Soul thirsting for God." [3]

[1] *Cinderella*, p xiv.   [2] Jacob Boehme.
[3] *Cantica Canticorum*, Sermon VII.

CHAPTER X

THE STAR OF THE SEA

"I must become Queen Mary and birth to God must give,
If I in blessedness for evermore would live."

SCHEFFLER.

IT is probable that the worship of the Virgin MARY did more to temper the unlovely ferocities of the dark ages than any other feature of the Catholic faith. The wildest swashbuckler thought it no slur upon his manhood to drop the knee before her wayside shrine, and the miserablest peasant derived some comfort from an *Ave Maria*.

The Church has endowed the Virgin MARY with other and more ancient features than the New Testament assigns her. From *The Song of Solomon* it has borrowed the titles : "Rose of Sharon," "Lily of the Valley," "Cedar of Lebanon," and "Tower of David"; and from the Apocalypse it has derived its conception of the Queen of Heaven standing upon the Moon, clothed with the Sun and crowned with the twelve Stars of the Assumption.

Religion grafts new conceptions on to ancient tenets, and no fresh creed has ever eradicated the older beliefs on which it has been imposed. The worship of the Queen of Heaven was flourishing long before the time of JEREMIAH,[1] and when the Christian Church appointed its festivals, it fixed upon 25th March as "Lady Day" for the reason that

[1] Jeremiah xliv. 16, 22.

232

this date was celebrated throughout the Grecian and Roman world as the festival of the miraculous conception of the "Blessed Virgin Juno." The month of May, now dedicated to the Virgin Mary, was likewise the month of the pagan virgin mothers.[1] The titles of "Our Lady," "Queen of Heaven," and "Mother of God" were borne by Isis the immaculate, and, Assumption-like, Isis was represented standing on the crescent moon and surrounded by twelve stars.[2]

The Virgin Mary is designated by the Catholic Church "Our Lady of Wisdom" and *Mater Sapientiæ*. When portrayed as Our Lady of Wisdom, she is represented reading the seventh chapter of the Wisdom of Solomon opened at the words, "For she is the breath of the power of God and a pure influence flowing from the glory of the Almighty."[3] According to the author of *Our Lady in Art*, "Mary from earliest Christianity has stood as a symbol of the Church and of the individual soul whose salvation is in her Son."[4] If this be so, the Latin Church has faithfully preserved some memory of the original and esoteric meaning of the parable.

Among the titles of Queen Mary is STELLA MARIS, the Star of the Sea—an appellation for which it is difficult to discern any Biblical justification. "Star of the Sea" was, however, one of the titles of Isis and other pagan goddesses, and one must assume that it was sanctioned by Christianity for the usual reason that the people obstinately refused to relinquish it.

The Star of the Sea is represented in the accompanying Water-Mother emblems, MARY, MARIA, MYRRHA, MIRIAM, or MARA, the sparkling light of the waters, the virgin daughter of LABISMINA, the Great Abyss.

---

[1] *Bible Myths*, A. W. Doane, p. 335.   [2] *Ibid.*, p. 328.
[3] *Our Lady in Art*, Mrs H. Jenner, p. 15.   [4] *Ibid.*, p. 196.

The circular mirror in the hands of figs. 500 to 503 is the Mirror of Perfection, which, even to-day, is the familiar attribute of " Truth."

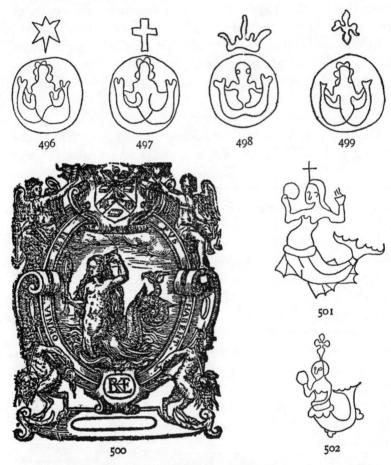

496

497

498

499

501

500

502

In the Wisdom of Solomon, Wisdom, clear and undefiled, is defined as the brightness of the everlasting light, the unspotted *mirror* of the power of God, and the image of His Goodness.[1]

[1] vii

Among certain West African tribes at the present day, the natives symbolise the Deity by a triangle surrounding a piece of looking-glass or something bright to represent Light, and this custom is supposed by Dr Churchward to have originated in ancient EGYPT.[1] Japanese mythology relates that the Sun goddess when taking leave of her grandchild, gave him a heavenly mirror, saying : " My child, when thou lookest upon this mirror, let it be as if thou wert looking upon me ; Let it be with thee on thy couch and in thy hall, and let it be to thee a holy mirror." [2] This mirror which is regarded by the Japanese as a symbol of

503 504 505

knowledge, is preserved at the shrines of ISE.[3] According to Indian poetry :

"There are two mirrors, where in bliss reflected lie
The sun of heaven, and the Spirit-Sun Most High ;
One mirror is the sea o'er which no storm-wind blows,
The other is *the mind* that no unquiet knows." [4]

There is hardly a nation whose history has come down to us that does not record the existence of some Saviour God born of an Immaculate Virgin, and not infrequently this Virgin Mother is named Maria or an equivalent word, pointing to the Sea. DIONYSOS was born of the virgin

[1] *Signs and Symbols of Primordial Man*, p. 132
[2] *The Story of Old Japan*, J. H. Longford, p. 22.
[3] *Ibid.*, p. 17.
[4] Translation from the German of F. Ruckhart by Eva M. Martin.

MYRRHA ; HERMES, the *Logos* of the Greeks, was born of the virgin MYRRHA or MAIA, and the mother of the Siamese Saviour was called MAYA MARIA.[1] All these names are related to *Mare*, the Sea, and the immaculate purity of the various Mother-Marys is explained by the mystic tenet that Spirit in its element was like water, essentially pure, and that sin and materialism being merely foreign bodies, would in the course of time settle into sediment and leave the Spirit in its pure pristine beauty. Thus Scheffler sings :

> "I must become Queen Mary and birth to God must give,
> If I in blessedness for evermore would live."

The knowledge that Mary the Virgin was symbolised by *Mare*, the Sea, seems to have been intentionally recognised by the Sienese painters, of whose Madonnas Mrs Jenner writes : "The excessive grace of the lines of her (Mary's) undulating figure recalls the wonderful curves of rolling waves."[2] In the rules laid down in 1649 by the Art Censor of the Holy Inquisition, it was ordained that Mary was to be portrayed in a scarf or mantle of *Blue*, her robe was to be of spotless white and her hair was to be *golden*.[3] In fig. 506 the Star of the Sea appears over the letter M ; surmounting fig. 510 are the three circles of perfect Power, Love, and Wisdom, and into fig. 508 have been introduced the six attributes previously associated with the Water Mother.

When the letter M was taken over from the Egyptians by the Phœnicians, it was supposed to resemble ripples and was christened Mem, "the waters."[4] The word *em* is

---

[1] *Bible Myths*, A. W. Doane, p. 332.
[2] *Our Lady in Art*, p. 44.
[3] *Ibid.*, p. 7.
[4] *Chambers's Encyclopædia*, vi. 760.

Hebrew for *water*, and in the emblems herewith the letter M is designed like the waves or ripples of Water.

Sometimes, as in fig. 515, the symbolists constructed it from two *esses* placed back to back, which, as on all previous occasions, read *Sanctus Spiritus*.

CINDERELLA, as we have already seen (*ante*, p. 191), is in various localities known as MARA, MARIA, MARY,

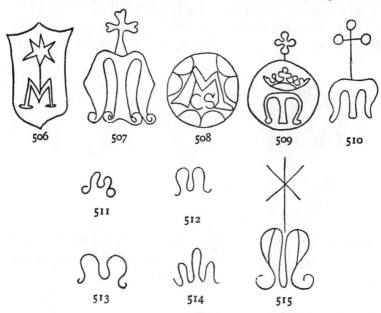

MARIETTA, and MARIUCELLA, all of which are said to be derivatives of the glittering light of the sea. The Indian Goddess of Beauty was, like APHRODITE, said to have been born of the Sea, and there is an inscription to Isis which hails her as :

" Blessed Goddess and Mother, Isis of the many names,
To whom the heavens gave birth on the glittering waves of the sea,
And whom the darkness begat as the light for all mankind." [1]

---

[1] *A Handbook of Egyptian Religion*, A. Erman, p. 245.

The arms of the parish of Marylebone consist of the Rose of Sharon and the Lily of the Valley, beneath which (fig. 516) appears what is heraldically described as a "barry wavy of six." These waves of the sea, *alternately black and white*, correspond in all probability to the six attributes of deity symbolised by the six hairs of figs. 488 to 492 (p. 209) and the six objects represented in fig. 508. These waves of the spiritual sea also appear on the summit of fig. 519 and on the millenniary emblem herewith. In fig. 518 the letter M by the addition of a fifth stroke has been extended into

517

518

516

a wavy zigzag of the waters. As the Millennium was to consist of the universal reign of Spirit and a fullness of the knowledge of the Lord, it is permissible to read M either as Millenarium or *em*, the waters, and it is plain that the symbolists employed it in both senses.

In the designs herewith the pure effluence from the Everlasting Light is symbolised by simple waves above and below fig. 521, by wavy lines surrounding fig. 522, and by the six snake-like forms of the letter M or S in fig. 523. In fig. 524 the waves (marked M) ascend and descend from the surmounting *Fleur-de-lys*, and at the base of this emblem they form themselves into the S S of *Sanctus Spiritus*.

Among all nations and from the remotest antiquity,

water, symbolised by a zigzag or wavy line, seems to have
been employed as a regenerative sacrament and as a representative of spiritual cleansing and rebirth.[1] The ceremony
among the ancient Mexicans was for the midwife to place
her moistened finger on the mouth of the newborn child,

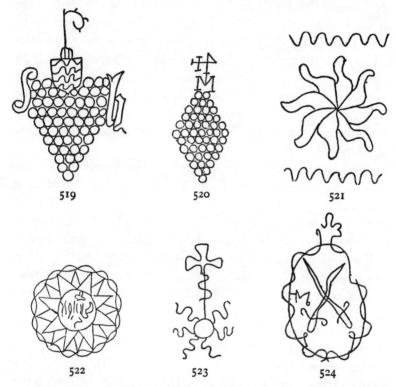

519   520   521

522   523   524

saying : " Take this ; by this thou hast to live on the earth,
to grow, and to flourish ; through this we get all things
that support existence on the earth ; receive it." Then,
with moistened fingers touching the breast of the child, she
said : " Behold the pure water that washes and cleanses
thy heart, that removes all filthiness ; receive it : may the

[1] *Bible Myths*, A. W. Doane, pp. 317, 323.

Goddess see good to purify and cleanse thy heart." Then the midwife poured water on the child's head, saying : " O my grandson, my son, take this water of the Lord of the World which is thy life, invigorating and refreshing, washing and cleansing. I pray that this celestial water, blue and light blue, may enter into thy body and there live. I pray that it may destroy in thee and put away from thee all things evil and adverse that were given thee before the beginning of the world. Wheresoever thou art in this child, O hurtful thing, begone ! leave it ; put thyself apart ; for now does it live anew, and anew is it born, now again is it purified and cleansed ; now again is it shapened and engendered by our Mother the Goddess of Water." [1]

The Latin Church has applied to the Virgin MARY the Solomonic image of the Bride as an " enclosed garden, a spring *shut up*, a fountain *sealed*." [2] This idea is paralleled by an Egyptian hymn to THOTH, in which he is compared to a well not to be found by the talkative and noisy : " Thou sweet spring for the thirsty in the desert ! It is *closed* for those who speak there, it is *open* for those who keep silence there ; when the silent man cometh he findeth the spring. [3]

The heroine of *The Song of Solomon* is further designated as " a fountain of gardens, a well of living waters, and streams from Lebanon." [4] The uncanonical Gospel according to the Hebrews relates that after the baptism of Christ " the entire fountain of the Holy Spirit descended and rested upon Him " ; [5] and this symbolic fountain is evidently a synonym for the symbolic Dove or Holy Spirit of the

---

[1] *Native Races*, Bancroft, iii. 372.
[2] *Song of Solomon* iv. 12.
[3] *A Handbook of Egyptian Religion*, A. Erman, p. 84.
[4] iv. 15.
[5] *Solomon and Solomonic Literature*, D. M. Conway, p. 183.

canonical Gospels. Among the Parsis the influence of
ANAHITA (the virgin of the Holy Spirit) is always described
as a fountain descending on the saints and heroes to whom
she gives strength,[1] and in the figure herewith [2] this fountain,
springing from the Goddess of the celestial waters, is seen
descending upon HERCULES (born 25th December) and
enabling him to cleanse the stable of Augeas. The popular

Hercules cleaning the Stables of Augeas
(From a Relief at Rome.)

525

version of this legend is that Hercules accomplished his
arduous task by diverting the river Alpheus, but the
designer of fig. 525 seems to have been acquainted with a
different version.

Stories of miraculous healing waters are common to
the folk-lore of most nations, and these waters are described
in fairy-tale as the " Well of the World," the " Well beyond
the World," the " Water of the Well of Virtues," the " Well

---

[1] *Solomon and Solomonic Literature*, D. M. Conway, p. 183.
[2] From Smith's *Classical Dictionary*. By kind permission of Mr J.
Murray.

of True Water," the "Reviving Cordial," the "Vessel of Cordial Balsam," and sometimes simply "Living Waters."[1]

The quest for this Water of Life is the chief incident in a large and important group of nursery tales. The magic elixir revives the dead, awakes the sleeping, cures the sick, opens the eyes of the blind, restores the petrified to life, causes a vast accession of strength to the strong, and imparts immortal youth and loveliness. The Maoris, Mongols, Indians, Slavs, and apparently every race on earth, have traditions of an inexhaustible Fountain of Youth, wherein it was sometimes maintained the Fairies dipped children in order to free them from mortality. Such fountains are spoken of in JAPAN, and one of them is said to be hidden on the top of Mount FUJI : whoever finds and drinks of it will live for ever.[2]

In BRITTANY, CINDERELLA is known as CÆSARINE,[3] and sometimes the magic fountain of Fairyland is called Cæsar's Well. In RUSSIA there is a Cinderella-type of story which relates how the youngest of three girls was killed by her jealous sister. The murdered maiden conveys a message to her father : "You will not bring me to life again till you fetch water from the Czar's Well." With this she is restored to life ; the Czar marries her and she freely forgives her unworthy sisters.[4]

Related to these Fairy-tales of a Magic Well is another large cycle of stories in which the heroine is undisguisedly called "Truth," and the villain "Falsehood." A Hungarian version describes how Truth, refusing to admit the superiority of Falsehood, has her eyes put out by the latter. Truth lying maimed overhears two devils boasting that they have cut off the water supply from the neighbour-

---

[1] *The Childhood of Fiction*, J. A. MacCulloch, p. 54.
[2] *Ibid.*, pp. 54–66.   [3] *Cinderella*, p. 373.
[4] *The Childhood of Fiction*, J. A. MacCulloch, p. 110.

ing town, and that they have just killed a physician who had discovered that if cripples rolled about, and the blind washed their eyes in the dew on the night of the new moon, they would be healed. Truth, taking advantage of this information, rubs her eye-sockets with dew and has her sight restored. Then she goes to the town, and, telling them how the supply of water may be recovered,[1] is received with gratitude and honour.

It is evident that WATER, whether in the form of sea, river, fountain, well, rain, or dew, has universally been employed as a symbol of the cleansing, refreshing, and invigorating qualities of Spirit. " My doctrine shall drop as the rain, my speech shall distil as the dew, as the small rain upon the tender herb, and as the showers upon the grass." [2] ISAIAH attributes to the dew exactly the same awakening properties as are met with in fairy-tale : " Awake and sing, ye that dwell in dust : for thy dew is as the dew of herbs, and the earth shall cast out the dead." [3] VIRGIL is represented as cleansing DANTE's face with dew, and it is eminently likely that the old idea that maidens were rendered beautiful by washing their faces in the dew of a May morning had its rise from a symbolic origin. The name DRUSILLA means " dew-watered," and it is a widely spread custom for old women to collect dew into a bottle and use it for washing the faces of children ; the superstition is that in this way the children will become as beautiful as angels.

The Bridegroom of the Song of Solomon, knocking at the door of his beloved, says : " Open to me, my sister, my love, my dove, my undefiled : for my head is filled with dew, and my locks with the drops of the night." [4] There is a Millennium prophecy in Deuteronomy concluding with the

---

[1] *The Childhood of Fiction*, J. A. MacCulloch, p. 68.
[2] Isaiah xxvi. 19.   [3] Deuteronomy xxxii. 2.   [4] v. 2.

promise that the " heavens shall drop down dew," [1] and in a similar prophecy in Hosea the Deity himself is identified with the Dew—" I will be as the dew." The Dewdrops here illustrated are not only marked with the wavy lines of water, but are further identified with the Spirit by the Heart of Love appearing on fig. 530, the three Rays of Light on figs. 528 and 529, and the threefold attributes on figs. 530, 531, and 532.

Dew was a singularly favourite emblem by reason of its symbolising the cardinal doctrine of Mysticism that every man is a " microcosmos " or world in miniature. In each

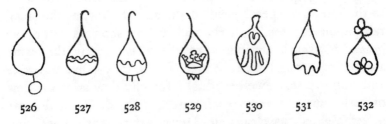

526   527   528   529   530   531   532

dewdrop everything is reflected, from the Sun itself down to the minutest object. It was believed that God was in every individual according to his capacity for reflecting God, and that each in his degree reflected God's image according to the development and purity of his soul.[2]

This idea, universally familiar to the poets, is expressed by Shelley in the lines :

> " What is Heaven ? A globe of dew,
> Filling in the morning new
> Some eyed flower whose young leaves waken
> On an unimagined world :
> Constellated suns unshaken,
> Orbits measureless are furled
> In that frail and fading sphere." [3]

[1] xxxiii. 26–28.   [2] *The Perfect Way*, pp. 61, 62
[3] *Ode to Heaven.*

" From Thy hand," says Oliver Wendell Holmes,

> " The worlds were cast ; yet every leaflet claims
> From that same Hand its little shining sphere
> Of star-lit dew." [1]

The Light of Asia concludes with an appeal to AUM :

> " I take my refuge in thy order ! OM !
> The dew is on the lotus !   Rise great sun !
> And lift my leaf and mix me with the wave ;
> OM MANI PADME HUM, the Sunrise comes !
> The dewdrop slips into the shining Sea."

533

In the above emblem Wisdom, the *Alma Mater*, is represented crowned " like the Tower of David builded for an
armoury." [2]

> " On the crown of her head the King throneth,
> Truth on her head doth repose." [3]

[1] *Wind Clouds and Stardrifts.*   [2] *Song of Solomon* iv. 4.
[3] *The Wedding Song of Wisdom.*

In one hand she holds the sunlight, in the other a chalice into which is distilling the dew of heaven. Representations of a fair and beautiful virgin clasping the symbolic chalice, set among evil spirits and beasts who try to drag her down, are common in mediæval art. In the uncanonical *Books of the Saviour*, Christ is said to be He who "bringeth a cup full of intuition and wisdom and also prudence and giveth it to the soul and casteth the soul into a body which will not be able to fall asleep and forget because of the cup of prudence which hath been given unto it ; but will be ever pure in heart and seeking after the mysteries of light

534   535   536   537   538   539

until it hath found them by order of the Virgin of Light in order (that that soul) may inherit the Light for ever."[1]

In the above cups the contents are indicated by the *Fleur-de-lys* of light, the letters I S (= Jesus Salvator), and by a circle representing either the pearl of price or a globe of dew. The designers of these emblems were presumably influenced by the words of the Psalmist, "The sorrows of death compassed me, and the pains of hell gat hold upon me : I found trouble and sorrow. . . . I will take the cup of salvation and call upon the name of the Lord."[2]

The mystic cups, flagons, vases, chalices, and vessels of Salvation, assumed an apparently infinite variety of form

[1] *Fragments of a Faith Forgotten*, G. R. S. Mead, p. 518.
[2] Psalm cxvi. 3, 13.

and size, and the symbolism with which they are decorated is so intricate that much of it I am unable to decipher. As a rule the embellishments indicate the contents, and it is probable that this is an artistic custom of extreme antiquity. Mr ANDREW LANG observes that anyone who is interested in the strange and universal identity of the human mind may examine American and early Greek pottery. "Com-

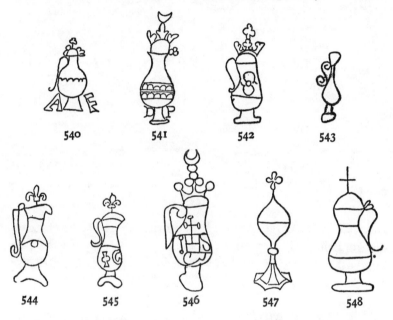

540   541   542   543

544   545   546   547   548

pare," says he, " the wave pattern on Greek and Mexican vases."[1] It may be that these ancient wave patterns are nothing more than natural ornament, but in the emblems herewith, the wavy lines certainly denote the dew of the Holy Spirit or the healing waters of Salvation.

The S of *Spiritus* encircling the Pearl appears on fig. 542 ; the handle of fig. 543 is an S, and of fig. 544 a J = Jesous. The letters J C on fig. 545 denote Jesous Christos, and on

[1] *Custom and Myth*, p. 288.

fig. 546 is the familiar I H S. On fig. 549 is the initial M, and the letters M R on fig. 550, supported by S S handles, presumably imply *Maria Redemptrix*. Surmounting figs. 551

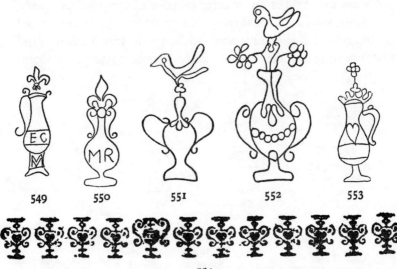

549   550   551   552   553

554

and 552 is the Dove of the Holy Spirit. The Heart of Love distinguishes fig. 553, and the bodies of the magnified vases herewith also consist of hearts supported by S S handles.

555   556

The flowers springing from the group below are *Fleurs-de-lys*, Lilies of the Field, and Marigolds, the latter symbolising the mystic gold of Mary.

Figs. 560 to 570 represent various forms of the Flame.
Note how in figs. 562 and 563 this divine fire forms at its
summit the trefoil and the crescent moon. Over fig. 561
the fire is burning like a six-rayed Sun, and the sign of the
Moon is on the body of the Vase.

557

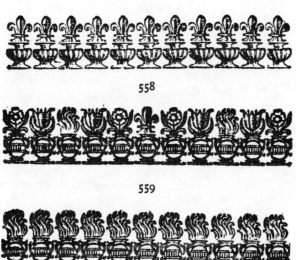

558

559

560

The triple arrangement on fig. 570 is presumably another
form of the three rays of Light, and the vessel with a spout
coincides in appearance with the emblematic vase that was
carried at the festivals of Isis. APULEIUS describes it as
" a small vessel made of burnished gold and most skilfully
wrought out into a hemispherical bottom, embossed ex-
ternally with strange Egyptian figures. Its mouth but

slightly raised, was extended into a spout and projected considerably beyond the body of the bowl."[1] By this

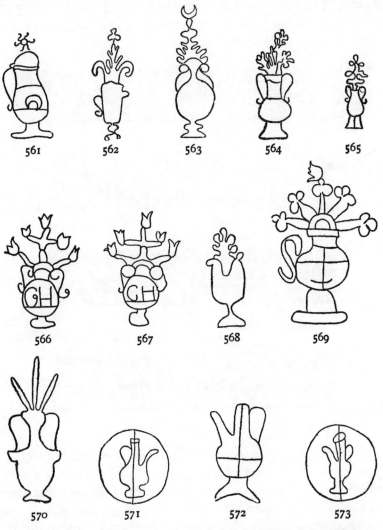

561   562   563   564   565

566   567   568   569

570   571   572   573

sacred vessel was typified the dead and risen Osiris.[2]

[1] *The Gnostics*, C. W. King, p. 111.   [2] *Bible Folk-Lore*, p. 324.

Sometimes these symbolic vases are loaded up with grapes typifying the new wine of Christ's Kingdom. BAHA ULLAH, the Arabian mystic, represents Wisdom as exclaiming:

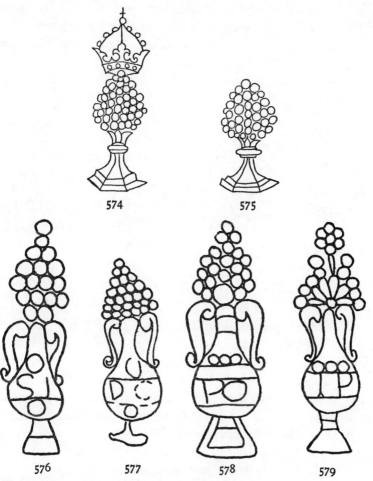

574   575

576   577   578   579

"O Son of Man; ascend to my Heaven that thou mayst drink of the pure Wine which has no likeness—from the chalice of everlasting Glory."[1]

[1] *Hidden Words from the Supreme Pen.*

In *The Song of Solomon* the Bridegroom is made to say :
" I have drunk my wine with my milk : eat, O friends ;
drink, yea, drink abundantly, O beloved."[1] This elixir of
life, this excellent and delectable liquor of Wisdom is again
mentioned in *The Song of Solomon* as that "best wine" that
"goeth down sweetly, causing the lips of those that are
asleep to speak."[2]

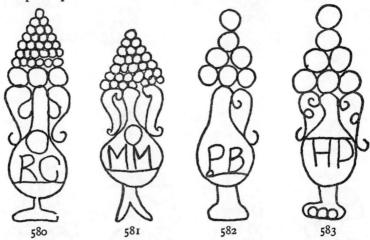

580   581   582   583

The honey and milk under the tongue of the Shulamite[3]
are doubtless identical with the "wine and honey" fabled
to flow from the mouth of Cinderella.[4] In one version
Cinderella's fairy visitors emerge from a vase, and from this
same vase they produce her exquisite dresses.[5] According
to another version wherein Cinderella gets her clothing
from an apple tree, she says :

> " Little golden apple tree,
> *With my vase of gold have I watered thee,*
> With my spade of gold have I digged thy mould ;
> Give me your lovely clothes, I pray,
> And take my ugly rags away."[6]

---

[1] v. 1.   [2] vii. 9.   [3] iv. 11.
[4] *Cinderella*, p. 188.   [5] *Ibid.*, p. 349.   [6] *Ibid.*, p. 139.

Among the vases herewith, figs. 552, 582, and 583 are decorated with seven circles, denoting probably the seven-fold gifts or perfections of the Holy Spirit. Occasionally these circles are arranged in three groups of three, thus forming the immutable number Nine. Nine is equivalent to the Hebrew word for *Truth* and has the peculiar property

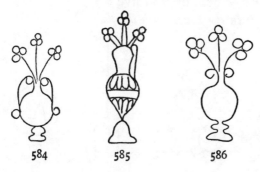

584   585   586

when multiplied of ever reproducing itself. Thus twice nine are 18 and $1+8=9$; thrice nine are 27 and $2+7=9$.

In figs. 587 and 588 the Vase of Truth is surmounted with seven nucleated cells, and Nucleolus, the divine *Nucleus*, the Germ of Life, was one of the appellations under which the Holy Spirit was known among the mystics.[1] The symbol N, used as in figs. 589 to 593 either separately or in combination, is merely a contracted form of M, and has been similarly derived from the Egyptian hieroglyph for water. In Palermo, Cinderella is named Nina and sometimes Ninetta.[2] The former, whence the city of Nineveh derived its name, was one of the titles of Ishtar. "Nina," says Dr Pinches, "another form of Ishtar, was a goddess of creation typified in the teeming life of the ocean, and her name is written with a character standing for a house or receptacle with the sign for 'fish' within."[3] When Nina

---

[1] See *The Perfect Way*, passim.   [2] *Cinderella*, p. 349.
[3] *The Religion of Babylonia and Assyria*, p. 75.

(CINDERELLA) has been dressed by fairies from the magic vase, the following curious dialogue takes place :

Prince : " Lady, how are you ? "
Nina : " As in winter."
Prince : " How are you called ? "
Nina : " By my name."
Prince : " Where do you live ? "
Nina : " *In the house with the door.*"[1]

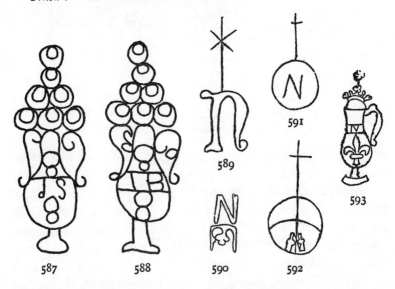

When the Phœnicians took over from EGYPT the letter N, they called it *nun,* the Fish. ISHTAR represented by a fish in a house is therefore clearly the same as NINA or CINDERELLA dwelling in the house with the door. In Egyptian theology this House of Wisdom appears in the name HATHOR = HAT-HOR, " the House of HORUS."[2] According to a Swiss variant of CINDERELLA, she is accosted by the curious title " gold Betheli,"[3] which immediately

---

[1] *Cinderella,* p. 349. [2] *Bible Folk-Lore,* p. 347.
[3] *Cinderella,* p. 502.

suggests Bethel and the vision of Jacob's Ladder. "And Jacob awaked out of his sleep, and he said, Surely the Lord is in this place ; and I knew it not. And he was afraid, and said, How dreadful is this place! this is none other but the house of God, and this is the gate of heaven. And he called the name of that place Beth-el : but the name of that city was called Luz at the first."[1]

"Luz" means Light,[2] and "Bethel," the House of God, may be identified with NINA's and CINDERELLA's "house with the door," *i.e.* the House of Wisdom. In fig. 594

594   595

note the prominent door and the trinity of doves upon the roof ; in fig. 595 note the circle of Perfection and the surmounting emblem of regeneration. In Egypt this symbol of Wisdom's Dwelling-place was sometimes known as the House of Anup, the circular window represented HORUS, the three-sided roof was typical of Heaven, and the square body denoted the Earth.[3] The mystics regarded the womanly element in humanity as "the *house* and *wall* of the man, without whose bounding and redeeming in-

---

[1] Genesis xxviii. 16, 17, 19.
[2] Luz is present-day Portuguese for *light*.
[3] *Signs and Symbols of Primordial Man*, Churchward, pp. 319, 327.

fluence he would inevitably be dissipated and lost in the abyss."[1]

This idea of Wisdom as a House and a Wall elucidates the otherwise absurd assertion of the Shulamite, "I am a wall."[2] It is also likely that the preceding passage, "The beams of our house are cedar, and our rafters are fir,"[3] has reference to this House of Wisdom, which is no doubt fundamentally identical with the Temple of Solomon.

The Latin Church teaches that "Mary is the mother of Grace" and the Star who guides and conducts us to the harbour of Salvation. One of the titles of Cinderella is ANNEMOR = Anna-mother = Anna-darling,[4] and the name ANNE means Grace of God.[5]

The Latin Church has also assigned to the Virgin Mary the title "Health of the Sick." By the sick, mystics have always understood ignorance and moral or mental sickness. "Turn again to the most high," says the writer of Ecclesiastes, "and turn away from iniquity, for he will lead thee out of darkness into the *light* of *health*."[6]

The five-pointed star described in the emblem herewith as the "Symbol of Health" is the Pentagon or famous Seal with which King Solomon is fabled to have worked his amazing marvels. It was with this potent talisman that he warded off all dangers and controlled the evil *genii*. Dr MACKEY states that among the followers of PYTHAGORAS— and PYTHAGORAS derived his philosophic ideas from EGYPT —the triple triangle represented *Light* and was an emblem of Health.[7] It is therefore probable that the letter S on fig. 601 stands for SANITAS and the letters S H on fig. 600 for SANITAS HOMINORUM.

---

[1] *The Perfect Way*, p. 273.　　[2] *Song of Solomon* viii. 10.
[3] *Ibid.*, i. 17.　　[4] *Cinderella*, p. 248.
[5] Similarly ANNABEL and HANNIBAL mean the Grace of BAL, BEL, or BAAL.　　[6] xviii. 2.
[7] *A Lexicon of Freemasonry*, p. 104.

Coloniae,
Joan. Soter epcudebat. MDXXXIII.

127.

596

597   598   599   600   601

The characters appearing in the angles of fig. 596 are unknown to me, but they appear to be Runic. Runes were the ancient alphabet of the Heathen Northmen, the old Norse word *run* originally meaning something secret or magical. The Runic alphabet was entirely angular, the characters being constructed from the forms taken by little sticks used for divining purposes.

In *The Song of Solomon* the Bride says to her Bridegroom, "Set me as a seal upon thy heart, as a seal upon thine arm."[1]

Among the Gnostics the seal of Solomon was assigned to the Virgin SOPHIA, and was regarded as the mark of, and passport to, the Kingdom of Light. At death it was believed that the soul would be brought to judgment before the Virgin and, provided the mark of her Seal were found upon it, would be admitted forthwith into the Treasury of Light.[2]

"Ignorance," says SHAKESPEARE, "is the curse of God ; knowledge the wing whereby we fly to Heaven."[3] The same idea was voiced by SADI, the Persian poet, who, in his *Scroll of Wisdom*, maintains that "without learning we cannot know God."

> "Go, seize fast hold of the skirt of knowledge,
> For learning will convey thee to everlasting abodes.
> Seek nought but knowledge if thou art wise,
> For it is neglectful to remain without wisdom.
> From learning there will come to thee perfection as
> regards religion and the world."

The Gnostics believed that SOPHIA typified that aspirational element in the soul which is constantly aspiring to

[1] viii. 6.
[2] *The Gnostics*, King, pp. 352–356.
[3] *Henry VI.*, iv. 7.

a higher world.[1] "This mystery," says an ancient commentator, "is the *Gate of Heaven*, and this is the House of God where the Good God dwells alone ; into which House no impure man shall come—but it is kept under watch for the Spiritual alone ; where, when they come, they must cast away their garments and all become Bridegrooms, obtaining their true manhood through the Virginal Spirit."[2] Here perhaps we have a clue to the meaning of the passage in the Song of Solomon, "I have put off my coat . . . I have washed my feet."[3]

The Church of Rome teaches that the Virgin Mary is the "Gate of Heaven"—a prerogative which, as we have seen, was claimed by the Virgin's various prototypes (*ante*, p. 177). "To open the lock of Heaven," maintains ISHTAR, "belongs to my supremacy." In the *Breviary* the Virgin Mary is addressed :

> "Hail, Star of the Sea !
> God's Gracious Mother,
> Thou happy gate of heaven.
>
> O Lady most glorious,
> Exalted above the heavens,
> Thou art become the window of. heaven ;
> 'Tis thou that art the gate of the King on high,
> And of bright light the portal art thou."

Fig. 602 consists of a large key surmounting what is now known as a Catherine Wheel. In fig. 603 this wheel is lettered with an inscription which Mons. Briquet believes to have originally read STELLA MARIS. Figs. 604 and 607 are surmounted with an M ; fig. 605 with the Pearl, and fig. 608 with M R = Maria Redemptrix ? The term

---

[1] *Early Christianity*, S. B. Slack, p. 711.
[2] See *Wedding Song of Wisdom*, Mead, p. 14.
[3] v. 3.

" Catherine Wheel "[1] arose, according to popular estimation, from the Legend of St Catherine, a Christian virgin of Alexandria, who publicly confessed the Gospel (A.D. 307) and was doomed to death on toothed wheels. No less than fifty pagan philosophers, sent by the Emperor to pervert her while she was in prison, were themselves converted to Christianity by her winning and irresistible eloquence : hence she was regarded as the patroness of philosophers

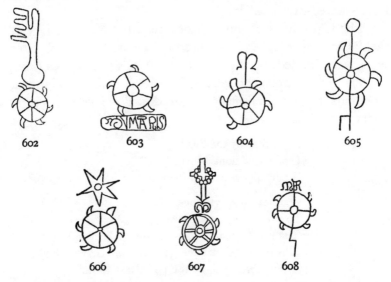

and learned schools. Having rejected all offers of earthly marriage, she was taken in a vision to Heaven and became the spouse of Christ, who plighted his troth to her with a ring.[2]

It is clear that this story is a Christianised version of some far more ancient legend. Catherine (from the Greek

---

[1] It would be interesting to trace how the blazing firework called a Catherine Wheel acquired its name. Sparks and fire have nothing in common with the Christian legend.

[2] *Chambers's Encyclopædia*, iii. 9.

word *Catharos* = pure) is clearly the all-pure, immaculate, and undefiled Bride of the Song of Solomon, and the toothed wheel with which she is identified is the four- or six-rayed Solar wheel. CINDERELLA is sometimes called *La Bella Catarina*,[1] and there are monuments to Isis bearing the inscription : " Immaculate is our Lady Isis."[2]

One of the Gnostic philosophers has left on record the account of an alleged vision of SOPHIA. "Truth," says he,

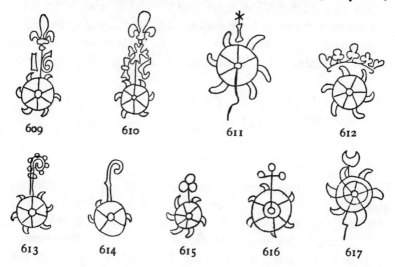

609   610   611   612

613   614   615   616   617

" looked upon me and opened her mouth and uttered a word, and that word became a Name ; a Name which we know and speak—JESUS CHRIST : and having named Him, she held her peace."[3] There is no doubt that the mystics of the Middle Ages identified CHRIST with SOPHIA, and this identity is reflected in the six-rayed Solar wheels herewith.

Over fig. 611 is the Holy ONE of JESUS, the True Light, and the meaning of the other examples is elucidated by the

[1] *Cinderella*, p. 93.
[2] See *The Gnostics*, King, p. 438.
[3] *Ibid.*, p. 288.

three circles of perfection, the pastoral crook of the Good Shepherd, the Moon of Heaven, and the Crown of Glory.

The equation of CHRIST and SOPHIA as both being incarnate, "Wisdom" is rendered the more complete by Christ's claim "I am the door; by me if any man enter in, he shall be saved, and shall go in and out, and find pasture."[1] In fig. 618 the trefoiled Hand is extending a key from Heaven—doubtless the key of David referred to in Isaiah xxii. 22 : "Woe unto you!" said Christ addressing the lawyers, "for ye have taken away the *key of knowledge* : ye entered not in yourselves, and them that were entering in ye hindered."[2] According to a German version of

618

CINDERELLA, the heroine catches sight of a glittering something, throws a stone at it, and a golden key falls into her hand. With this key she unlocks a cupboard full of the most exquisite clothes ; dons a silver dress ; finds a magic steed waiting her behests, and goes to the dance.[3]

From the emblems herewith it is easy to see how the mystics understood this magic key. The handle of figs. 619 to 621 is the Heart of *Love*, and of figs. 622 and 623 it is the Pearl of *Wisdom*. The Serpentine waves of LABISMINA formed into the letter M constitute the base of fig. 622, and the initials S S are seen on the cross keys in fig. 624. In fig. 625 the keys of heaven are identified with the heart of Love, and the fourfold heart-shaped meander over fig. 626 is presumably the flaming rose of Love.

[1] John x. 9.   [2] Luke xi. 52.   [3] *Cinderella*, p. 399.

The diamond that constitutes the handle of figs. 627 and 628 was the emblem of "light, innocence, life, and joy."[1] Sometimes this stone was employed as a separate and distinct emblem, and on fig. 630 there appears the letter D. It is eminently likely that the Diamond was

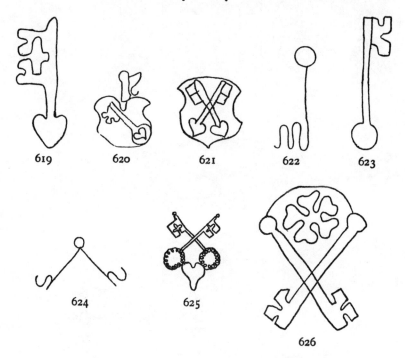

619   620   621   622   623

624   625

626

regarded as the gem of Dionysos or Day, and that the name *Diamond* is affiliated with the Sanscrit *dyu*, "to be brilliant." The hard and indestructible character of diamond is expressed in its alternative name *adamant*, derived from the Greek *adamas*, unconquerable. A diamond surmounts fig. 631 and was no doubt the emblem of brilliant, victorious, and unconquerable Light. Note the Cross of Light on figs. 629 and 630.

[1] *Romance of Symbolism*, S. Heath, p. 217.

Associated with the diamond-handled key of fig. 628 is the Hawk or Dove of the Holy Spirit. There is a striking

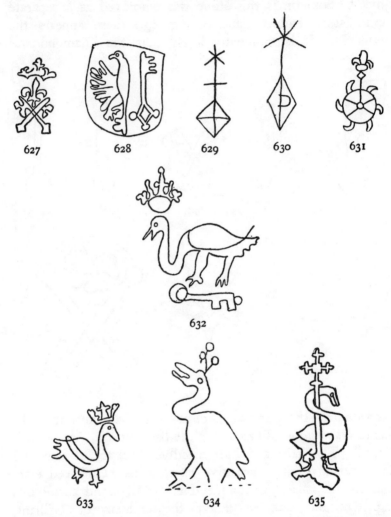

627   628   629   630   631

632

633   634   635

similarity between this design and the Egyptian Dove reproduced on page 104, vol. ii. The Dove was the attribute of ISHTAR and VENUS, and in *The Song of Solomon* is likewise associated with the Bride : " My *dove*, my undefiled is but one." [1]

In the figure herewith the key of knowledge is associated not with the dove but with the Holy Goose or Ghost. In fig. 634 the Goose is crowned with the triple Perfection ; in figs. 632 and 633 with the diadem of beauty, and in fig. 635 it appears in combination with the cross.

The conjunction of Goose, Dove, and Key appears to indicate that *Spirit* was regarded as the only opener of the Doors of Heaven. " God is a spirit, and they that worship him *must* worship him *in spirit* and in truth."

With poetic intuition Mrs Katherine Tynan sums up most of the time-honoured symbols or similes of Stella Maris, the Bona Dea, the immaculate Magna Mater, in her poem entitled " The Mother." The italics are mine.

> " I am *the pillars* of the house ;
>   *The keystone* of the arch am I.
> Take me away, and roof and wall
>   Would fall to ruin utterly.
>
> I am *the fire upon the hearth*,
>   I am *the light of the good sun.*
> I am the heat that warms the earth,
>   Which else were colder than a stone.
>
> At me the children warm their hands ;
>   I am their light of love alive.
> Without me cold the hearthstone stands,
>   Nor could the precious children thrive.
>
> I am *the twist* that holds together
>   The children in its sacred ring,
> Their *knot* of love, from whose close tether
>   No lost child goes a-wandering.

---

[1] vi. 9.

I am *the house* from floor to roof.
　I deck the walls, the board I spread ;
I spin the curtains, warp and woof,
　And shake the down to be their bed.

I am their *wall* against all danger,
　Their *door* against the wind and snow.
Thou Whom a woman laid in manger,
　Take me not till the children grow ! "

CHAPTER XI

ONE-EYE, TWO-EYES, AND THREE-EYES

"Language has been called by Jean Paul 'a dictionary of faded metaphors': so it is, and it is the duty of the etymologist to try to restore them to their original brightness."—MAX MÜLLER.

THE window of the house of Wisdom (*ante*, p. 255, fig. 594) was constructed of *five* perfect circles, and these five circles were the Mayan and Egyptian symbol for "daylight and splendour."[1] In the school of PYTHAGORAS *five* typified Light;[2] among the Greeks it was the number sacred to APOLLO, and among modern Freemasons it stands for the Five Virtues or Points of Fellowship. The simple practice of these Five precepts constituted, I have little doubt, the mysterious potencies of Solomon's five-pointed Seal. The Five virtues were sometimes symbolised separately and sometimes, as in fig. 637, they constitute an ornament of grace and splendour.

Occasionally four circles are linked to a fifth and larger central one, thus constituting an illustration of the words of Wisdom : "I am the mother of fair love, and fear, and knowledge, and holy hope.[3]

The two children associated with WISDOM, the Water Mother, in fig. 500 (*ante*, p. 234) are respectively distinguished

---

[1] *Signs and Symbols of Primordial Man*, Churchward, p. 128.
[2] *A Lexicon of Freemasonry*, Mackey, p. 104.
[3] Ecclesiasticus xxiv. 20.

by the Heart of *Love* and the Book of *Knowledge* ; *Hope* is also expressed by the Anchor, and *Fear* by the Scales of Justice.

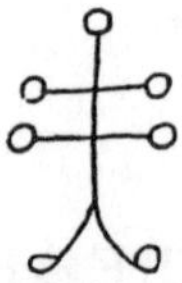

636    637    638

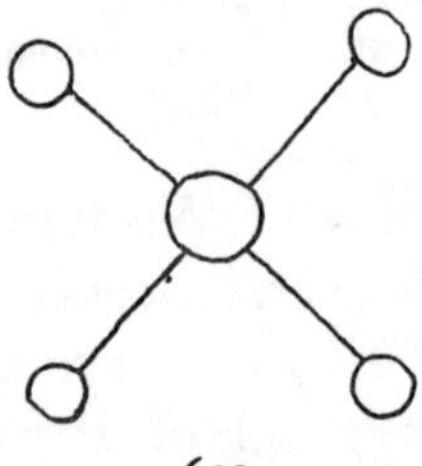

639

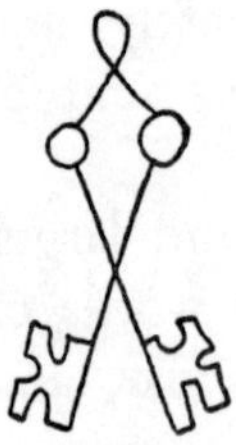

640 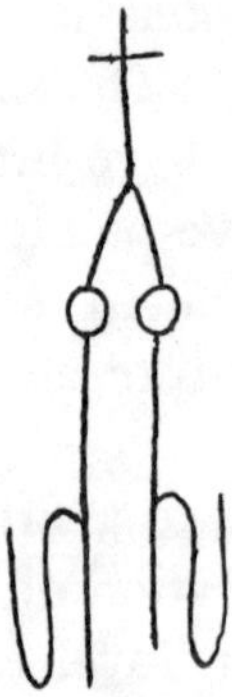   641 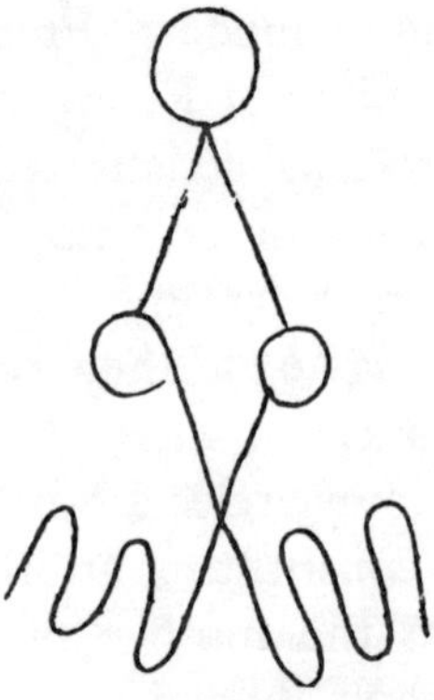   642 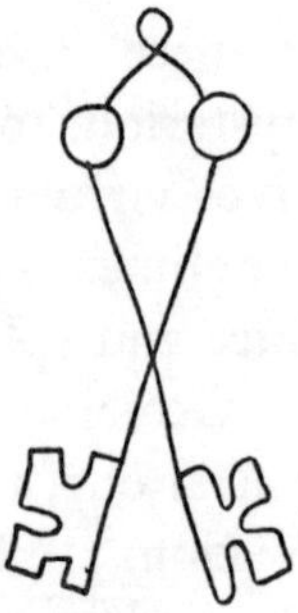   643

Of WISDOM's children, two were regarded as incomparably the chiefest, and these two, "Knowledge" and "Fair Love," were symbolised by multifarious forms and methods. The streams of milk flowing from the *Alma*

Mater represented in fig. 533 (*ante*, p. 245) probably denote them and in the Cross Keys herewith they are represented by two Pearls or Circles.

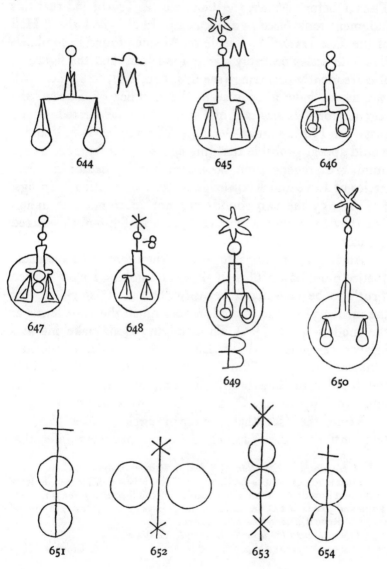

644   645   646

647   648   649   650

651   652   653   654

Sometimes the twin circles themselves form Scales or are poised within the scales. The Egyptians believed that at death the action of the disembodied soul was weighed by THOTH before MAAT, the Goddess of Truth, and that this judgment took place in a Heavenly Hall called the "Hall of the *Two Truths*."[1] The letter M when found in combination with scales probably stands for Maat,[2] and the figure 8, also frequently occurring (see figs. 646, 647, 648, and 650), was, as we have already seen, the number of THOTH, the regenerator. It was said of CHRIST by a celebrated mystic that "in His essential elements His number is 8,"[3] and it would appear probable that this figure 8 was regarded as the number of regeneration because it is composed of the twin circles of Love and Knowledge in close imposition. In figs. 651 to 653 the two rounds are not touching, but in fig. 654 they form into a perfect 8, and in fig. 646 this sacred number appears as the goal of Vision.

Among inscriptions to Isis is the claim, "I have made Justice more powerful than silver and gold. I have caused Truth to be considered beautiful,"[4] and it is evident that the mediæval mystic aspired in very much the same terms as the modern poet. "O Thou mighty God, make me as a balance of rubies and jet that is cast in the lap of the sun. I beseech thee, O Thou Great God, that I may flash forth the wonder of Thy brightness, and melt into the perfect poise of Thy Being, O Thou God my God."[5]

From the fact that the twin circles appear not infrequently on the Vase of Wisdom, one may infer that

---

[1] *A Handbook of Egyptian Religion*, A. Erman, p. 108.

[2] Maat is represented as the Daughter of RA, Mistress of Heaven, Ruler of Earth, and President of the Nether-World. "The Egyptian *maat* is not only Truth and Justice but Order and Law in the physical as well as in the moral world."—Renouf, *Hibbert Lectures*, p. 120.

[3] *Life of Louis Claude de St Martin*, A. E. Waite, p. 411.

[4] *A Handbook*, Erman, p. 245.   [5] A. Crowley.

"Wisdom" was regarded as a perfect blend, or equipoise of Love and Knowledge.[1] The letter G on fig. 656 stands either for GNOSIS—*i.e.* inspired, revealed, divine, and charitable knowledge—or not improbably for GESU. Notice with

what ingenuity the stem of fig. 657 forms the regenerative 8.

It was evidently the aim of the emblem makers to concentrate manifold meanings within a single form, thus illustrating the maxim that "That Scripture is the more

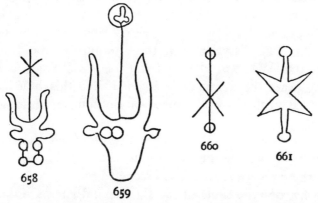

excellent which brings forth abundant signification. For God is able to say many things in one, as the perfect ovary contains many seeds in its chalice."[2] The bodies and faces of symbolic animals are, more often than not, ingeniously symbolic to the minutest detail. In fig. 658 the Four

[1] "Knowledge bloweth up, but charity buildeth up."
[2] From a Hermetic fragment quoted in *The Perfect Way*.

children of Wisdom appear as eyes and nostrils. In fig. 659 the eyes have deliberately been placed in juxtaposition, and when drawn as perfect circles there is little doubt that they symbolised the regenerate eyes of Perfect Love and Perfect Wisdom.

The Egyptians imagined the Deity as possessed of two eyes, the Sun and the Moon ; and these they termed the eyes of the North and South or the eye of Horus=Light, and the eye of Sut=Darkness. They believed that the regenerate man would have this dual sight bestowed as a Gift from the Gods, and that eventually " two eyes are given to him and he becomes glorious therewith." [1]

In fig. 660 these symbolic eyes are associated with the star of Light, and in fig. 661 they form its northern and its southern points. In fig. 663 the twin circles have been combined with the three light-rays, and in fig. 664 these three rays are flowing from the mouth of a Bull. The Supreme Spirit was very widely represented as being bearded. The Assyrian Sin, the Illuminator, the God of Light and Wisdom, the " Heifer of Anu," [2] has a long flowing beard the colour of *lapis lazuli*,[3] and this blue beard was in all probability a symbol of outpouring, descending Truth.[4]

In fig. 662 the symbolic light flowing from the mouth is expressed by a design combining the T cross, the Latin cross, the Triangle, and the Crescent Moon.

In fig. 666 the circle of the Perfect and Eternal One has

[1] See *Signs and Symbols of Primordial Man*, Churchward, pp. 201, 202, 330, 345.

[2] Anu was also the name of a Gaelic goddess of prosperity and abundance.

[3] *Religion of Babylonia and Assyria*, Jastrow, p. 76.

[4] The amenities of Theology seem always to demand that the Gods of one's neighbour should be regarded as Demons. Our term Devil is cognate with *devel*, the Gypsy for God ; " Ogre " was originally a Northern Deity, and the " Bluebeard " of fairy-tale is probably a perversion of blue-bearded Sin.

been made to do duty as a mouth, and in fig. 667 this
mouth has significantly been misplaced. The Stag was not

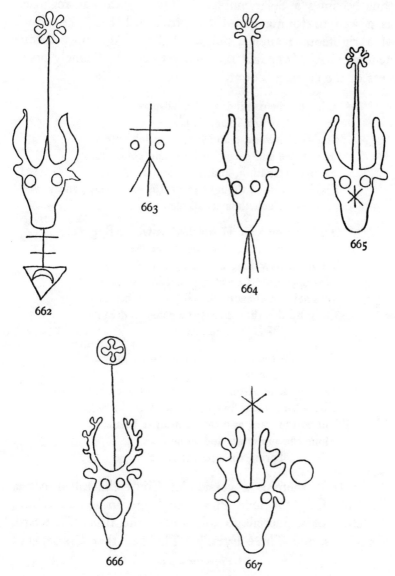

663

662

664

665

666

667

only a symbol of Solitary Purity, but its branching antlers were likened to the rays of the rising Sun, and the Stag thus becomes a Solar emblem. The mouth was regarded as a well or fountain, and it is proverbial that "the mouth of a righteous man is a well of life." [1]   Fig. 666 will thus denote what MATTHEW ARNOLD termed the "lonely pureness of the all-pure Fount."

> " If, in the silent mind of One all-pure
> At first imagin'd lay
> The sacred world ; and by procession sure
> From those still deeps, in form and colour drest,
> Seasons alternating, and night and day,
> The long-mused thought to north, south, east, and west
> Took then its all-seen way :
>
> O waking on a world which thus-wise springs !
> Whether it needs the count
> Betwixt thy waking and the birth of things
> Ages or hours : O waking on Life's stream !
> By lonely pureness to the all-pure Fount
> (Only by this thou canst) the colour'd dream
> Of Life remount.
>
> Thin, thin the pleasant human noises grow,
> And faint the city gleams ;
> Rare the lone pastoral huts : marvel not thou !
> The solemn peaks but to the stars are known,
> But to the stars, and the cold lunar beams :
> Alone the sun arises and alone
> Spring the great streams."

In Italy there is a version of Cinderella called Mona Catarina, *i.e.* "the lone Pure one," and in some localities the story of Cinderella is told under the title " One-Eye, Two-Eyes, and Three-Eyes."   The fact that CINDERELLA

[1] Proverbs x. 11.

appears as the "Two-Eyes" of this version supports the suggestion that WISDOM was regarded as the equipoise of Love and Knowledge. Sometimes the Gods were described as having Three Eyes ; the Third Eye representing that mysterious faculty we call Intuition, or what the ancient poets termed the "inner eye of Reason." Greek myth attributes three eyes to JUPITER ; sometimes three eyes were assigned to THOR, and three-eyed characters in folk-lore are not uncommon.

The authors of *The Perfect Way* state that in the symbolism of the face the two eyes denote respectively Intelligence and Love,[1] and it is probable that right and left eye had each its own proper significance. ZECHARIAH fulminating against contemporary priestcraft exclaims : " Woe to the idle shepherd that leaveth the flock ! . . . his *right* eye shall be utterly darkened,"[2] and the still prevalent expres-

---

[1] " As man, made in the 'image' of Adonai, is the expression of God, so is the expression or countenance of man the express image of God's nature, and bears in its features the impress of the celestial, showing him to be thence derived. Thus, in the human face, by the straight, central, protruding, and vertical line of the organ of respiration, is denoted Individuality, the divine Ego, the I AM, of the man. Though single exteriorly and constituting one organ in token of the Divine Unity, within it is dual, having a double function, and two nostrils in which resides the power of the Breath or Spirit, and which represent the Divine Duality. The duality finds its especial symbolisation in the two spheres of the eyes, which, placed on a level with the summit of the nose, denote, respectively, Intelligence and Love, or Father and Mother, as the supreme elements of Being. Though exteriorly two, interiorly they are one, as vision is one. And of the harmonious co-operation of the two personalities represented by them, proceeds, as child, a third personality, which is their joint expression or 'Word.' Of this the Mouth is at once the organ and symbol, being in itself Dual—when closed a line, when open a circle ; and also twofold, being compounded of line and circle in the tongue and lips. And as the place of issue of the creative breath, it is below the other features, since creation, in coming from the Highest, is in its direction necessarily downwards. Thus, in the countenance of the 'Image of God,' is expressed the nature of God—even the Holy Trinity. For 'these three are one,' being essential modes of the Same Being."—P. 205.   [2] xi. 17.

sion "one-eyed" has, in all probability, descended from an immemorial past. Fable records the existence of a one-eyed race of men, who, it is said, were constantly endeavouring to filch the hoarded gold over which certain griffins kept watch and ward.

These one-eyed people were entitled "*Arima*spians"—a word suggestive of ARIMANES, the Persian Lucifer.[1] Griffins, lion‑bodied monsters with eagle‑heads and wings are known to have typified Wisdom and Enlightenment,[2] and the gold that it was their mission to watch over and defend was probably the gold of Wisdom. In the cut herewith a pair

668

of griffins are supporting Wisdom in her form of the Water Mother. Griffins decorate the helmet that protects the head of Minerva—a name generally attributed to the same root as *mens*, the Mind—and they are often represented guarding the Vase of Wisdom.[3] In sculpture the Griffin usually appears holding a ball under its claw, and pseudo-griffins may be seen in this attitude on the parapet of Holborn Viaduct. This ball, the Pearl of Wisdom, is the same Ball of Perfection as is held by the seven-starred BONA DEA who appears over the portico of the British Museum as the

---

[1] It is said that from ARIMANES, the Prince of Darkness, we derive our expression "old Harry," meaning the Devil.—*Mythology of the Aryan Nations*, Cox, p. 567.

[2] *Horns of Honour*, J. C. Elworthy, p. 116.

[3] On Stationers' Hall there is a replica of a classic medallion thus representing them.

central figure to the group of Gods and Goddesses. In fig. 669 [1] the Great Mother holds a ball and a ring. The magic ring figuring so largely in Solomonic mythology had probably the same significance as our modern wedding ring, the Heathen origin of which nearly led to its abolition during the Commonwealth.[2] Some of the Griffins here illustrated are crowned with the Fleur-de-lys of Enlightenment. Fig. 672, who is marked with the sign of the cross, has his tail twined into the form of the Pearl, and in fig.

Rhea, or Cybele. (From a Roman Lamp.)

669

673 the circle has been imposed in the centre of the body. Jesus Christ was regarded as the Master-Griffin,[3] and the 1 and 8 under fig. 674 will thus stand for the Holy *One* who manifests Himself as the number 8.

On fig. 676 there is an indistinct inscription in which the letters S H are prominent. The inscription on fig. 677

[1] From Smith's *Classical Dictionary*. By permission of Mr. J. Murray.

[2] "The form of the ring," says an old writer, "being circular, that is round and without end, importeth thus much that their mutual love and hearty affection should roundly flow from the one to the other as in a Circle, and that continually and for ever."—*The Origins of Popular Superstitions*, T. Sharper Knowlson, p. 99.

[3] See Dante's *Purgatorio* : cantos xxx. and xxxi.

(a Great Bear) reads I S S, and the wording on fig. 674 concludes with the letters I S.

According to the authors of *The Perfect Way*, the words Is and Ish originally meant Light, and the name Isis, once Ish-Ish, was Egyptian for Light-Light.[1] Those who were

[1] P. 111.

initiated into the mysteries of Isis were known as Issa,[1] and the legendary " Issedones," who were said to have been evicted from their country by the ever-encroaching, one-eyed Arimaspians, may probably be identified as the enlightened followers of Ormuz, the Lord of Light and adversary of Ahriman,[2] the Prince of Darkness.

There is a Northern tale of " Old Harry " that bears a remarkable resemblance to the Greek legend of Ulysses and Polyphemus. The Devil noticing a man moulding buttons, asks what he may be doing, and when answered that he is moulding eyes, asks him further whether he can furnish him with a new pair. The workman undertakes to do so, but instead of furnishing new eyes " Issi," as he terms himself, pours into the sockets a deadly stream of molten lead, and the frenzied Devil rushes away, exclaiming : " Issi did it, Issi did it." The word Issi being ambiguous, meaning also " himself," the neighbours, instead of sympathising with the outwitted Devil, jeeringly bid him lie on the bed he has " himself " made.[3]

The syllables isse occur in the name Ulysses, and again in its equivalent Odysseus. According to Greek legend, Ulysses, when asked his name by Polyphemus, answered wilily : " My name is Noman." Subsequently Ulysses, with four select friends, heated the end of a stake until it glowed like a living coal ; then, poising it over the giant's solitary eye, buried it deeply in the socket. The neighbouring Cyclops disturbed by the monstrous bellowing of Polyphemus flocked from their surrounding caves and inquired what grievous hurt had caused him to sound such a horrible alarm and break their slumbers. He replied :

---

[1] *The Perfect Way*, p. 111.

[2] " His name and epithets import essential wickedness ; a being occupied in perverting and corrupting everything good."—*Persia*, J. B. Fraser, p. 128.

[3] *Mythology of Aryan Nations*, Cox, p. 570.

"O friends I die, and NOMAN gives me the blow." They answered : "If *no man* hurts thee, it is the stroke of JOVE, and thou must bear it." So saying, they left him groaning. On the following morning ULYSSES, safe from the clutches of the giant, shouted in derision : "Cyclops ! the Gods have well requited thee for thy atrocious deeds. Know it is ULYSSES to whom thou owest thy shameful loss of sight."

The Tartars have a story of a one-eyed, man-eating giant, and the hero BISSAT, as usual, burns out the monster's eye with a red-hot knife.[1]

Celtic legend relates that a certain hero named LUGH blinded a one-eyed giant[2] by means of a red-hot iron, and this name LUGH is always equated with LLEU, the Welsh word for *Light*.[3]

The ambiguous ISSI, YSSE, ISSE, or ISSA is related to ESSE, the Latin verb "to be," and from *esse* is derived the word Essence, a philosophic and poetic synonym for the Soul or "Light within."

It would thus appear probable that the Odyssey is to some extent an allegory of the Soul, and that ODYSSEUS, the wanderer, is truly NOMAN, no historic personage, but, like Cinderella, a personification of the soul, the spark, the "God within," or "Dweller in the Innermost." The word-play upon ISSI, "the Light," and ISSI, "himself," is comparable to Cinderella's amazed awakening to the fact that the glory of her dazing radiance is "herself."

The syllables ISSE or ISHI appear to have anciently meant *Light* in many directions. We meet them in NYSSA, the name of the nymph who was said to be the mother of the Sun ; in NYSA, the mountain where DIONYSOS was born, and

---

[1] *Cinderella*, p. 489.
[2] *Celtic Myth and Legend*, Charles Squire, p. 239.
[3] Rhys, J., *Hibbert Lectures*, pp. 239, 409.

in Mount Nissa of Ethiopia,[1] where Osiris was born. The sacred Stone Lanterns or Light receptacles of Japan are still called *Ishidoro*, and the Japanese Heavenly Grandchild is said to have descended to earth upon Mount Kirishima. Isis was known in Northern Europe as Zizi ; the Chaldean solar hero was Izdubar ; and the last of the Japanese twin-deities were named Izanagi and Izanami.

In Lapland the goddess corresponding to Isis was worshipped under the name Isa, and this word must be related to Isia, a Greek variant of Isis, signifying, according to Plato, " Holy One," " Intelligence," and " Perception."[2]

678

The name Isis was understood by Plutarch as meaning " Knowledge."[3]

In Hebrew the syllable is becomes jes, and thus the Jews term Isaiah Jesaiah ; conversely the word Jesse is presumably identical with Isse. In the collection of mystic literature grouped together in our Bible under the significant title Isaiah, is a prophecy of the future, when " the earth shall be full of the knowledge of the Lord, as the waters cover the sea." " In that day," says Isaiah, " there shall be a root of Jesse. And there shall come forth a rod out of the stem of Jesse, and a Branch shall grow out of his roots."[4] The root of Jesse, as represented herewith, is *five*-limbed, and is thus the root of Light.

[1] *Things Seen in Japan*, Clive Holland, p. 209.
[2] *Cf.* Plutarch's *Isis and Osiris*.
[3] *Ibid.*   [4] xi.

In Hosea there is a Millenniary prophecy wherein occurs the enigmatic passage : " And it shall be at that day, saith the Lord, that thou shalt call me Ishi ; and shalt call me no more Baali.   For I will take away the names of Baalim out of her mouth, and they shall no more be remembered by their name."[1]   The Baalim were secondary divinities into which the Phœnician Great God El was subdivided, and Ishi was probably a synonym for the primal Light.   The Celtic giant blinded by Lugh, the Light, was named Balor, the *Bal* of which may perhaps be equated with the *Baal* of Baalim.

The animal upon which the letters I S S are inscribed (*ante*, p. 278) is a Bear, and the Seven Stars of the Golden Bear were known as the Seven *Rishis* or shining Lights.   From this word an initial vowel has evidently worn off.   As the Seven stars are very like a plough, and the constellation was sometimes known as the *Seven Ploughing Oxen*, it is probable that the lost vowel was *A*, making *Ar-ishis*.   The syllable AR, which is Irish for Plough, is the root of many terms relating to ploughing, such as *Arable, Aryan*, etc.[2]   *Arishis* will thus simply and reasonably resolve into *Plough Lights*.

Ursa, the Latin for Bear, is from the same root as Ushas, the Dawn ; and the shining Ushas (the *usher* of Day) is identical with Isis.   The Vedic Man in the Sun, corresponding to the generic term Adam, was entitled Purusha.   Shri, the wife of Vishnu, before descending from the Sun, was known as Anushayini,[3] and the wife of

---

[1] ii. 16, 17.

[2] The name *George* means a plough or husbandman.   English rural folk still pronounce this "Jaarge," wherein they unconsciously preserve the primitive radical AR.

[3] The Mountains of Kirishima are situated in the Island of Kiushio, and it is recorded of a certain Japanese God that he established himself under the name of Okuninushi at a place named Izumo.   In Sanscrit the root Ush means "to burn."

KRISHNA, "the nocturnal Sun," is named LUXMEE. The knowledge that *Is* or *Ish* meant *Lux*, the light, not only elucidates the meaning of ISHI, but it also unravels the etymology of many other obscure titles, *e.g.* the Goddess ISHTAR, whose name has hitherto proved an insoluble enigma, may be resolved into *Ish*, the Light, and *Tar*, "daughter of." [1]

The name of the prophet ELISHA (a burning and a shining light) resolves itself naturally into ISHA, "the light of," EL, "God." In the authorised version of the New Testament ELISHA is rendered ELISEUS, and it may safely be inferred that ELISSA, an alternative name of DIDO, has also the same signification. DIDO is generally accepted as a mythical personification of the Sun, and her famous suicide is equivalent to the flaming death of the sun on the funeral pyre of the sunset. The term ELISSA, which was also borne by an Arabian Goddess whom Herodotus identifies with the Persian Mitra,[2] leads suggestively to ELISYON, and there is little doubt that the Elysian Fields of the Greeks may be equated with ZION, the Holy City of the Hebrews.

One of the lesser Elizabethans who dedicates a sonnet sequence entitled *Diana*, "Unto Her Majesty's Sacred Honourable Maids," leads off:

> "Eternal Twins that conquer Death and Time,
> Perpetual advocates in Heaven and Earth ;
> Fair, chaste, immaculate, and all-divine,
> Glorious alone before the first man's birth." [3]

---

[1] The syllable TAR occurs again in the Finnish name ILMATAR, supposedly meaning "Daughter of the Air." It is well recognised that the language of Finland abounds in Chaldean survivals, and the Finnish suffix "tar," equivalent to "the daughter of," is seemingly one of these. Cf. *Popular Poetry of the Finns*, C. J. Billson.

[2] i. 131.

[3] *Elizabethan Sonnets*, Richard Smith. Ed. S. Lee.

"Her Majesty" has here been supposed to mean Queen Elizabeth, but the Elizabeth in the poet's mind was evidently the Daughter of Zion, who was "all glorious within"—EL-IZZA-BETH, *i.e.* the House of the Light of God.

It is obvious that *Jeshurun* or "ISRAEL" refers frequently to something more than an historic tribe of Semitic demon-worshippers, and that ISRAEL, he or she, is sometimes a personification of the individual soul wandering in the wilderness. I suggest that the name ISRAEL resolves itself naturally into Is, "the Light of," RA, "the eternal Sun which has existed for ever,"[1] EL "the First Cause, the principle or beginning of all things."[2] The poetic "ISRAEL" thus appears as an extension of the name EZRA, "Rising of Light,"[3] and as another personification of the Divine Essence, Light, or Colony in the soul.

It was said of Wisdom, "She is the brightness of the everlasting Light, she is more beautiful than the Sun and above all the order of Stars."[4] In some parts of Italy Cinderella is entitled L'ISABELLUCCIA,[5] a name obviously akin to ISABELLA, which may mean either "Beautiful Light" or "The Shining of the Light." The syllables ELLA, as in Cinderella, are found in *stella*, a star; and *aster*, an alternative word for star, is related to ASHTAROTH. ASHTAROTH and ASTARTE are appellations of ISHTAR, and ISHTAR has been identified with ESTHER, a name which is radically identical with the Zendic *stara*, a star. The Greek version of the Book of Esther contains the remarkable passage : "*A little*

---

[1] Compare the names EZRA and ZERAH, both said to mean "rising of Light."—*Christian Names*, Helena M. Swan.

[2] *A Lexicon of Freemasonry*, Mackey, p. 229.

[3] This is the definition given in Mrs Swan's *Christian Names*. Primarily it probably meant EZ or IZRA, the Light of RA.

[4] Wisdom of Solomon vii.

[5] *Cinderella*, p. 281.

fountain became a river, and there was light, and the sun, and much water. This river is ESTHER, and the two dragons are I and HAMAN." In Ecclesiasticus a similar piece of

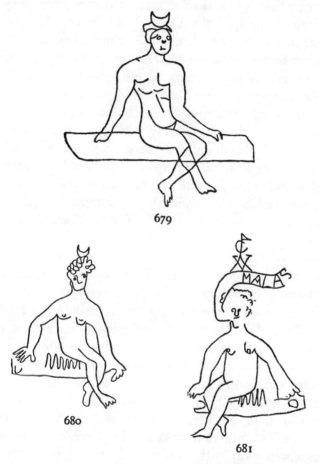

679

680

681

autobiography is put into the mouth of *Wisdom.* "I also came out as a brook from a river and as a conduit into a garden. I said, I will water my best garden, and will water abundantly my garden bed : and lo, *my brook became a river,* and my river became a sea. I will yet make my doctrine to shine as the morning, and will send forth her light afar off. I will yet pour out doctrine as prophecy and leave it to all ages for ever."[1] The Rabbis seem to preserve some tradition of a similar interpretation when they call Esther the "hind of the Dawn," and in the Talmud it is stated that her complexion was the colour of gold.[2]

In the above emblems of L'ISABELLUCCIA or CINDERELLA she is seated on the zigzags of effulgence and is adorned with the hair jewel of the Dawn goddess.

On the scroll emerging from the mouth of fig. 681 is a word that was almost certainly " MANAS," but two strokes of the letter N have unfortunately broken away. MANAS in Sanscrit means " mind," " organ of thought," " function of cognition and action," " the ego or individualising principle sometimes called the rational or human soul." The Crescent Moon was the badge of blue-bearded SIN, the Assyrian God of Light, and the word Cinderella is indubitably related to SIN. The etymology of our word *Cinder* is so suggestive that I quote it verbatim from WEDGWOOD's *Dictionary of English Etymology*. " It should be written *Sinder*, corresponding to German *Sinter*; Dutch *Sindel*; *Sintel*, Old Norse : *Sindr* signifying in the first place the brilliant sparks which are driven off when white-hot iron is beaten on the anvil, then the black scales to which they turn when cold, and the slag or dross of iron of which they are composed. The origin of the word is seen in Old Norse *Sindra*, to sparkle, to throw out sparks—a parallel form with *Tyndra*, to sparkle. In Germany *Zunder* is used as a synonym with *Sinder*." The Old Norse of our word TINDER is SINDRI = a flint for striking fire associated with a tinkling sound.

The name SINDBAD is doubtless of similar derivation to

[1] xxv. 1.
[2] *Bible Folk-Lore*, anon., p. 198.

Sindrella and to the Teutonic names Sindbald, meaning "sparkling prince," and Sindbert meaning "sparkling bright." The Seven voyages of Sindbad were once allegoric, and their symbolism has been worked out in considerable detail by E. A. Hitchcock.[1] In the third of the Seven voyages Sindbad, like "Issi," Ulysses, and Bissat, blinds a one-eyed monster.

[1] *The Red Book of Appian*, New York, 1866.

CHAPTER XII

THE EYE OF THE UNIVERSE

"On the earth the broken arcs, in the heavens the Perfect Round."
BROWNING.

"Let us then acknowledge man a born poet. . . . Despite his utmost efforts, were he mad enough to employ them, he could not succeed in exhausting his language of the poetical element which is inherent in it, in stripping it of blossom, flower, and fruit, and leaving it nothing but a bare and naked stem. He may fancy for a moment that he has succeeded in doing this, but it will only need for him to become a little better philologer, to go a little deeper into the study of the words which he is using, and he will discover that he is as remote from this consummation as ever."—TRENCH.

THE expression "one-eyed" was not used invariably in an unfavourable sense, and the Eye of SHIVA, the Eye of HORUS, and the Eye of ZEUS were time-honoured symbols of Divine Omniscience. WOTAN, the blue-cloaked All-Father of Northern mythology, was said to possess a solitary eye, understood by mythologists to point "beyond all doubt to the Sun, the one eye which all day long looks down from Heaven upon the Earth."[1] In the mind of ST MATTHEW the single eye was the equation of Light. "The light of the body is the eye : if therefore, thine eye be single, thy whole body shall be full of light."[2]

In fig. 682 a reconciliation or atonement of the two circles is in progress and the dual sight is merging into the single eye of Light.

[1] *Aryan Mythology*, G. W. Cox, p. 193.   [2] Matthew vi. 22.

288

The similitude of God to a circle is common to theologians and philosophers. In the picture writing of ancient Mexico the Deity is represented by a circle precisely as was ORMUZ by the Persians,[1] and ASSUR by the Assyrians.

The Egyptians considered God as the Eye of the Universe ; and a point within a circle was regarded by them as a symbol of the Deity surrounded by eternity : a globe typified the supreme and everlasting God.[2]

The Greek for Sun is *Helios, i.e.* the " Shining Light." The Assyrian Sun-God SIN, the English " sun," and the Dutch " zon " were probably once *is-in, is-un,* and *iz-on,*

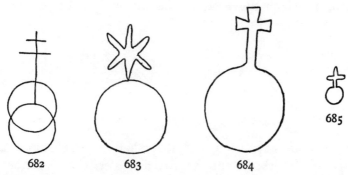

682   683   684   685

the " Light of the One " or " Light of the Sun." It is one of the axioms of Philology that vowel sounds are equal to one another and have little, if any, individual importance ;[3] the *ol* of *sol* must therefore be equal to EL, meaning God and Power, and the Icelandic, Swedish, Danish, Latin, and

---

[1] *Great Cities of the Ancient World,* T. A. Buckley, p. 367. Emerson in his Essay on circles refers to the Unattainable as " the flying Perfect " around which the hands of man can never meet.

[2] *A Lexicon of Freemasonry,* Mackey.

[3] Voltaire defined etymology as a science in which " vowels signify nothing at all and consonants very little." Upon this Max Müller comments : " It is only in the present century that etymology has taken its rank as a Science, and it is curious to observe that what Voltaire intended as a sarcasm has now become one of its acknowledged principles."—*Science of Language,* 2nd series, p. 258.

Portuguese *sol* may be equated with Is EL, the "Light of EL." Italians call the Sun *il Sole*, "the solitary one," and the French *soleil* may be equated with *sole il* or EL, the Sole and Solitary God, the Monocle or Lone Great EYE.

The Chaldees symbolised EUSOPH, the Light of Life, by an equilateral triangle, and by the Hindoos the great AUM dwelling in the infinite is similarly figured. The Egyptians regarded the Triangle as "Nature" beautiful and fruitful, and the encircled Triangle herewith will thus express the words of PLUTARCH : "The area within this triangle is the common hearth of them all, and is named the 'Plain of Truth,' in which the Reason, the forms, and the pattern of

686   687

all things that have been, and that shall be, are stored up not to be disturbed ; and, as Eternity dwells around them, from thence Time, like a stream from a fountain, flows down upon the worlds."[1]

The Z of ZEUS, forming the centre of fig. 687, "the EYE of ZEUS which sees all and knows all," consists of three strokes answering to the Triple ray. A common but hitherto undeciphered symbol on Gnostic gems is the letter S or Z *thrice* repeated and traversed by a straight rod through the middle.[2] This is again the Holy One and the triple rays corresponding to the three exclamations, *Sanctus !* *Sanctus !* *Sanctus !* The characters surrounding fig. 687 consist of *five* diamonds and the letters A U O M. The three strokes attached to the right of the A are again the

[1] *On the Cessation of Oracles.*   [2] *The Gnostics*, p. 218.

three rays, and these three rays when attached to the Holy
ONE constitute our letter E.

There was a world-famous "E" inscribed over the
Oracle at Delphi.[1] Because this character has five points,
the Greeks considered it to be equivalent to the numeral 5,
"but," says King, "others more profoundly interpreted the
letter as meaning by its proper sound in the Greek alphabet
the declaration Ei, *Thou art*, as addressed to the Godhead,
thus making it equivalent to the title O ON, 'the living
God,' so frequently given to JEHOVAH."[2]

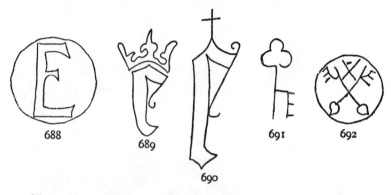

The five points of E caused it to be regarded as
equivalent to the five-pointed Solomon's Seal. It was
esteemed to be the letter of Light, and its appearance in fig.
688 stamps that emblem as another example of the Single
Eye of Light. The letter E, which by design or coincidence
is the *fifth* character in the Egyptian, Phœnician, Greek,
and Latin alphabets, forms the *Key of Light*[3] in figs. 691
and 692.

---

[1] See Plutarch's Essay, *On the E at Delphi.*   [2] *The Gnostics*, p. 297.
[3] Compare: "And Mary answered and said to the Saviour, ' Now we know,
O Master, freely, surely, plainly, that thou hast brought the Keys of the
Mysteries of the Kingdom of Light, which remit the sins of souls that they may
be cleansed and be transformed into pure light, and be brought into the
Light."—*Pistis Sophia.*

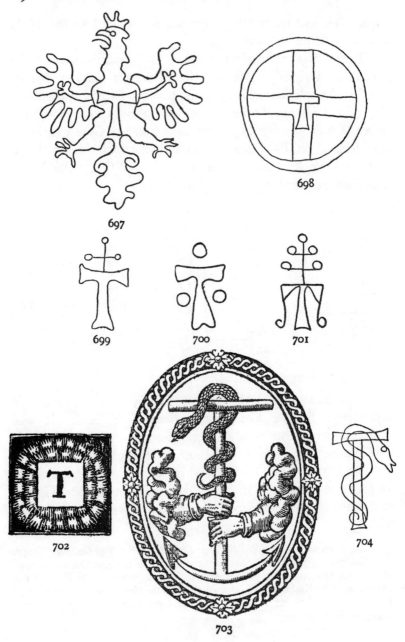

697

698

699

700

701

702

703

704

The character T, whether in its large or small form, was similarly the letter of light.   T or the Tau cross was the *signa tau*, the *signature* or mark of enlightenment mentioned in EZEKIEL as being branded upon the foreheads of the elect,[1] and its sanctity is exemplified in the emblems here preceding.

The Latin T was originally written +, it was subsequently altered to ×, and the stroke with which we now cross our small t's is a reversion to the original cross.[2]

The Circles herewith exhibit all four characters : fig. 693

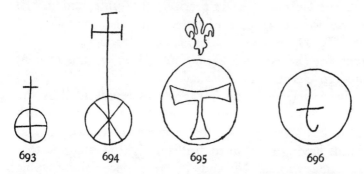

693   694   695   696

the original plus sign + ; fig. 694 the subsequent X of Lux ; and figs. 695 and 696 the modern large and small T.

In the Mayan alphabet T was expressed by the same sign as the Latin T and also by an equilateral triangle.[3]   In the Greek alphabet D or *delta* is expressed by a triangle, and it would seem that the meaning expressed by T and D was originally identical.   This identity may explain the interchangeability of T and D formulated in Grimm's Law, as for example, in *Tius* and *Deus*, the Teutonic and Latin terms for Deity.   The Greek for God is *Theos* and the *Th* of this word is simply a variant of T or D.   In the

---

[1] ix. 4.

[2] See *The Alphabet*, Dr Isaac Taylor.

[3] *Sacred Mysteries among the Quiches*, Le Plongeon (A.), p. xii.

Phœnician and Greek alphabets *Th* was denoted by a circle divided into four quarters.[1]

The Sanscrit word *dyu*, meaning *brilliant* and *resplendent*, is supposed to be the root of DEUS, DIES, DIANA, DIEU, and so forth, but *dyu* is a word of two syllables and is incorrectly described as a root. The true root is the *dee* or *dy*, and it is evident that this monosyllable carries in itself the idea of brilliance, light, and splendour. Thus the Latin *Deus* or *Dies* and the Spanish *Dios* resolves into the "Shining Light." The meaning expressed by the Greek *Theos* or the German *Tius* is precisely the same, and in the name *Zeus* we are again confronted with the variability of Z with T, D, or Th. The same interchangeability is apparent in *Tuesday* and *Ziestag* or *Dienstag*, the ancient and modern German for Tuesday.

In fig. 687 (*ante*, p. 290) Light was represented by the letter Z, and judging from the significant frequency with which this character enters into the names of Sun-Gods and into words having relation to brilliant light, I suggest that in the same way as M and N were once hieroglyphic representations of sea waves, so Z was at one time understood to express the descending zigzags of the lightning flash.

Our word *Zed*, borrowed from the Phœnicians, is probably the Persian word *ized* with the *i* worn off. The IZEDS were, according to Zoroastrian theosophy, the thirty arch-angels of ORMUZ, the Lord of Light, and they presided as guardian spirits over the thirty *days* or *dies* of the month.

[1] In the Greek alphabet this letter was also expressed by a point within a circle, and in the old alphabet of Italy it is expressed by X in a circle as at base of fig. 705. The Quakers are said to have adopted the dental "thou" and "thee" of their everyday speech as a constant reminder of the Primal Breath or Spirit, and in fig. 705 the symbolic *th* or X forms the handle of the Key of Life.

705

The letter X, the cross of *Lux*, was known to the Greeks as *xi*, and the syllable *xi*, *zi*, or *si* evidently once meant Fire or Light. It occurs significantly in XIUTLECUTLI, the Mexican God of Fire; in XILONEN, a Mexican Goddess ; in ZIZI and ZIZA, European equivalents of ISIS ; in ZIO, the old High German for ZEUS ; in the Hebrew ZION or Light of the Sun ; in the Greek equivalent ELISYON or Shining Light

706

of the Sun ; in the Hindoo SIVA, the fiery sunlight, and in the Greek ZEUS.

The French for lightning, *éclair*, is phonetically *ak-clare*, the "great shine " ; the Italian for lightning, *baleno*, is evidently derived from BELENUS, the name of the Celtic APOLLO ; the German for lightning, *blitz*, we may legitimately restore into *belitz*[1] or *beliz*, the " brilliant light of BEL." An older form of *blitz* was *blicze*, which resolves into *bel-ik-ze*, the "great fire of BEL " or the " fire of great BEL." The Portuguese for lightning, *raio*, and the Spanish *rayo*, are suggestive of RA.

---

[1] In the Mayan alphabet the sound TS was expressed by the sign ×.

The French word for blaze is *rayon*, and as *az* is equivalent to *iz*, our word *blaze* may like *blitz* be restored into *belaze*, " the Fire of BEL." We have here perhaps the origin of the words *blast*, *bliss*, *blush*, and *bless*, and of the proper names BLAISE and BELASSES. There was evidently some close connection between the pagan BAAL or BEL fires and the Christian ST BLASE, BLAISE, BLAYSE, etc. In ENGLAND ST BLASE's Day was formerly marked by several significant observances—the lighting of tapers, bonfires on hills, etc., and at BRADFORD in YORKSHIRE a festival is still held in his memory every *five* years.[1]

It was customary among the ancients to employ divine names as adjectives—as nowadays we also do when using *good*, *gaudy*, *jovial*, *martial*, *mercurial*, *saturnine*, and *venereal*. It is also evident that divine names served and still serve not infrequently as nouns. Of a certain Irish divinity named BRESS, which means beautiful, it is recorded that every beautiful thing in Ireland " whether plain or fortress, or ale, or torch, or woman or man," was compared with him, so that men said of them, " that is a BRESS." [2] This custom is still apparent in JAPAN, where the word *Kami*, God, is used also to mean anything and everything that is in any respect God-like.

Thus it is probable that to BEL, the God of Light, the Conqueror of the Dragon, we owe the French adjective *bel*, meaning beautiful, good, and honest. In the East *Bel* was used as a generic term for Lord or Ruler.

The Anglo-Saxon word for bright, white, and shining was *blac*, evidently BELAC, the Great Bel ; and just as the Greeks used *Knepha*ios to denote darkness or inscrutability and the Hindoos KRISTNA to mean *black*, so we now

---

[1] *A Book of the Saints*, L. H. Dawson, p. 24.
[2] *Celtic Myth and Legend*, C. Squire, p. 50.
[3] *Shinto*, W. G. Aston, p. 5.

employ the term *black* in its secondary sense, *i.e.* the direct opposite of the Saxon *blac*.

In fig. 707 the letter Z surmounts the head of an ox or

707

BULL, the animal that is said to "bellow," and whose name *Bull* or *Bullock* is affiliated to BEL or BELLOC.[1] That *oc* is radically the same as *ac* is shown by abundant evidence, such, for instance, as the identity between our *Oak*-tree and

---

[1] Compare the proper names BLACK, BLAKE, BULLOCH, and BELLOC ; also the Highland place-name BELLOCHANTUY. "In the case of local names the raw materials of language do not lend themselves with the same facility as other words to the processes of decomposition and reconstruction, and many names have for thousands of years remained unchanged, and some- times linger round the now deserted sites of the places to which they refer. The names of four of the oldest cities of the world—HEBRON, GAZA, SIDON, and HAMATH, are still pronounced by the inhabitants in precisely the same manner as was the case perhaps thirty or forty centuries ago, defying often- times the persistent attempts of rulers to substitute some other name. During the three hundred years of the Greek rule, an attempt was made by the conquerors to change the name of HAMATH to Epiphania, but the ancient appellation lingered on the lips of the surrounding tribes, and has now resumed its sway, while the Greek name has been utterly forgotten. The name of Accho, which we find in the Old Testament, was superseded for some time by the Greek name of Ptolemais. This is now forgotten, and the place goes by the name of AKKA. The Greeks attempted to impose their name of Nicopolis on the town of Emmaus, but in vain ; for the modern name, AMWÂS, still asserts the vitality of the ancient designation. We read in the Book of Chronicles that Solomon built TADMOR in the wilderness. The Romans attempted to impose on it the name of Adrianopolis, but this appellation has utterly perished, and the Bedouins still give the ancient name of Tadmor to the desolate forest of erect and prostrate columns which marks the site of the city of the palms."—*Words and Places*, Dr Isaac Taylor, p. 256.

the Anglo-Saxon *Ac*-tree. Similarly, the Devonshire River Ock is known alternatively as the Exe, both names, according to Baring-Gould, being traceable to the same Celtic roots, and the difference being due to there having been two distinct branches of the Celtic family planted on the river one above the other.[1] The letter X, which I have systematically decoded as the symbol of light, is named *exe*, and phonetically this is *ecse*, "the Great Light." X is employed by mathematicians as the first of the unknown quantities, and among Christians it is an abbreviated sign for the name of Christ.

At the Dionysiak or Great Dionysian Festivals it was customary for the assembled worshippers to raise loud shouts of *Axie Taure !*—understood by Plutarch to mean "Worthy is the Bull."[2] But the *ak*clamation or great clamour of *Axie !* seemingly once meant *Acze*, "Great Fire or Light"—a meaning to which many other cheers and glorias of the present day are traceable. The modern Christian chants somewhat unwittingly about "raising the *Trisagion* for ever and aye."[3] *Trisagion*, equivalent to Latin *Ter-sanctus*, is *tris-agion* ; *i.e.* a thrice-repeated shout of *agion !* Great Sun or One. The German *Hoch !* is still to-day understood to mean "High day."[4] The war-cry of the ancient Greeks was *Eleleu !* i.e. *ele lu*, "the shining light," and to this the Hebrews seem to have added Jah, making it *Hallelujah !* or *Alleluia !* The Nuns of St Mary's, Chester, used to sing a Hymn, *Qui creavit cælum, lully, lully lu*, and this mysterious *lully, lully lu* is a survival of the ecstatic cry, *Ialuz ! Ialuz !* i.e. the Ever-existent Light ! the Ever-existent Light !

The Semitic for Fire and Light is *Ur*, whence Christian

---

[1] *Devon*, p. 16.   [2] *Greek Questions*, 36.
[3] *Hymns Ancient and Modern*, No. 423.
[4] *Origin of Popular Superstitions*, T. Sharper Knowlson, p. 53.

names such as URIAH (URJAH) and URIEL are both defined
in name-dictionaries as meaning " God is my Light or Fire."¹
The British *Hooray !* or *Hurrah !* may in all probability be
resolved into *Ur-ray* or *-Ra*, " the light of RA." At the Sun
Festivals of PERU the worshippers raised triumphant shouts
of *Hailli !*² which is seemingly a later form of our more
primitive *Hail !* and one may picture the primitive Britons
on Salisbury Plain and other sites of prehistoric Sun-worship,
waiting in silent expectation for the Dawn and raising
ecstatic shouts of URRAH ! as the great Eye of Day rose
over the horizon and opened upon them.

The British *three* cheers or Trisagion may be compared
with the expression *Selah*, which occurs at intervals in the
Hebrew Psalms and is nowadays supposed to have meant
"a pause." It is phonetically *Silah !* the " Fire of the
Everlasting."

The *Vive !* or *Vivas !* of the Latin nations is related to
VIVASVAT, a Sanscrit name for the Sun, the Source and
Giver of Life. The word *laus*, as in *Laus Deo*, before it
meant "praise," must have been *la us*, the " Light of the
Everlasting," and we may again recognise it in this prehistoric
sense in SANTA CLAUS or, as it should be written, SANT
ACLAUS, the " Holy Great Light that has existed for ever."

These same two syllables *la-us* are the conclusion of
the name ELELEUS, one of the surnames of APOLLO and
DIONYSOS.

"Wherever," says Max Müller, "we analyse language
in a truly scholarlike spirit, whether in Iceland or in Tierra
del Fuego, we shall find in it the key to some of the deepest
secrets of the human mind, and the solution of problems
in philosophy and religion which nothing else can supply.

¹ IAH or JAH is similarly apparent in UZZIAH, ZEDEKIAH, HEZEKIAH,
OBADIAH, JEREMIAH, KEZIAH, and JEDEDIAH.
² *Peru*, Prescott, Ch. II.

Each language, whether Sanscrit or Zulu, is like a palimpsest, which, if carefully handled, will disclose the original text beneath the superficial writing, and though that original text may be more difficult to recover in illiterate languages, yet it is there nevertheless. Every language, if properly summoned, will reveal to us the mind of the artist who framed it, from its earliest awakening to its latest dreams. Every one will teach us the same lesson, the lesson on which the whole Science of Thought is based, that there is no language without reason, as there is no reason without language."[1]

An analysis of the several terms for *man, soul,* or *spirit* reveals the time-honoured belief that the human race emerged in its infancy from the Great Light, and that every human soul was a spark or fragment of the Ever-Existent Oversoul. The Egyptian for *man* was *se,* the German for *soul* is *seele* — cognate with *Selah !* — and meaning likewise the "Light of the Everlasting." The Dutch for *soul* is *ziel,* the fiery light of God, and the English *soul* was once presumably *is ol,* the essence or light of God.[2] The Hebrew for *man* is *ish* and for woman *isha.* The Latin *homo* is OM, the Sun, as also is the French *homme* ; and *âme,* the French for *soul,* is apparently the Hindoo AUM. The ancient Mexicans traced their descent from an ancestor named Coxcox, *i.e. ack ock se, ack ock se,* the "Great Great Light, the Great Great Light."[3] The Teutons claim to have descended from TIU or TUISCO, an Aryan God of Light, and the name TUISCO may be restored into *tu is ack O,* the "brilliant light of the Great O." A German

---

[1] *Biographies of Words,* Intro.

[2] We may see similar vowel erosion going on at the present day, and the word *cute* will soon take its place in the dictionaries in addition to *acute,* its proper form.

[3] This doubling of a title is a world-wide commonplace, similar to our "King of Kings and Lord of Lords, Very God of Very God."

name for the first-born man was ASKR, *i.e. as ack ur*, the "light or essence of the Great Light." The word *askr* means also ash-tree, and the Greeks imagined that one of the races of men sprang from ash-trees. The ASH- or ISH-tree was the symbol of Light and sacred to the sole-eyed WOTAN, and the expression "son of the ash-tree" was used as synonymous with "man."[1]

Not only do the generic terms for man, soul, and spirit reveal the ancient conception, but the same aristocracy of thought is manifest in many individual names and surnames.

The Scotch URE is the Hebrew *ur*; ERIC or HERRICK is *ur ik*; HARRIS and RHYS were once *ur is*. HAWKER or HOCKER are in all probability the same names as KERR or CARR. The Persian OMAR is parallel with the Greek HOMER, and both names may probably be equated with *amor* and *amour*, primarily meaning *sunlight* or *sunfire*, and secondarily *love*. The name ANN is *an*, the Sun ; and ANNA is the same as *ana*, the Assyrian word for *heaven*, and ANU, the Assyrian name for the All-Father. The Scotch IAN or ION is identical with the Continental HAHN and the English JOHN, pronounced in country districts JAH-ON. JAH or JE is Hebrew for the Ever-Existent, and JOHN, JOAN, and JANE mean the ever-existent One or Sun. So likewise does the European JOHAN or JEAN and the Persian JEHAN express the Egyptian tenet, "Thou hast been born a god, Son of the One," and the Hebrew, "Ye are gods : and all of you are children of the Most High."[2]

The names JESSE, JESSIE, and JOSE mean "Ever-Existent Great Light." The Cornish JOZON is the "ever-existent Sunlight," and this same meaning underlies JANUS, JONAS, JONES, JOHNS, and HANS. HICKS is the "Great Light," HOCKEN, HACON, and HAAKON are the "Great Sun or Great

---

[1] Müller, *Science of Language*, ii. 478.
[2] Psalm lxxxii.

One," and HACO, HUGO, and JAGO, the "Ever-Existent great O."

The high ancestry of the human *Ego*, the "I myself," the "I" of the first person singular is reflected in the Greek and Latin term *Ego*, the "Great O." The Anglo-Saxon for "I" was *Ic* and the Old English *Ik*. The Dutch is *Ik*, the Icelandic is *Ek*, and the German *Ich*. The French *Je* means the ever-existent, and in the Danish and Swedish *Jeg* and *Jag* we are again confronted with "ever-existent great one." The Lithuanian for "I myself" is *Asz*, *i.e.* the "light of the strong Light," and in the Sanscrit *Aham* there is, as it were, an *echo*[1] of the words "I AM."

The *Je* of *ever-existent* occurs in JAHWE or JEHOVAH; in JOVE, which is the same word as JEHOVAH; in JUPITER, *i.e. Ju pitar*, the "ever-existent Father"; in the Japanese JIMMU;[2] and in JUMALA, the Finnish ALL FATHER. The latter name may be resolved into JUM, the "ever-existent Sun," ALA or ALLAH, the "God who has existed for ever."

In Germany SANTA CLAUS is known alternatively as Knecht (Knight) CLOBES. CLOBES is the same word as our *globes*, and the root of both is the syllable *ob*, once meaning the same as *Orb*. *Ob*, meaning a *ball*, is the foundation of *obus*, a *ball*, and also of *obolus*, a little ball. The word *bolus* or large pill is *obolus* with a lost initial, and to the same root are traceable *bowl*, a round ball, and *bowl*, a circular utensil. *Globe* must originally have been *ag el obe*, the "Great Orb of God." CLOBES will therefore, like ACLAUS,

---

[1] Presumably so called with the pleasing fancy that Echo was the voice of the Great O.

[2] On ascending the throne of his fathers, A.D. 1868, Mutsuhito, the late Emperor of Japan, thus addressed his people :—"My house, that from Jimmu Tenshi has ruled over Japan according to the will of the gods, is the oldest dynasty on earth, and is carried back ten thousand years beyond Jimmu to the time when our Divine ancestors laid the foundations of the earth." JIMMU is the same as the English JIMMY, a form of JAMES, or, as it used to be pronounced, JEAMES, *i.e.* the Everlasting Sunlight.

have meant the "light of the Great Orb of God," and we may equate "Knight CLOBES" with OBERON, the Fairy King.[1] *Hob* was a word used long ago to denote a sprite, and it survives in "Hobgoblin."

As O is interchangeable with A, it follows that *ab*, the Hebrew term for Father, is the same as *ob*.[2] The word *abyss*, so frequently applied to God, is fundamentally *ab is*, and the Babylonian for *abyss* was *abzu*, the Fire and Light of *ab* the Father or the *orb* of Day.[3] It is also probable that *ob*, as in *observer*, is the *hub* of the Universal Wheel, and the root of the term *ubique*, meaning here, there, and everywhere.[4]

Oabl is the Celtic word for *heaven*, and the French for *heaven* and for *sky* is *ciel*, *i.e.* the "Light of God."

The ancients had a custom for which philologists have coined the pleasant term "onomatopoësis." "This," says Max Müller, "is one of the secrets of *onomatopoësis*, or name poetry, that each name should express not the most important or specific quality but that which strikes our fancy."

It apparently struck the ancient fancy that anything round or circular was like the Orb of Day. Thus the Lithuanians called an apple *obolys*, which is simply *obolus*, a little ball. The Irish for apple is *abhal*, the Gaelic *ubhal*, and the Russian *iabloko*, a word which resolves into *iabel*, the "orb of god," *oko*, "the great O."

Among the ancient Mexicans the word *on* served to denote anything circular.[5] The Celtic for *circle* is *kib*—

---

[1] Compare names: JOB, JOBSON, HOBBS, HOBSON, OBEN, OBADIAH, HOBDAY, etc.

[2] Compare ABNER, ABSALOM, ABDIEL, etc., and as vowels are interchangeable, also the Scandinavian IB and the German IBACH.

[3] Compare ABYSSINIA (old capital AXUME) and ARABIA.

[4] The red Ruby was probably named after *ur ube*, the fiery orb.

[5] Le Plongeon, *Queen Moo*, p. 151.

ak ib, the " great orb," and for *round, krenn—ak ur en*, the
" great fire sun."

It would appear to be one of the prime clues to language
that sharp and blunt consonants, such as S and Z, T and D,
P and B, were originally identical or at all events had a
value so nearly identical that they may be grouped together
like male and female of one species. This fact is recognised
in the alphabet of Pitman's Shorthand, where P and B, T
and D, Ch and J, K and G, etc., are represented by the same
signs, but light and dark, thus : \ =p, \ =b ; | =t, | =d ;
/ =ch, / =j ; — =k, — =g. In accordance with this
rule the *ob* of the Russian, Gaelic, Irish, and Lithuanian
"apple" becomes the *ap* of the English *apple*, the German
apfel, the Icelandic *epli*.[1] The knowledge that *ap* is equal
to *ob* or *orb* enables us to reduce the name *Apollo* into
Ap ol lo, the " orb of the Lord Everlasting."[2]

> " I am the EYE with which the universe
> Beholds itself and knows itself divine,
> All harmony of instrument or verse,
> All prophecy, all medicine are mine,
> All light of Art and Nature :—to my song
> Victory and praise in their own right belong."[3]

Ap must be the root of the Greek *apo*, meaning " far
away," and it may also be equated with our *up* and *upwards*,
both meaning towards the orb : it is also the foundation of
optimus, the best, and of *optimism* or faith in the highest.[4]

[1] This etymology of "Apple" is confirmed by the French *pomme*, i.e.
op om, the Sun Ball ; also by *pomolo*, the name for a giant orange. The word
orange resolves into *or-an-je*, the golden everlasting Sun.
[2] Among the Peruvians *capac* was not only an adjective meaning *great*
and *powerful*, but it was also a name for the Sun. APSU and APASON were
alternative forms of ABZU, the Babylonish great Abyss.
[3] Shelley, *Hymn of Apollo*.
[4] "High" may similarly be equated with towards the I or Eye.

Country people pronounce *up* " oop," and the child's *hoop* may have been so named because it was a circle like the Sun.   *Op* is not only the root of *hope* and *happy* but it is also the foundation of *optics*, *optical*, and other terms relating to the eye or eyeball.   The word *eye*, phonetically " I," may have arisen from the fact that the eye is a ball like the Sun, and this idea runs through the etymology of " eye " in many languages.[1]

Ops or Opis[2] was one of the names of Juno, the " unique, ever-existent O," or, as she was sometimes known, Demeter, the " Mother of brilliant splendour."   Ops was the giver of *ops*, riches, whence the word *opulent* ; *plenty* is fundamentally *opulenty*, and the Latin for *plenty* is *copia*, *ak-ope-ia*.   A synonym for *plenty* is *ab-un-dance*.

The syllable Op, meaning Eye, occurs in many proper names[3] and place-names, notably in Ethiopia and Europe. Cox translates Europe as meaning " the splendour of morning," and the word is alternatively rendered " the broad-eyed."   But the two syllables of Europe are simply a reversed form of the English surname Hooper, the Eye or " Hoop of Light," *i.e.* the Sun.   It is a curious coincidence that in the Island of Lewis (Llew = light) there is a place named Erropie, close to which is Eye Peninsula.

Within the Ope or Hoop or *Agape*[4] of fig. 708 appears the letter P.   The earliest form of P—judging from figs. 709 to 711, which are reproduced from Mons. Briquet's collection of archaic P's—was a shepherd's crook, and P in these emblems stands seemingly for Pa, the Father, the Shepherd, and Bishop of all souls.

---

[1] The Sanscrit for Eye is Akshi (=Akishi ?), Lithuanian Akis, Latin Oculus (diminutive of Ocus), Greek Omma, Swedish Oga, Russian Oko Spanish Ojo (=ever-existent O), Portuguese Olho (Lord O).

[2] Pinches (T. G.), *Religion of Babylonia and Assyria*, pp. 17, 93.

[3] Compare Hopps, Hope, Opie, Jope, Jeppe, Joppa.

[4] *Agape* is the Greek for *Love*.

Pa, which according to Max Müller means not to *beget* but to *protect* and to *nourish*,[1] is the root of the Greek and Latin *pater*, of the Italian *padre*, and of *parens*, a parent. The Persian for "Father" is *pidar*, the Sanscrit *pitar*, the Maori *pata*, and in seemingly all languages *pa* or *pi* once meant the Parent, the Protector, and the Feeder. ST NICHOLAS—a synonym for SANTA CLAUS or Father Christmas —is said to have been born at PATARA; and in Italy the Festival of ST NICHOLAS is called ZOPATA,[2] *i.e.* the "Fire Father." A symbol of the Supreme Father was the Peacock,

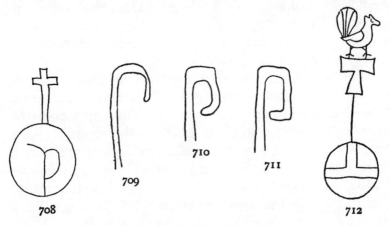

708   709   710   711   712

and this emblem may be seen embroidered on the vestments of Catholic ecclesiastics. The Peacock, like the Goose, was the Bird of JUNO or OPS obviously because of the blue iridescent[3] eyes of its wonderful plumage. It is fabled that ARGUS, surnamed PANOPTES or "the All-seeing," was changed into a Peacock, and if the name ARGUS be analysed, it yields *ar goose*, the "Fire Ghost or Spirit." In the figure herewith ARGUS standing upon a T or Tau Cross surmounts the Orb. The French for Peacock is *paon*, i.e.

---

[1] *Chips*, ii. 22.   [2] Brand, *Antiquities*, p. 226.
[3] Compare the blue iridescent *opal*.

Father-Sun, and if we knock off the negligible *cock* or *hen*, the name *peacock*[1] resolves into *pea* or *pi*, the Father.

The Holy Ghost is symbolised in Christianity by a Dove, and the Hebrew for *dove* is *jonah*. The *jon* of *jonah* reappears in the English and French *pigeon*, a word resolving into *pi ja on*, the "Father of the Everlasting One." The Celtic names for a *pigeon* are *dube*, the "brilliant orb," and *klom*, i.e. *ak el om*, "Great Lord the Sun."[2] At the Baptism of Christ the Heavens are said to have opened and a Dove or Pigeon to have descended to the words, "This is my beloved Son in whom I am well pleased." *Pi* or *pa*, the Father, is the root of *pity*, *peace*, *patience*, and of the names PAUL, PAULUS, etc.[3] The two syllables of PAUL coalesce frequently into POL, whence POLLOCK, POLSON, POLLY, POLDI, etc., and innumerable place-names, such as POLDHU or BALDHU, POLTON and BOLTON, POLPERRO, and BELPUR. POL was a title of BALDUR,[4] the APOLLO of Scandinavia, and BALDUR seemingly once meant the "enduring BALL" or the "enduring BAAL." The Eastern BAAL may be equated with the Druidic BEAL, which, according to Celtic antiquaries, means "the life of everything" or "the source of all beings."[5] *Pais*, i.e. the "essence of the Father," is the Greek for *son*,[6] and *paour*, again the "light of the Father," is Celtic for *son*. *Pa ur*, the Father of Light, is the origin of *power*, which in French is *puissance*, the light or essence of PA. The Celtic for *spirit* is *poell*, and *poële* is the French for *stove*; German, *stube*. Even to-day in Japan the domestic cooking-furnace is considered as a Deity.[7] *Patriarch* must originally have been

---

[1] Compare surname POCOCK or Great Great Father.
[2] Compare *colombe* and *columba*.
[3] Paul is equal to POEL, God the Father. Compare also JOEL and JAEL, the Ever-Existent God.   [4] Bartholomew (J. G.), *Gazetteer of British Isles*, p. 884.
[5] Peacock, *Age of Fable*, p. 375.
[6] PAISH is a Cornish surname.   [7] W. G. Aston, *Shinto*, p. 44.

pater-arch, and meant Great Father. The patron saint of Ireland is presumably a corrupted form of PATERICK, the Great Father, and the Shamrock or Clover leaf may be regarded as the threefold symbol of *ac lover,* the Great Lover.

In fig. 713 the letter P embellished into a pastoral staff surmounts the Solar Wheel or Sun Flower, the Golden Bull's Eye of the Universe.

The Daisy or "dyzi," formed like a little yellow sun encircled by radiating white florets, was held to symbolise

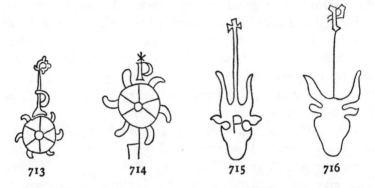

713	714	715	716

the Eye of Day, and the giant variety of Daisy is called an *Oxeye.*

In figs. 715 and 716 the P of the Great Parent appears upon the head of an Ox. In Egypt the sacred Ox was known as APIS, *i.e. opis,* the Eye of Light.

Our word Ox, phonetically *ok se,* was evidently bestowed because apparently from the dawn of human life the Ox was regarded as a symbol of the Creator, the Solar Saviour, the Great Light. The Sanscrit for Bull is *ukshan, i.e. ukishan,* the great Sunlight. The Greek for Bull or Ox, *tauros,* is radically *tau* or T, and means the brilliant and strong Light.

The giant Ox of Central Asia is called a *Yak, i.e. Y-ak* or *J-ak,* the Ever-existent Great One. The most ancient term for Dionysos was Iakchos, of which the syllable chos, as in Argus, is evidently cognate with our *goose* and *ghost*. Iakchos will thus resolve itself into the Ever-existent Great Ghost, Spirit, or Breath, and this high symbolism of the Goose will perhaps account for its otherwise inexplicable Italian names *oca* and *papero*.

In fig. 717 the Z is blazoned on the Eagle of Omnipotence, the Bird of Fire, the Hawk of Gold. East and west the Eagle-hawk was invariably the symbol of the sun. In Egypt Hawks were kept in the Sun-god's temple, where the Deity himself was represented as a man with a hawk's

717

head and the disk of the Sun over it.[1] The Greek for Hawk is *hierax*, a word that has much puzzled philologers, but which obviously is *hier*, sacred or holy to —, *ak se*, the Great Light. The Latin for *hawk* is *accipiter*, a word containing the *piter* of Jupiter and resolvable into *ak se pitar*, Great Light Father. The Latin for Eagle is *aquila*, and the Spanish *aguila*. The core of both these words is evidently Huhi, an Egyptian term for God the Father, and both thus read *ak* Huhi *la*, the Great Father Everlasting.[2] The Irish for Eagle was *achil*, probably *ak el*,

---

[1] Frazer, *Golden Bough*, iii. p. 112.

[2] "In the Egyptian the One God Ptah or Atum Ra was *Huhi*, the Eternal in the character of God the Father."—Churchward (A. W.), *Signs and Symbols of Primordial Man*, p. 365.

the Great God, with which we may compare the French *aigle* and the English *eagle*.[1]

One of the surnames of DIONYSOS was PURIPAIS, a word understood to mean "Son of Fire." *Pur* or *pyr* is Greek for Fire, and the Greeks sometimes called the Lightning PUR DIOS, *i.e.* the Fire of DIOS or DYAUS, the Shining light, the Sky. *Pyre* in English means a funeral fire, in Umbrian *pyr* means light, and in Tahitian *pura* means "to blaze as a fire." In Sanscrit *pramantha* means the stick with which one kindled fire, and the *pur* of *pramantha* is no doubt identical with the *pur* of PROMETHEUS, the traditional Bringer of Fire.

It is recorded by one of the Greek historians that "the Slavs knew only one god, the *fabricator of lightning*, whom they look upon as the ruler of all." This God, represented with *three* heads, was named PERUN and was portrayed with a fiery-red face, surrounded by flames. He was worshipped by the Russians, the Bohemians, the Poles, and the Bulgarians. A perpetual fire was maintained in honour of PERUN, which, if extinguished, was rekindled by sparks struck from a stone held in the hand of the God's image.[2] The name PERUN evidently meant either Fire of the Sun or the One Fire ; *un* being still the French for *one*[3] and the root of *unus, unit, unique,* etc. PERUN[4] was also

---

[1] *Eeg* is Scandinavian for *Oak*=AC. The Portuguese for Hawk is ACOR Great Fire). Our *Hawk* is almost identical with ORK, Gaelic for "whale,") the *Great* fish. Compare also *Hag*, Old Scandinavian for a Hawk. There is a variety of Hawk known in England as a "Hobby," another as a *Goshawk* or Great Light *Hawk*.

[2] Cf. *Religious Systems of the World*, p. 261.

[3] There is no doubt that the English *one* ; the French *on, un,* or *une* ; the Scotch and Anglo-Saxon *ane* or *an* ; the German *ein* ; Latin *unus*, the "one light"—all meant the Sun, the sole one. The Finnish for *one* is *ik* or *yksi*, "the great light" ; the Sanscrit is *ek* ; the Breton *unan*, "the one sun." The Anglo-Saxon for "only" was *anlic, i.e.* one-like, unique.

[4] Compare the English surname PERRIN.

known as Peraun, *i.e.* the Solar Fire ; as Perkunas, which we may restore to Per-ak-un-as, the Blazing Great Sun Fire ; and as Perkuns, *i.e.* Per-ak-ince,[1] the Sparkling Great Fire.[2]

The Greek word *paraclete* used by St John to denote the Holy Ghost the Comforter, is radically *per ak el,* the Fire of the Great God, and it was perhaps from Perak, the Great Fire, that the East Indian Perak and the American Paraguay derived their names.[3]

Perun must be allied not only to Perugia or Perusia, but also to Peru, the land of the self-termed " Children of the Sun." The Peruvian Solar hero was named Pirhua Manca, a term translated by Spence as " Son of the Sun,"[4] and by Donnelly as "revealer of *pir,* light."[5] The syllable Per, either a coalesced form of *pa ur* or a contracted form of *op ur,* is still to-day a Scandinavian Christian name, and is obviously the root of Percy, Perceval, and Parzifal, —names once meaning the light or strong light of the Fire. In Persian *persica* means Sun, and the Founder of the Persian Monarchy was termed Persica.[6]

The English surname Purvis may be equated with Peredur, an alternative form of Percevale or Parsifal ; the suffixes *-vis, -dur,* and *-val,* each meaning strong or enduring.

The Son of Helios the Sun was named Perses ; the daughter of Perses was Perseis ; and the wife of Helios was Perse. Per, the Fire or Light, was doubtless also the root of Percides, Perseus, and of Persephone or Peroser-

---

[1] Compare the English surnames Perrins, Prince, and Perkins.
[2] *Ince* = " sparkling," as in *etincelle* and *tinsel.*
[3] Perak may well have been the origin of our adjective *perky,* meaning sprightly and full of fire.
[4] *Mythologies of Ancient Mexico and Peru,* p. 53.
[5] *Atlantis,* p. 391.
[6] Payne-Knight, *Symbol. Lang. of Ancient Art and Mythology,* p. 145.

PINE, who is here represented[1] with the Fleur-de-lys-tipped sceptre of Light and is crowned with the tower of Truth.

The famous PERSEPOLIS, one of the wonders of the Eastern world, must have meant PER-SE-POLIS, the City of PERSE, the light of PER ; and the land of PERSIA, originally PERSIS,[2] clearly owes its name to the same root. The

Persephone (Proserpine) enthroned. (Gerhard, Archäolog. Zeit. tav. 11.)

718

Spanish surname PEREZ may be equated with the Italian PERIZZI, and with the PERIZZITES of the Old Testament. The Fire-worshipping PARSIS were originally—like the PARISII, the founders of the City of PARIS[3]—the followers or children of PER. In PERU there is a town named PER,

---

[1] From Smith's *Classical Dictionary*, by permission of Mr J. Murray.

[2] Alternatively ELAM, " Lord Sun."

[3] The name PARIS, the light of the Sun, may be contrasted with HELEN or SELENA, the Moon. The French once had a girl's name SELENISSA, *i.e.* the light of the Moon.

in Cornwall a place named PAR,[1] and PARR is a familiar English surname. Close to Stonehenge is PERHAM, and elsewhere in England we meet with PERTON, PYRFORD, PURBECK, PURFLEET, PERBOROUGH, and PIRBRIGHT.

The Sun-God PERUN is probably the Godfather of the Stone amphitheatre in Cornwall called PERRAN ROUND, which is situate at PERRANZABULOE, a ruined settlement abounding in prehistoric remains. In Cornwall there is a PERRAN WELL and also a PERRANPORTH.

In South America is the city of PARA, in Asia is PERA, and in Devon is PARACOMB, all probably owing their nomenclature to a Shrine of the Father Fire.

PAR, the foundation of our word *parent*, may be equated with the French *père*, which means "father," and the Sun-God PERUN may probably be equated with *père un*, the one Father.

Pur is French for *pure* and is the root of *prime, primal, primitive, premier*, and *progressive*. *Perfect*, or as the French have it, *parfait*, must originally have implied made by or like PER. PER, meaning *through* or *thorough*, is the foundation of the adjectives *permanent, permeating, persevering, pervasive, pertinacious, perennial*, and *present*. *Pardon* means the *donation* or gift of PER, and just as *laus* was primarily the light of the Everlasting, so must its English equivalent *praise* have meant *per az* the light of PER. The Sanscrit *Purusha* is the equivalent of the generic term ADAM. The French for *spirit* is *esprit* and the Portuguese for *light* is *esperti, i.e.* the light of shining PER. In our word *spirit* and in the Latin *spiritus* the initial vowel has phonetically decayed. Many words now commencing with *sc, st, sp*, etc., were originally spelled with an initial vowel, and native races often find it impossible to pronounce such a syllable as our

[1] Close to PAR are LUXULYAN and St BLAZEY. PARIS is a Cornish surname.

school without saying "ischool" or "sukool."[1]   The Greek word *peri*, meaning here, there, and everywhere, is equivalent to the Latin *ubique*.   A Persian name for radiant and winged spirits is *peri* or *pari* ; the New Zealand Maoris

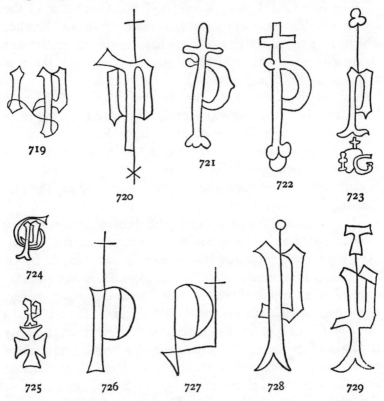

719   720   721   722   723

724   725   726   727   728   729

speak of the fairies as *paiarehe*, whom they state dwell on the fiery mountain named Pirongia,[2] a word suggestive of Ever-Existent Perun and also of Parnassus.   The Home[3] of the Persian *peri* was Paradise, and the Garden

[1] See Müller, *Science of Language*, ii. 209, 210.
[2] Cowan (J.), *Maoris of New Zealand*, p. 203.
[3] The Germans term Death *Heimgang*, "a going home."   The words *Home* and *Heim* both mean Om, the Sun, or Omma, the Eye.

of the HESPERIDES cannot differ from PARADISE, the Shining
Light of PER.   HYPERION was the Father of the Sun;
HESPERUS was the Morning Star who heralded the Dawn;
and *espérance* means *Hope.*[1]   The French for dawn is *aube*,
i.e. *orb* or *hoop*, the opening of the radiant Eye.

In figs. 719 and 720 the I or Holy One is combined
with P, forming the word IP.[2]   In figs. 721 and 722 the

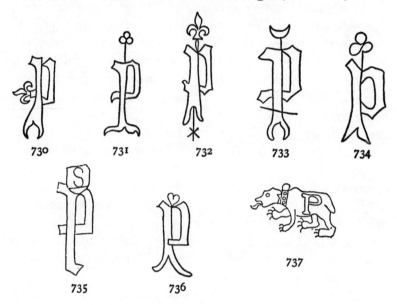

| 730 | 731 | 732 | 733 | 734 |

| 735 | 736 | 737 |

I forms part of the P; in fig. 723 this sacred initial is
identified with " JESUS CHRISTUS "; and in fig. 724 with the
C of CHRISTUS.

In fig. 735 the P of the All-Parent is surmounted by
the S of *espiritus* and *essence*; in fig. 736 with the Heart of
Love; and in fig. 737 it is identified with the Great Bear.
The Old German for Bear was *pero* or *bero*.   The modern

[1] Compare also *espoir, spire, spero,* and *aspiration.*
[2] Possibly this word has survived in HIP (Anglo-Saxon *Heope*), the name
for the little round or eye-shaped berries of the Hawthorn.

German is *bar*, the Dutch *beer*; and as *b* is apparently everywhere interchangeable with *p*,[1] our English *bear* will resolve into *baur*, the Father of Light. The Bear, symbol of the Self-Existent, was figured upon the Bird of Fire in fig. 312 (*ante*, p. 115), and in all languages the equivalents to Bear mean also Light or Fire. The French *ours* and the Latin *ursa* resolve into *ur se*, the Fire light, and the Sanscrit *riksha* expands into *ur ik isha*, the fire of the great ISHA. The similarity of this word *riksha* (bear) to *rishi* (shiner) was the peg upon which Max Müller hung his once all-popular theory that mythology was due to a "disease of language." In order to find some explanation for the Bear being named "shiner" or "brilliant," he was driven to the futile suggestion that it was because of the animal's "bright eyes, or from his brilliant tawny fur."[2]

Sometimes the Bear is called BRUIN, a name which may be equated with PERAUN or PERUN. The colour *brun* or *brown* may have been named after the colour of Bruin's fur.

The All-Father of Teutonic mythology was named BUR; *bra* is Hebrew for *create*, *brao* is Celtic for *good*, and the Sons of BUR are said to have slain the primeval giants and to have created the Celestial Spheres.[3] The root *bur*, meaning "fire," will account for such words as *burn, burnished, brass, brazier, bright, brilliant,* and *breeze* (cinders). The German for *fire* is *brennen* and the Spanish *brillo*.

In Scandinavian mythology BRAGI Son of ODIN was the brilliant gleaming Lord of the Sky and Day, and the chief of the Fire Maidens was named BRUNHILDE.[4]

---

[1] The most ancient form of the name BERTHA was PERAHTA; the Breton for *pardon* is *bardone*. There is a hill in Cornwall known as PERTINNY or BARTINE. Innumerable instances of similar interrelation can be adduced.

[2] *Science of Language*, ii. 379.

[3] Rydberg, *Teut. Mythology*, 389, 418, 425, 428.

[4] VALKYRE or WALKURE, the Fire Maidens, resolves into VAL'K UR—strong great Fire.

The name BRIDGET is traceable to BRIGHIT, the Irish Goddess of Fire, who is sometimes referred to as "the Presiding Care"; and the husband of BRIGHIT was named BRESS. One of the titles of OPS or CYBELE was BERECINTHIA; and AGNI, the Indian God of Fire, is alternatively known as BRIHASPATI.[1] The Son of BRAHMA was named BRIGHU, and BRIGHU was the "Discoverer of fire."[2] In Sanscrit the word *bhrama* means whirling, leaping flame, and *bhrama* must be identical with the divine names BRAHMA and BRAHM. The latter resolves into *bur aum*, the Fiery Sun or Solar Fire. The name ABRAHAM is admittedly BRAHM; the German BRAHMS will mean the light of BRAHM, with which may also be compared the English surnames BRAM, BRAHM, and BROUGHAM.[3] The latter is pronounced *Broom*, and the *Broom* and *Gorse* bush of Europe were presumably so christened because their flamelike flowers have the appearance of *ag or se*, the "Great Golden Fire Light." In Hebrew *Bram* means "father of a multitude."

BRAHMA is represented as riding upon a goose—*ag oos*, the Great Light; or a gander—*ag an dur*, the Great Enduring Sun;[4] and one of the titles of BACCHUS, the Father Goose, was BROMIUS. The old Scotch for goose[5] was *clakis*, i.e. *ak el akis*, the Great God, the Great Light; and in seemingly all languages the names for "goose" meant also Sun.

The root BUR is responsible for innumerable place-names and proper names, and for adjectives such as *burly* (or bur-

[1] PATI, the Shining Father; BRIHAS, Fire Light.
[2] M. Müller, *Biogr. of Words*, p. 190.
[3] Compare BARR, BURRUP, BORIS, BARUCH, BARKER, BERNARD, etc.
[4] GANDER may be equated with CONDOR, the gigantic eagle of South America. The *gan*net or "Solan goose" is a sea goose.
[5] Sw. *gas*, Icel. *gas*, Dan. *gaas*, Du. and G. *gans*, L. *anser*. The name *brandt* is applied to a variety of goose; also *barnacle*, L. *bernacla* or *bernecha*, Fr. *bernache*.

like [1]), *brisk* and *brave*. The shout of *Bravo* ! was, it may be assumed, originally *Buravo* or *Bur ave*, " I hail thee, BUR ! " The word "applause" points suggestively to the conclusion that it was originally *op laus*, a *laus* or lauding of the beneficent Hoop.

The names *burr* and *burdock*,[2] applied to the spiky little seed-vessels of the hedgerow, were evidently bestowed with the poetic notion that the clinging burr was a miniature Sunball. The same notion underlies the nomenclature of the hedgehog, which rolls itself into a prickly ball. The Spanish for hedgehog is *erizo*,[3] and the French *herisson*,[4] both

738

of which resolve into *ur is on*, *i.e.* Fire Light Sun. Our hedgehog is phonetically *ejog*, everlasting great one ; and as *ch* must be equivalent to *j*, its alternative name of *urchin*— Walloon *urechon*—will mean Fire of the Ever-existent Sun. In the emblem herewith the urchin is surmounted by the fivefold light of the Parent Flame.

Sea-Urchins—round shellfish with multitudinous spikes most exquisitely coloured—seemingly derive their name for the same reason as the hedgehog ; and the Swedish name for sea-urchin is *borre*.

---

[1] Barley was in Anglo-Saxon times written *Baerlic,* i.e. *Bur*-like or *Baer*-like, Father-of-Fire-like. The bearded firelike spike of barley is obviously the cause of its name.   [2] " Burr, the Great Shiner."

[3] *Erezu* is Zend for *right*.   [4] Compare surname HARRISON.

One of the appellations of BACCHUS, the Father of Great Light, was LIBER = LA-BUR, the Everlasting BURR. LABUR must have been Lord of the fire-like *Laburnum* tree, and in Latin *liber* means free—whence *liberty*. Our word *free* is almost identical with FRO, the name of the ancient All-Father of Northern Europe—whence Friday. Cox observes : " In the oldest Teutonic mythology we find a god Fro or Friuja, which is worshipped as the Lord of all created things. If we may judge from the name, the conception of this deity was probably far above the ideas formed of any of the Vedic or Olympian gods. If the word is connected with the modern German *Froh*, it expresses an idea which is the very opposite of the Hebrew tendency to worship mere strength and power. For Fro is no harsh taskmaster, but the merciful and eternal God. He is, in short, the bene-ficence and long-suffering of nature. Fro is thus the power which imparts to human life all its strength and sweetness, and which consecrates all righteous efforts and sanctions all righteous motives." [1]

The foundation of the name FRO is *fer*, whence our English word *fire*. The same root is evidently responsible for the German *feuer*, the Dutch *vuur*, and the English *furnace*, *forge*, *frizzle*, and similar terms relative to fire. FORNAX was the Latin goddess of the Oven, and *fornax* was the generic term for a *furnace*. *Formus* is Latin for *warm*, and *fourneau* is French for *stove*. *Fervour* means warmth, and to *fry* an article was presumably to expose it to the Fiery One. *Phare* is Greek for a lighthouse, and *fair* is a double-barrelled English word meaning *just* and *beautiful*. The word *sphere* in mediæval English was written *spere*, and the Old French was *espere*, and these terms are evidently related to the light of Père, the Father, or the great Phare of Day. *Fairies*, the light or essence of THE FIRE, may be

[1] *Mythology of Aryan Nations*, p. 198.

equated with the *peri* or pixies, [1] and the term *fairies* is cognate with the Persian word *Ferouers*. The Ferouers were the grade of Divine beings next in rank below the Izeds, and in Celtic *izod* means *fair*. Infinite in number, the Ferouers protected man during his mortal life and purified his soul on the Day of Ascension.

The Old Irish *fer*, like the Latin *vir*, was the generic term for *man*, and FRIUJA, the alternative name of FRO, is the Teutonic adjective *frija*, meaning *free*, *dear*, and *beloved*. It may be compared with the Sanscrit *priya*, meaning *wife* or *loved one*, and with the Gothic *frijon*, *to love*—whence, it is assumed, our word *friend*. The adjectives *fresh* and *frisky* are equivalent to *brisk* and *perky*, and *force* is akin to *power*. PHARE, the Primeval POWER, the foundation of our terms *firm*, *firmament*, *first*, and *foremost*, is the root of the dynastic title PHARAOH [2] and of the names PHRA, PHARAMOND, FARADAY, FRAZER, FERGUS, FARQUHARSON, FREDERICK, FRITZ, etc. The Town of PHERENICE, alternatively BERENICE and originally HESPERIS, is the fabled site of the garden of the Hesperides. PHORONEUS is Greek for " discoverer of fire," and the FORTUNATE Islands might legitimately be spelt PHORTUNATE. In the word *ophthalmia oph* is obviously a form of *op* or *ob*. The FAROE Islands were probably named after FRO, who was doubtless also the origin of *franc*, meaning *free* ; of *frank*, meaning *open* ; and of FRANZ and FRANCE. The ancient town of FIRAN was alternatively known as PHARAN, and this, according to Lepsius, is the same as the PARAN of the Old Testament. [3]

As the acute F must be equal to the blunt V, the Indian VARUNA expresses the same idea as PERUN, the unique

---

[1] Pixy=Pickze. Their leader was PUCK. Compare also *Brownies*, *Sprites* (sepurites), and *sprightly*.

[2] Or PERAA.

[3] *Egypt, Ethiopia, and Sinai*, p. 304.

POWER or PERE. The Frisian term for Father is *vaar*, to whom we may attribute the city name VERONA and the Christian name VERONICA.[1]

The original identity of VER with BER may be deduced from place-names apparently all the world over. Mount BEROMA in Mashonaland is alternatively Mount VEROMA. In Cornwall is a ST BURYAN and a ST VERYAN; the former is no doubt identical with the Christian name BRYAN or BRIEN.

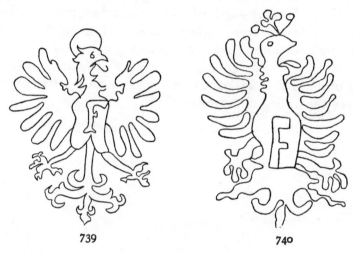

739   740

VER is the French for Spring, *i.e. se puring*, the fire of PERE, and is the root of *verdure*. VIR is Latin for *strength*, and in Sanscrit the word *vrishan*, according to Max Müller, means "the strong rising sun."[2] In French *vrai* means true, and the same root is responsible for *verité*, *verax*, *veracity*, *virtue*, *virility*, and *very*. The expression "Very God of Very God" is still in *frequent* use.

The consort of ODIN, the Scandinavian ONE EYE, was said to be FRIG, the "Great Fire," and the means by which

[1] The *Vera Icon* legend must have been an afterthought.
[2] *Science of Language*, ii. 463.

the ancients obtained fire was *friction*. FURICK is also evidently the root of the name AFRICA; a conclusion strengthened by the fact that Africa was alternatively known as APARICA. In Peru the word VIRACOCHA, besides meaning the Great Father, was a generic term for all divine beings.[1]

Sir John Maundeville mentions in his *Asiatic Travels*[2] a place named PHARSIPEE, *i.e.* PHAR, the Fire Father. At PHARSIPEE there was said to be a marvellous Sparrow-hawk —we may call it a *Peregrine* (*per-eg-ur-un*, the Fire of the One Great POWER)—and whosoever watched this bird for seven days and seven nights—some said three days and three nights—would have every desire granted by a " fair lady of fairie." In fig. 739 the letter F is figured on the Bird of Fire, and fig. 740 is designed in such a way as to convey the notion of a flaming Fire.

[1] *Myth. of Ancient Mexico and Peru*, Spence (L.), p. 48.
[2] Chapter XIII.

CHAPTER XIII

THE PRESIDENT OF THE MOUNTAINS

"Every beast of the forest is mine, and the cattle upon a thousand hills."
PSALM l. 10.

THE first Deity that looms out of the prodigious antiquity of Egyptian history is PTAH, the Creator. Under the symbolism of a Bull—"the beautiful Bull of the Cycle of the Gods"—PTAH was worshipped as HAPI or APIS. He was also typified by a Bull known as the KA-NUB or KANO-BUS; a name resolving easily into *ak-an-obus*, the "great Sun, the obus." A third Bull was known as BAKH or BAKIS, *i.e.* "*Ob*, the Great Light," or, in other words,. BACCHUS. The Egyptians also symbolised the Creator under the form of a fourth Bull named UR-MER. The first syllable of this name probably, as among the Semites, meant *Fire*, and the word is probably allied to MER, one of the names of the Assyrian God of Lightning. One of the titles of the Assyrian Fire-god was NIN-IP and NINIP or NERIG— *on ur ig*, the one Great Fire, was also known as URAS.[1] The giant Bull of primitive Europe was known to the Latins as *urus*, the "light of the Fire," and this word is practically identical with HORUS or ORUS, the Egyptian APOLLO. So widespread was the cult of HORUS that in Egypt the word *horus* was used as a generic term for "God."[2] *Urus* is

[1] Pinches, *Religion of Babylonia and Assyria*, 97.
[2] Tiele (C. P.), *Religious Systems of the World*, p. 6.

323

evidently the foundation of *tauros* the Greek, *taurus* the Latin, and *toro*[1] the Spanish, for Bull. The Chinese have still a Temple called the Palace of the Horned Bull, and the same symbol is venerated in Japan and all over Hindustan. THOR, the Scandinavian Jupiter, was represented in the Temple of UPSAL (OP-CIEL[2] ?) with the head of a Bull upon his breast ; and in Old Scandinavian, as in Phœnician and Chaldee, *thur* was the generic term for *bull* :[3] *tur* was Chaldee for *sun*.[4] At MIAKO (OM-YAK-O ?) in Japan, the

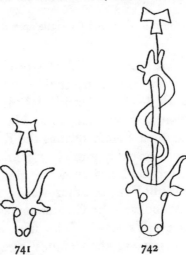

741   742

creation of the world is represented under the image of a Bull breaking the shell of an egg and animating the contents with his breath.[5]

The name PTAH must have been pronounced either

[1] The city arms of TORINO or TURIN are a rampant *Bull*.

[2] Upsal, the Eye of the Fire of God, was also called UPSALA. This name is almost identical with *upsilon*, the Greek name for their letter *v*. Compare also *epsilon*, the Greek name for E. One of the titles of BACCHUS was PSILAS.

[3] Payne-Knight (R.), *Symbol. Lang. of Ancient Art and Mythology*, p. 20.

[4] Higgens, *Anacalypsis*, i. 607.

[5] Payne-Knight (R.), *Symbol. Lang. of Ancient Art and Mythology*, p. 20.

OPTAH, the " shining Eye," or PATAH, the " shining Father,"
and Egyptologists have commented upon the fact that the
images of PTAH closely resemble the *pataikoi* or small
figures carried about by Phœnician sailors. The word *pata*
is related to *pehti*, the Egyptian for *strong* or *strength*, and to
patu the Maori term for *father* ; and the *pataikoi* or *pataiks*
were presumably small symbols of St Patrick, the Great
Strong Father.

In subsequent ages the term PTAH was extended by
the addition of later God-names, such as SEKER,[1] whose
symbol was a Hawk. The name SEKER, SOKAR, or SEGER,
is clearly the same as the English word *saker*, a kind of
Falcon. The French and Spanish call this bird *sacre*, and
the Arabians *saqr*. At the town of OPIS in Assyria was the
chief shrine of the Deity ZAKAR, and this name, identified
with the Biblical ISSACHAR, the Son of JACOB,[2] is the foundation of our word *sacred* (French *sacre*). The Supreme God
of Buddhism is known as SEKRA.

In addition to the title PTAH-SEKER the Egyptian All-
Father was named also PTAH-SEKER-OSIRIS. An earlier
form of the name OSIRIS, the Watcher, the Many-Eyed, the
Good Being, was ASAR or ASIR. ESAR is the Turkish, SIRE
is the Persian, name for God—and *sire*,[3] which is English
for *father*, is Chaldean for *light*. The presiding Deity of
ASSYRIA was named ASSUR. ASURA was one of the appella-
tions of VARUNA, and ASURA has been equated with AHURA-
MAZDA, *i.e.* ORMUZ.[4] In Hebrew the name AZUR means
" He that assists " ; ASSER is an English surname ; and in
Assyrian ASSUR or ASUR means *Holy*. There is an inscrip-

---

[1] Varying into SOKAR, SEGER, etc.
[2] JACOBUS is Latin for JAMES.
[3] Our English title *Sir* has the same meaning. At one time all priests
were entitled *Sir* or *Sir reverence* ; sometimes as *Sir John*. The King is
addressed as *Sire*.
[4] Cox, *Aryan Mythology*, p. 156.

tion at NINEVEH where the word *asur* occurs three times, suggesting the exclamation, " Holy ! Holy ! Holy !" or " Holy ! Holy ! Holy One !" [1] *Azure* is the Sky-blue of the Heavens, and in Scandinavian mythology the Twelve self-existent spirits who dwelt in ASGARD were termed the AESIR. ASARI was one of the appellations of MERODACH, " the young steer of Day," who is described as " pasturing the Gods like sheep," [2] and it is obvious that ASARI and correlative terms may be equated with OSIRIS. Thus PTAH's later appellation of PTAH-SEKER-OSIRIS resolves into the idea, " Shining Father, the light of the Great Fire, the blaze of the Fire light."

AUF

743

OSIRIS was known alternatively as UNNEFER, the one or Solar Fire, and in fig. 743 the sun is subscribed AUNF, a contracted form of this term. The inner circle of the Eye is called the *iris*, and the name OSIRIS is generally interpreted to mean " the Many-eyed." IRIS, the Rainbow, was the iridescent messenger of the gods, but more particularly of JUNO ; and *eros* is the Greek for *Love*. OSIRIS was also known as UNBU, *un* meaning *one* or *sun*, and *bu*, *Father*. That BA is interchangeable with and equivalent to PA is obvious from many considerations ; such, for instance, as the fact that the city of PABAST was alternatively known as BUBASTIS ; that the Turkish *Pasha* is equivalent to *Bashaw*,

[1] Pinches, *Religion of Babylonia and Assyria*, p. 87.
[2] *Ibid.*, p. 61.

and that the town of PAPHOS was alternately BAFU. *Ba* was the Mayan word for *father* and the Egyptian for *soul*.[1]

BE is our verb *to be*, *Being*, or *Existence*. The Latin for *to be* is *fore*, *i.e.* the *fire*, and in French *beau* means *beautiful*.[2] The Cornish for *pity* was *byte*, whence it may be inferred that the "Father Resplendent" was esteemed to be a god of *Pity* and of *Beauty*.

In fig. 744 the P of PTAH is surmounted by his symbol, the Scarabæus or beetle. The Egyptian for scarabæus was *chepera*, and the word *chepera* signified also *being*. "No words," says RENOUF, "can more distinctly express the notion of 'self-existent Being' than *chepera cheper t'esef*,

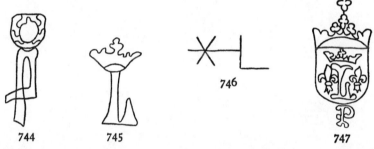

746

744   745   747

words which very frequently occur in Egyptian religious texts."[3] At one time the morning Sun was worshipped under the name KHEPERA,[4] and CHAFURA was a name among the Egyptians for their kings or "Sons of the Sun." We English have this term *chafura* in its more primitive form, *chafer*, meaning a beetle. In the ancient hieroglyphic

---

[1] The negligibility of vowel sounds is conspicuous in our words *pope*, i.e. *papa* or *pape*, and in *babe*, *baby*, or *bébé*. The word babe (Anglo-Saxon *bab*, earliest form *baban*) is described by Skeat as "probably due to infantile utterance." A baby was no doubt called *baby* because it cried *baba* or *papa*, and it is not unlikely that the lamb's cry of *Baa* was one reason for that animal's symbolic sanctity. PEPI and BABA were kingly names in Egypt; BABYLON was alternatively BABILU.

[2] The Hebrew for *beautiful* is *joppa*.   [3] *Hibbert Lectures*, 1879, p. 217.

[4] Petrie (Flinders), *Religion of Ancient Egypt*, p. 54.

alphabet of Mexico a beetle was the sign of the letter L,[1] and *El* was presumably so called because it symbolised El, meaning Power or God. The Mayans represented L by a dot within a circle and by an acute angle. In the emblems herewith the letter is glorified with the crown and cross, and in fig. 747 it is associated with the P of PA.

The word *chafer* meant primarily " Ever-existing Fire," and the *pera* of *chepera* may be rendered *père* or *power*. The term *scarab* may be compared with *escarbot*, the French for beetle, and extended into *is-ac-ar-ab* or *es-ac-ar-bo*.

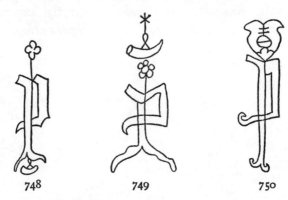

748   749   750

The Egyptian *chepera* is almost the English *shepherd*, and the German for *shepherd* is *schafer*. The French for *shepherd* is *berger* (*bur-zhay*), " Baur, the ever-existent," and the Sanscrit is *payu*. The Italian for shepherd is *pecorajo*, i.e. *op-ek-ur-ajo*, " the Eye, the great Fire ever-existent," and the Celtic for shepherd was *bugel*. In figs. 748 and 749 P is associated with a bugle, and in English *bugle* has two additional meanings. It implies a wild ox and also a circular or oval-shaped ornament. The root of *bugle* is *bug*, and *bug*[2] is an English term for all the tribe of beetles.

---

[1] Donnelly (I.), *Atlantis*, p. 219.
[2] There is a River BUG in Russia and another in Austria. BUGGE is an English surname.

One may surmise that, apart from symbolism, they were so called because they are round shaped like *ob ug*, the Mighty Orb. Fig. 750 is surmounted by an Orb.

Among the Celts the beetle was named *chouil* or *chuyl*, and in some districts *huyl*. The word *huyl* is equal to *heol*, *haul*, or *houl*, the Celtic name for the *Sun*. It is seemingly from *heol*,[1] the eternal EL, that we derive our adjectives *hale*, *whole*, and *holy*. The Teutonic for Holy is *hel*, *heli*, *heil*, or *ala*, *i.e.* ELLA, God that has existed for ever, the ALL and the WHOLE. In apparently all languages the word signifying *holy* has been derived from the divinely honoured sunlight.[2]

The Latin P has the same form as the Greek letter named *Rho*. One of the most famous emblems of early Christianity—known as the LABARUM, the seal of Constantine, or the *Chi-Rho* monogram—is the letter X surmounted by a P. The two letters *Chi* and *Rho* are assumed to read *Chr*, a contraction for the name CHRIST, but the symbol was in use for long ages prior to Christianity, and it probably stood for X, the Great Fire, and P, Pater or PATAH. The word *labarum* resolves into *la bar um*, the "everlasting Father Sun." The *Pe Ekse* of this famous symbol was also doubtless understood to mean *Pax=peace*. The ancients personified PAX as a divinity and built temples to his honour. As the mystic forms of *pi* represent a shepherd's crook, the letter was doubtless understood also to mean *Payu*, the Good Shepherd. From the emblems herewith it is evident that R was similarly derived from a shepherd's crook. Our letter R is *Ar*, the Fire, and in fig. 142, *ante*, p. 59, AR formed the centre of the Solar Eye. The Egyptian word for *eye* was *ar* ; HAR was one of the names of the one-eyed ODIN, and in

---

[1] Compare surnames HULL and HOOLE.

[2] Compare Greek *Hagios* and *Hieros*. The word *saint* or *santa* was primarily *san*.

Norse *harr* meant *high*, doubtless because HAR[1] was up on high. The Greek *Rho* probably derived its name from RA, and the Italian word *papero*, a *green goose*, was presumably "Father RA." *Ra* is no doubt responsible for the English words *ray* and *radiant*, and for innumerable place-names and surnames.[2] The Danish for *goose* is *radgaas* or *raygaas*, and

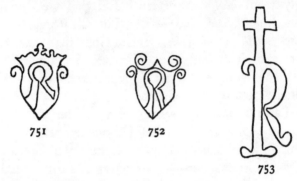

751   752

753

in Northern Europe the principal Deity was at one time RADGOST or RADEGOST.[3]

The P of the Great Shepherd is the foundation of PAN, the God of all Shepherds, and the name PAN may be understood indifferently as *opan*, the Sun Disk, or *paan*, Father Sun.[4] APOLLO, who was particularly worshipped at the

[1] Compare place-names HARBOROUGH, HARBY, HARGRAVE, etc., and surname HARDY, "the resplendent HAR."

[2] Compare RAY, WRAY, REAY, RAOUL, REAN, REHAN, REJANE, RENE, RABAL, RACKHAM, RACKSOLE, etc.

[3] The chief seat of his worship was among a people named the OBOTRITES, whose territory corresponded roughly to present-day MECKLENBURG (*Burg* means a stronghold, and the remaining MECKLEN looks curiously like OMEKA or OMEGA-LEN). In BOHEMIA several places are supposed to have been named after RADEGOST, and the OBOTRITES are also believed to be responsible for the names BERLIN, BREMEN, LE-IP-SE-IC, and many others.

[4] In every ancient language there is a certain ambiguity: thus of Sanscrit Mr F. W. Bain in the preface of one of his Indian stories writes: "The name of the little Indian fable, here presented to the lover of curiosities in an English dress, is ambiguous. We may translate it indifferently, either *The New Moon in the Hair of the God of Gods*, or else *She that reduces*

city of PATARA, was surnamed PÆAN, and the songs sung at his festivals were thence named *pæans*. The word *patara* meant a round or disk, and the word *pæan* was used also to mean *Healer* and *Physician*.

> " Shepherds, rise and shake off sleep ;
> See, the budding morn doth peep
> Through the window, while the sun
> To the mountain tops is run.
>
> Sing His praises that doth keep
> Our flocks from harm,
> Pan, the Father of our sheep ;
> While arm in arm
> Tread we softly in a round,
> While the hollow neighbouring ground
> Fills the music with her sound.
>
> Pan, O Great God Pan, to Thee
> Thus do we sing !
> Thou that keep'st us chaste and free
> As the young Spring ;
> Ever be thy honours spoke,
> From that place the morn is broke,
> To that place day doth unyoke." [1]

---

the Pride of Gods, Demons, and all the Rest of Creation; that is the Goddess of Beauty and Fortune. To those unfamiliar with the peculiar genius of the Sanscrit language it might seem singular that two such different ideas should be expressible by the one and the same word. But it is just in this power of dexterous ambiguity that the beauty of that language lies. As there are butterflies' and beetles' wings, of which we find it impossible to say that they are positively this colour or that—for according to the light in which we view them they change and turn, now dusky red, now peacock blue, now it may be dark purple or old gold—so a well-formed Sanscrit compound word will subtly shoot and coruscate with meaning, as do those wondrous wings with colour : and this studied double, treble, manifold signification of its words lends to the classic tongue a sort of verbal sheen, a perpetual under-current of indirect suggestion, a by-play of allusion, a prismatic beauty, of which no other language can convey the least idea. For translation must split up what in the original is a unity. And so our title, according to the value which we choose to assign to its component elements, can be taken to denote either the hair-jewel of the moon-crested god or the universal pre-eminence of world-wildering Aphrodite." [1] Fletcher.

It is usually assumed that PAN was a divinity of Greek conception, but HERODOTUS records that the Egyptians, contrariwise, regarded PAN as "exceedingly ancient" and belonging to those whom they called "the eight Gods," *i.e.* the original OGDOAD. He states : "These Egyptians who are the Mendesians consider PAN to be one of the eight gods who existed before the twelve, and PAN is represented in Egypt by the painters and the sculptors just as he is in Greece, with the face and legs of a goat. They do not, however, believe this to be his shape or consider him in any respect unlike the other god, but they represent him thus for a reason which I prefer not to relate." [1]

PAN and his consort MAYA were adored in CENTRAL AMERICA, and at the town of PANUCA or PANCA [2] in MEXICO the Spaniards on their entry found superb temples and images of PAN. [3] The names PAN and MAIA enter largely into the Mayan vocabulary, MAIA being the same as MAYA, the name of the Peninsular, and PAN combined with MAYA forming the name of the ancient capital MAYAPAN.

Among the Greeks the name PAN was used to mean the *All*, the *Everything*, and the *Universal*. PAN, the root of PANACEA, the Goddess of Health, must be equal to *Ban* ; and *ban*, *bon*, or *ben*, meaning *good*, are the roots of *benign*, *benevolent*, *benison*, etc. *Bonheur* is the French for *happiness*.

PAN would appear to have been an original Deity of JAPAN or JAPON. The Japanese call their country NIPPON (*on ip pon*), and their national cheer is BANZI ! the light of the great FIRE or LIFE. In modern Japanese NIPPON is understood to mean "Fountain or Source of Light."

PAN is recorded to have been the son of AITHER, the all-permeating *ether*, and the Mother of PAN is said variously

[1] Bk. ii. p. 46.
[2] Compare surname PANKHURST.
[3] Brasseur's Introduction to Landa's *Relacion*.

to have been DRYOPE,[1] the "Enduring Great Unit or EYE," or YBIS or ONEIS, the "One Essence or Light," or PENELOPE. According to Greek mythology the first-born woman was PANDORA.

Pente in Greek means *Five* ; *panch* or *punj* is Sanscrit and Gypsy for *Five*, and the PUNJAB or *Punj orb* is supposed to be so named because it is watered by *Five* Rivers. Off the coast of ARABIA or UROBIA is an island called PANCHEA whereon was a magnificent Temple of Jupiter. It is a most curious fact that the form of our numeral " 5 " is identical with the letter P in the Indian alphabet, from which have also been derived certain other of our numerals.[2]

The Welsh for Great Spirit is MAWR PEN AETHIR, which cannot but be related to the North-American-Indian term for Great Spirit MAHO PENETA ;[3] indeed, so numerous are the similarities between the language of WALES and that of certain tribes of AMERICA that the Welsh have claimed the honour of being the first European settlers in MEXICO. READE states : "We have it on the authority of a Captain Davies and Lieutenant Roberts of HAWCORDEN in Flintshire and from an MS. entry in William Penn's journal, evidence collected by the famous Dr Owen Pughe, that the tribes of the Illinois, Madocantes, the Padoncas, and Mud Indians spoke the Welsh language."[4] It is not improbable that the " White PANIS," now called PAWNEES, were originally a tribe of PAN worshippers.

PAN, in the fearful majesty of his higher aspects, is the source of the word *panic*. Similarly, the word *fear* may be equated with FIRE, *appalling* with APOLLO, and the French *peur* with POWER.

PAN is the Godfather of SPAIN—a contracted form of the older HISPANIA, and to the same root are no doubt traceable

---

[1] DROPE is an English surname.   [2] *Chambers's Encyclo.*, i. 188.
[3] *Atlantis*, p. 115.   [4] *The Veil of Isis*, p. 196.

the Latin *panis*, bread, and the French *pain*. PAN is evidently also the root of *pensive* and of *pensée*, the French for thought. The Gypsy for "to think" is *penchava*, and the Persian is *pendashten*. The time-honoured emblem of remembrance and kind *thought* is the flower we call a *pansy*, from which one may deduce the fact that the ancients defined *thought* as the "light or fire of God.'

PAN was particularly styled "President of the Mountains,"[1] and in many languages his name has become a generic term for hills and mountains. The Chinese for *mountain* or *hill* is *pan*,[2] and the Phœnician was *pennah*, whence, it is supposed, was derived the Cornish *pen* and the Scotch *ben*. All over the world the root *pen* or *ben* enters into mountain names, from the APENNINES to the PENNINE RANGE and from the Grecian PINDUS Mountains to the Peruvian PINRA.

The Chinese regard mountains as the symbol of Constancy and Firmness, and, according to SWEDENBORG, "in the ancient Church divine worship was upon mountains, because mountains signified celestial Love."[3]

In Egypt PAN was known as MIN, and *three* gigantic limestone figures of MIN have been found at the town of KOPTOS, the chief seat of his worship.[4] "MIN," says Professor Petrie, "was the *male* principle," and it is probable that MIN is the same as *man*,[5] in contradistinction to *woman*. *Man*, in Scotland pronounced *mon*, is the root of the Latin *mens*, the English *mind*, the Sanscrit *manas*, and of the Greek *monos*, meaning *single*, *solitary*, *alone*. It was originally, perhaps, *om on*, the "One Sun," or it may have been a coalition of *ma on*, the One Mother, as in *moon*, the symbol

[1] *Wisdom of the Ancients*, Bacon.
[2] Knox (A.), *Gloss. of Geogr. Terms*, p. 303.
[3] *Arcana Celestia*, n. 4288.
[4] Petrie (Flinders), *Religion of Ancient Egypt*, p. 59.
[5] In Gypsy language *man* is the personal pronoun "I."

of the Magna Mater. RA, the Sun, was AMON or AMUN ; the Greeks entitled Zeus AMMON[1] or HAMMON ; and the word *Amen !* means *firm, true, verily.*

The Anglo-Saxons termed the Moon *mona*, and at the present day *Moon-* or *Mona-day* is called " Monday." Anglesey,[2] a famous sanctuary of the British Druids, was anciently known as MON, MONA, or MENAI ; and MONA and MINNIE are familiar Christian names.[3] MONA is an alternative name of the Isle of Man, which was also known as MONABIA.

The town of BODMIN was originally " the abode of MIN," and in nomenclature may be equated with the Indian ALLAHABAD, " the 'abad' or abode of ALLAH."[4]

IRMIN was the name of a Saxon Deity,[5] and his title— whence *harmony* (?)—suggests that he was a male aspect of MINERVA, the Sole Strong Fire. There is again this same connection in the names of the little animal known as the *ermine*[6]

---

[1] Compare surname HAMMOND.

[2] The place-names in Anglesey are of great interest. BEAUM-AR-IS= " Father Sun, the Sunlight." In fig. 746 EL was represented as a right *angle.* The word angle or *an ag el* is the root of modern ENGLAND.

[3] Compare surnames MANN, MANNING, etc.

[4] *Cf.* Taylor, *Words and Places*, p. 332.

[5] Doubtless related to the Saxon and Anglican Deity ER or IR. The surname ACKERMANN is the great ERMIN. MONRO is a reversed form of RAMON or RAYMONDE, and MUNDAY, SIMON, SIMEON, SYMON, and SIMMONDS are all from this same great root.

[6] ERMINE Street is the ancient British highway northward from the English Channel to Yorkshire. Ermine fur is still an emblem of British royalty, the bench, and the peerage. " The ermine was believed to prefer death to defilement, and if placed within a wall or ring of mud, would kill itself rather than contaminate its spotless fur. It is on this account that ermine is selected as the robe of prince and judge—an emblem of unspotted purity."—Hulme (F. E.), *Nat. Hist. Lore*, p. 176.

> " Said an envious, erudite ermine :
> ' There's *one* thing I cannot determine ;
>   When a *man* wears my coat,
>   He's a person of note,
> While *I'm* but a species of vermin ! ' "

or *miniver*; within the boundaries of BODMIN is the parish of ST MINVER.

It was believed by the ancients, and is still an ingrained idea among native races, that kings and rulers are "Sons of the Sun," the living images and viceregents or "shadows" of the Holy Sun.[1] This divinity of kings is reflected not only in generic terms like *monarch*, Sanscrit *chunig*, German *konig*, "great unique one,"[2] but particularly in dynastic names.

According to priestly traditions the original king of Egypt was a certain MEN, MENA, or MENES—and *Menes*, the "sole Light," was a generic term for the white or golden Sun Bull of OSIRIS. MENUR, the "sole Fire," was a name of the Sacred Bull of MNEVIS. JUNO was termed MENA, and in Old Latin *manis* meant *good* and *propitious*; *manes* is the Latin for *ancestors*. MENES of Egypt may be equated with the name MINOS, a kingly name in CRETE, and CRETE was the seat of the *Minotaur*, a fabulously monstrous Bull.

---

[1] "The early monarchs of Babylon were worshipped as gods in their lifetime. . . . The kings of Tyre traced their descent from Baal, and apparently professed to be gods in their own person."—Frazer, *Adonis, Attis, Osiris*, pp. 10, 11.

In New Zealand a Tampo chief said to a missionary: "Think not that I am a man, that my origin is of the earth. I come from the heavens; my ancestors are all there; they are gods and I shall return to them."—Thompson, *The Story of New Zealand*, i. p. 95.

In ancient Egypt it was the "belief that the ruling king or sovereign of Egypt was the living image and viceregent of the sun-god (Ra). He was invested with the attributes of divinity, and that in the earliest times, of which we possess monumental evidence."—Renouf, *Religion of Ancient Egypt*, p. 161.

[2] Compare *Rajah, Rey, Rex, Anax, Archon*, etc. *Shah* is a contracted form of *padishah*—*pad*, as in *padre*, meaning, no doubt, Father, and *isha*, the Light. Kshi (*akishi*) is Sanscrit for "to rule." *Shiek* was probably ISHI EK, the Great Light; *Kaiser*, phonetically *Kysur*, may be restored to *ak yz ur*, the Great Light of Light; and *Akbar* is simply *ak bar*, the Great Fire. The word *emperor* or *empereur* is, as the French pronounce it, *om per ur*, "Sun, Father, Fire."

In Ireland are the Ox Mountains, and TAURICA was a surname of DIANA. Mount TAURUS, also known as AMANUS, ANTITAURUS,[1] and AMARANTHA,[2] is the largest mountain in ASIA.

MENA, the original King of Egypt, must be related to MANU, the Noah and first ancestor of the Hindoos. The original of the German race is said to have been MANNUS, and *manus*, *manush*, or *monish*, are the Gypsy words for *man*. The Sanscrit for *man* is *manasha*.

MON, the root of *monocle*, *monopoly*,[3] etc., is the base of the Egyptian royal name MENEPTAH, " sole Eye resplendent," and it is also the foundation of *monde* and *mundus*, the round world, the universe.

MIN, who was particularly worshipped at the city of MENDES, was also reverenced in Egypt under the name of MENTU.[4] The principal shrine of MENTU, who was figured with the head of a Hawk, was at the city of ERMENT, which is akin, not only to the Saxon IRMIN, but also to HERMON, an alternative name for Mount Zion. It is evident that MIN, like PAN, became a generic term for *mountain*. The Japanese for *mountain-peak* is *mine*, and in English *min* once meant the " brow of a hill."[5] The great mountain called MONCH[6] was doubtless named after MON, the Ever-Existent, and the same root is responsible for the generic terms *mons*, *mont*, *mount*, *mound*, and all their numerous correlatives. *Mons* is the Latin for *above*, and the verb *mount* means to *rise upward*. With the words *mountain* and *montagne*

---

[1] Compare name ANTIPATER.
[2] AMARANTHA means *immortal* and *unfading*.
[3] Compare Italian place-name MONOPOLI.
[4] Compare surname MINTO.
[5] Edmunds, *Names of Places*, p. 237.
[6] Compare MANCHURIA and MANCHESTER. The latter town, known also as MANIGCEASTER and MANCUNIUM, was founded by the BRIGANTES, a tribe from YORKSHIRE.

may be compared the names MONTAIGNE, MONTAGUE, MONICA, MONACO, MONIGUE, and MUNGO. The word *mungo* is Celtic for *lovable*, and the Irish Province MONA-GHAN is nominally related to the Asiatic MONGOLIA, the country of the MONGULS. A dynastic title of the Mexican emperors was MONTEZUMA, meaning the Mount of the Blazing Sun, and the *Ezuma* of this name may be equated with IZUME, a Japanese Goddess, and with the Assyrian ISUM, "seemingly a name of the fire God."[1]

The site of PAN's ruined city of MENDES is now marked only by the mounds of ASHMOUN, a name in which is retained

754

moun, the root of *mound* and *mount*. In the emblem herewith a fourfold cross is poised upon a threefold Holy Mount.

There is a Christian tradition that when the angelic hosts heralded the birth of JESUS CHRIST, a hollow groan reverberated through the Isles of Greece, intimating that great PAN was dead, and that the erstwhile divinities of OLYMPUS were dethroned and outcast. This story originated from the incident recorded by PLUTARCH, that while cruising near the island of PAXOS—note the name—an Egyptian pilot named THAMUS heard coming from the shore repeated cries of THAMUS! the voice subsequently announcing that "Great Pan was dead." As Dr Frazer has surmised, the true inference from this story appears to be the equation of

[1] Pinches, *Religion of Babylonia and Assyria*, p. 93.

PAN with TAMMUZ, the Syrian Shepherd-God whose demise was annually and noisily bewailed.

The root of the name THAMUS, TAMMUZ, or THOMAS, is *Tham, Tam,* or *Thom,* and just as *pan* and *mon* were generic terms for *hill* or *mountain,* so also was *thom.* In Welsh and Gaelic *tom* is a hillock—whence the Old English word *tump,* a hillock. *Tom* is the root of *tumulus,* a mound, and one of the famous sights near Carnac in Brittany is "the Butte de THUMIAC or Grand Mont, a Celtic mound 70 feet high and 800 feet round."[1]

THUM or TOM should originally have meant the "resplendent Sun," and in Egypt it did so, TUM being the title of the Sun-god at the great city of ANU, ON, or HELIOPOLIS. *Tambo* was Peruvian for *the dawn.*[2] RENOUF equates MENTU with TMU as being merely two different aspects of the same great Sun.[3] "I am TMU," runs an inscription, "who have made Heaven and have created all the things which are, and I exist alone."[4]

The Egyptian TM, THOM, or TUM, is the root of *tempus* or *time,* and the one lone, solitary lock of hair represented on the bald head of FATHER TIME is what was known in Egypt as the lock of HORUS.

At the festivals of BACCHUS, as at all other solar or Bacchanalian orgies, it was customary for the worshippers to raise a most joyful din upon cymbals and tambourines. The word *tambourine* or *timbrel* is an extended form of *tambour,*[5] a drum, and *tambour* has developed from the native *tom-tom* or *tan-tan.* All these words point to the conclusion

---

[1] Cook's *Handbook to Normandy and Brittany,* p. 277.
[2] Spence, *Mythologies of Ancient Mexico and Peru,* p. 51.
[3] *Hibbert Lectures,* p. 88.
[4] *Ibid.,* p. 198.
[5] Compare name TAMBURLAINE or TAMERLANE; also the English THOM, TOMS, TOMLEY, THOMPSON, and TOMPKINS. In Celtic *tam* meant *gentle.*

that the circular drum was so named after *dur oom*,[1] the Enduring Sun. The Latin for drum is *timpanus.*

There is a kind of small drum known as a *tabor* or *tabour* which suggests Mount TABOR, a mountain doubtless thus named because it is " of a remarkably round shape."[2] The Byzantine mystics used to sit watching their navels, or "circles of the Sun," in the hope of witnessing the far-famed "Light of TABOR" streaming therefrom, as from a focus.[3]

The brightly-coloured ribbons of the tambourine, like the many-coloured streamers from the ring at the summit of the Maypole, symbolised the all-radiant, streaming sunshine.

Layard in his account of a solar festival near NINEVEH describes how the natives in their exultant frenzy hurled tambourines into the air, while the women made the rocks resound with shrill cries of *tahlehl.*[4]

This cry of *tahlehl* appears to be *ta el ale*, " Hail resplendent God ! " The word *hail* is the Celtic *hael*, the *Sun*, and is radically the same as the word *yule*. *Hiul* in Danish and Swedish means *wheel*, and if we discard the differences of spelling, *hueel* and *hiul* are the same word. In Yorkshire, people, until comparatively recently, used to cry *Ule ! Ule !* in the churches as a token of rejoicing, and the common sort ran about the streets singing :

> "*Ule ! Ule ! Ule ! Ule !*
> Three puddings in a pule,
> Crack nuts and cry *Ule !*"[5]

---

[1] Compare surname DRUMMOND and place-names such as MINDRUM, DUNDRUM, DRUMLISH, DROMORE, DRUMOD, etc.
[2] Wright (T.), *Early Travels in Palestine*, p. 9.
[3] King (C. W.), *The Gnostics*, p. 300.
[4] *Nineveh*, p. 186.
[5] Brand's *Antiquities*, p. 252.

In MEXICO *Hool* meant the Head, the Deity, and *ho* meant *five*.[1]

In all probability the word *hubbub* arose from the exhilarating cries of HOB-HOB! raised at the solar festivals. In Hebrew *hobab* means *beloved*, and one of the world's most sacred trees is the *baobab*, the Father HOBAB.

Jobb and *chop*, *i.e.* the Ever-Existent Orb, are ancient British words for a *hill-top*, and are thence traceable in place-names such as EVANJOBB or EVANCHOP in RADNORSHIRE.

The Syrian TAMMUZ has been equated, notably by Mr Baring-Gould,[2] with our patron saint, ST GEORGE. In the Russian province of GEORGIA, whose southern boundary is the mountains of ARMENIA (*Harmonia* ?), ST GEORGE is not regarded merely as a saint, but is worshipped as the Deity. Addressed as "God Saint George of IKHINTI," he occupies in the minds of the Georgians precisely the position of Mediator and Intercessor, as does Christ in the minds of Christians.

The Cross of ST GEORGE, who was said to have been born at the city of DIOSPOLIS, appears in fig. 754, and that St George was identified with *mountains* is plain from the fact that in GEORGIA " there are no hills nor small mountains without churches in honour of St George."[3]

The most famous chapel in the world is perhaps that of St George on the Hill at WINDSOR.[4] At the neighbouring ETON there is still held a *triennial* festival called MONTEM—originally in honour of *Mon Tem*, the Sole Sun? The Egyptian "TEM, the Lord of Light," and the gentle-flowing, life-giving River THAMES,[5] THAMISE, or TAMESIS, are presumably allied

---

[1] Le Plongeon, *Sacred Mysteries*, p. 63.

[2] *Curious Myths of the Middle Ages.*

[3] Javakhishvili (J.), "Folk-Tales of the Georgians," *The Quest*, January 1912.   [4] The name *Windsor* means "winding shore."

[5] Towards OXFORD is the village of THAME. The original names of Oxford were CAER (the seat of) MEMPHRIC, afterwards BELLOSITUM, and CAER PEN HALGOIT.

to TAMMUZ, the light or essence of TAM or Father TIME. In the THAMES valley TIMMS is a familiar surname.

ETON in Bucks once held a great annual Fair upon ASH-Wednesday. The cult of ST GEORGE was noticeably practised at the town of ASHBY DE LA ZOUCHE : ASHBY was anciently called ESSEBY, and ASHBURY near OKEHAMPTON was also originally known as ESSEBURY.[1]

The famous "Furry Dance" at HELSTON[2] (Heol's Town ?) in Cornwall was, and still is, a "Fair," "Highday," "Eyeday," or "Holyday" of ST GEORGE, a stanza in the old Furry Song running :

> " As for Saint George O,
> Saint George he was a Knight O;
> Of all the Kings in Christendom,
> King Georgie is the right O,
> In every land O,
> Each land where'er we go ! "

The word *furry* might equally well be *verry*, a fire or spring dance, and the same root reappears in PHARNAVAS, a kingly name in GEORGIA. The most celebrated Queen of Georgia was THAMAR or TAMARA.

The play upon O in the Furry Song of King Georgy O is suggestive of the Italian GEORGIO. In Russia the saint is known as YURGEN, *i.e. yur-ag-en*, the "Ever-existent Fire, the Mighty Sun." Among Mussulmans his name is EL KOUDR ; and EL KOUDUR (*ak-o-dur*), the Great Enduring O, they say, is not yet dead, but still flies round and round the world.[3] At URMI, in Persia—and URMI cannot but be related to URMIN—the Churches of St George are frequented by those suffering from fear, *i.e. panic*.

The Rose, St George's flower, symbolises Love, and the

---

[1] Wilson, *Imperial Gazetteer.*
[2] Near HELSTON is MANACCAN.
[3] H. O. F., *St George for England*, p. 28.

word *rose* is an inflected form of EROS, the God of Love. The Greek for *rose* is *rhode* or *rhoda*, the resplendent RHO or RA.[1] In Hungarian *eros* means *strong*, and is evidently the same as *eros*, the Greek for *hero*. There is a close connection between *heroic* and *erotic*, which means *loving*. The French for *love* is *amour*, " fire or light of the Sun," and this word, like the Latin *amor*, is the same as the first two syllables of AMARUDUK, the oldest form[2] of the name MERODACH. MERODACH, " the young steer of day," the "life of the whole of the gods," is the same as MERIADEK,[3] the patron saint of BRITTANY. The Breton for *love* is *minoniach* ; the Breton for *ami*, a friend, is *minon* or *minoun* ; and there is also a Breton word *orged*, meaning *love*.[4] *Orged* resolves into " resplendent ORGE," or the " Ever-existent Golden Light," and the word ORGE, whence *gorgeous* and *urge*, is evidently the root of GEORGE. *Georgia*, the Greek for *husbandry*, probably was derived from GEORGE and not GEORGE from *georgia*. *Ge*, as in *geography*, meant *earth*, so that the true meaning of *George* may legitimately be surmised as *Ge urge*, the urger or stimulator of the Earth.

On Good *Friday* or " *Furry* Day " it is customary to eat

---

[1] Compare surname MONTROSE ; place-names MONTROSE, MONTREUX.

[2] Pinches, *Religion of Babylonia and Assyria*, p. 59.

[3] " As it was quite impossible to destroy these pagan customs, Christianity tried, as we know, to turn them to her own account. She raised chapels near the fountains, placed figures of the Virgin in crannies of the sacred oak trees, sanctified the old myths by adopting them as her own, substituting the names of saints for those of the old gods. And so, no doubt, it came to pass that good Meriadek, fabulous Bishop of Vannes, was called upon to receive the worship hitherto addressed to the sun in this corner of Tregor. There are many things about him that justify this theory. A certain Mystery Play—precious remnant of a lost dialect—shows him to us endowed with the gift of light, dissipating the darkness of sightless eyes, opening the shadowed understanding to behold the Light of Lights."—Anatole le Braz, *The Land of Pardons* [Brittany], p. 134.

[4] Gonidec, *Vocab., French-Breton*, p. 12.

hot cross-buns, which are round cakes stamped with the signature of St George. This custom is traceable to Egypt, where sacrificial cakes, made of the purest and most delectable ingredients, were on sale outside the Temples. The word *bun* was originally *boun*, and the Greeks changed it slightly into *bous*.[1] The word *bous* in Greek also means an Ox, and the sacred buns were sometimes made with a representation of two horns. At Yuletide it is usual to eat *mince* pies, or, as they are also named, " *happy months.*" In Scotland little troops of boys and girls were wont to perambulate the villages at Christmas time crying, " Hagmena, Hagmena, give us cakes and cheese and let us go away." This most remarkable word *Hagmena*, used on these occasions, is supposed, says the cautious Brand, to be of an antiquity prior to the introduction of the Christian faith.[2] It would seem to be more aged than AG-Mena, the Great Mena, the traditional prehistoric ancestor of Egyptian royalty. To account for the words *bun* and *pie*, one may assume either that these comestibles were originally circular, or that the ancients believed, as many Christians still believe, that in the sacrament of the *bun*, wafer, or *pie*, they were eating the veritable and substantial body of their Spiritual Father. The Book or Ordinale of Church Service is called the *pie*, and the little chest that holds the consecrated Host is known as the *pix*. Pius, a standard Papal name, means the same as *pious*. *Pikkis* in Gypsy language means the female breasts, which are also termed by the gypsies *birk* and *bark*. Bir or Birqu was a title of the Assyrian Mer, the Father, Fire, or *Amour* ; and the idea of the Great Feeder is retained in *piept*, the Wallachian for *breasts* ; and in our English *pap*, food for infants, and *paps* or *bubs*, the female breasts.

At the Egyptian city of Thebes, whose name originated

---

[1] Brand, *Antiquities*, p. 81.
[2] The festival survives to-day under the name of " Hogmanay."

from a sanctuary called AP,[1] AMON-RA was worshipped under the guise of a Ram, and in fig. 757 the Head of a Ram appears in the centre of the Eye.

The Ram, figuring as ARES in the Zodiac, was the symbol of Creative Heat. The Egyptian for *ram* was *ba*, and this same word also signified *soul*. *Belus*, the Latin for *ram*, is allied to BELENUS, the Celtic APOLLO, and *tup*, the English for a male sheep, may be equated with *top*, the

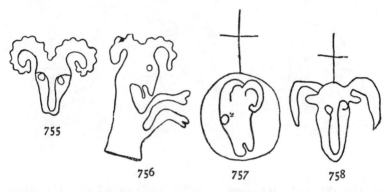

755   756   757   758

resplendent Eye. *Ares* is identical with URAS, EROS, HORUS, etc., and our *ram* was evidently once *uram*, the Solar Fire.[2] *Ramr* is Icelandic for *strong*, and the idea of strength, straightness, and power is retained in the word *ramrod* and the verb *to ram*. In Hebrew *ram* means *high*, and *ramah* a *lofty place* ; in Sanscrit RAMA is the Sun. RAM

---

[1] "*Ap*, along with the feminine article *Tap*, from which the Greeks made THEBE, was the name of one particular sanctuary of AMMON."—Lepsius, *Egypt, Ethiopia, and Sinai*, Bohn's Library, p. 248.

[2] The gypsies of England call their language, as the gypsies of many other countries call theirs, *Romany* or *Romanes*—a word either derived from the Indian *Ram* or *Rama*, which signifies a husband, or from the town Rome, which took its name either from the Indian *Ram* or from the Gaulic word *Rom*, which is nearly tantamount to husband or man ; for, as the Indian *Ram* means a husband or man, so does the Gaulic *Rom* signify that which constitutes a man and enables him to become a husband."—George Borrow, *Romano Lavo-Lil*, Intro.

is the root of the royal name RAMESES,[1] translated by the authorities to mean "Son of the Sun," and of RAMADAN or RAMAZAN, a great Feast among Mahommedan peoples. The word RAMADAN, implying consuming fire, is allied to the Arabian root *ramed, it was hot; Ramazan* is *san rama*,[2] the Holy Sun.

RIMMON, BER, or BIRQU, the Babylonish Almighty, was alternatively known as RAMMANU, and as *Urim* is the plural

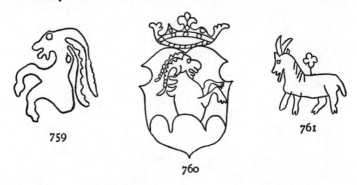

759   760   761

of *Ur*, the title RIMMON may be understood as *Urim Mon*, "Sole Lord of Fires and Lights."

> "Whatever lamps on Earth or Heaven may shine
> Are portions of ONE POWER which is MINE." [3]

The principal towns in the Isle of MAN, MANOBIA, or MANXLAND (*manikseland*), are RAMSEY and PEEL.

In fig. 760 a Goat is ramping on a mountain-peak. At MENDES, in Egypt, MIN was worshipped under the form of a goat, and in that district *mendes*[4] was the generic name for *goat*. In GREECE, as in EGYPT, Pan was figured as having the countenance and limbs of a goat. The choral odes sung

---

[1] The glories of RAMESES II. were sung by an Egyptian poet named PENTAUR. In Cornwall is a RAME Head and a PENTIRE Point.

[2] Compare Republic of SAN REMO.   [3] *Hymn of Apollo*, Shelley.

[4] Compare English MENDENHAM.

in honour of BACCHUS, who is also said to have appeared as a goat, were called *tragodiai* or goat songs, and a goat was the symbolical prize given on those occasions.

The emblematic distinction of the goat arose partly because the *habitat* of this animal is hilly and mountainous districts, but mainly because the Goat typified Generative Heat or the Vital Urge. The word *urge* will be recognised, as in GEORGE, and in *Demiurge*, a Gnostic term for the Deity, to mean the Ever-Existent Fire, the Solar *en-urgy*.

The French for a he-goat is *bouc*, which means exactly the same as *bauk*, the Egyptian for hawk. It is also the same as our English *buck*, and is perhaps traceable in place-names such as Box,[1] BUXTON, and BAXENDEN. The Latin *caper*, Italian *capra*,[2] and Spanish *cabron*, need merely their initial vowel to restore them into " Great Eye of Fire." There is a long-horned mountain goat known as the *ibex*, a word resolving into *ib ek se*. The French *chèvre* is almost the same as our *chafer*, and meant similarly the Ever-Existent Fire. The Greeks have two terms for goat—*tragos*, the enduring great light, and *aix*,[3] the great fire of A. In the Mayan alphabet A was represented by *three* alternative signs—a dot within a circle, a diamond-shaped square, and a peak, which was no doubt intended as the hieroglyphic of a mountain or hill. The Greek for a mountain-peak was *akra*, and our word *peak* similarly contains the notion of Great Father. In the North of England *pyke* is a generic term for pointed hill, and *pic*, the same word, occurs on the Continent, as in PIC DU MIDI. KRISTNA is recorded to have affirmed, " I am the letter A "; and in the Revelation of

---

[1] The Gloucestershire Box is a hamlet in MINCHINHAMPTON. The Box near CHIPPENHAM, the hamlet of CHEOPPEN, includes ASHLEY. South of SALISBURY is an eminence called BUXBURY. Compare also BEX in Switzerland and BUXAR in India. BAX, BEX, and JEX are English surnames.

[2] Compare CAPRI off the coast of CAMPANIA.

[3] AIX is a common place-name.

Jesus Christ it is asserted, "I am Alpha and Omega, the beginning and the ending, saith the Lord, which is, and which was, and which is to come, the Almighty."[1] In all languages the great A seems to have stood for a symbol of the Aged, Unaging, Constant, and Everlasting HILL, the Immutable EL, the Unchangeable First Cause.

That a mountain-top was regarded as a symbol and a physical similitude of the sacred A[2] is evidenced to some extent by generic terms for mountain, such as the Greek *akra*, the great Fire A; Savoyade *crau*; Slavonic *gara*; Anglo-Saxon *law*, i.e. *el aw*, "Lord Aw"; Japanese *jama* or *yama san*, "Holy unique Sun A"; Latin *montana*;[3] Spanish *montanha* and *sierra*.

The names JAH and YAH resolve into the Existent or

---

[1] Rev. i. 8.

[2] That the letter A had some recondite significance is evident from the words of Jesus found in the Apocryphal Gospel of Thomas : " And he looked upon the teacher Zacchæus, and said to him : Thou who art ignorant of the nature of the Alpha, how canst thou teach others the Beta ? Thou hypocrite ! first, if thou knowest, teach the A, and we shall believe thee about the B. Then he began to question the teacher about the first letter, and he was not able to answer him. And in the hearing of many, the child says to Zacchæus : Hear, O teacher, the order of the first letter, and notice here how it has lines, and a middle stroke crossing those which thou seest common ; (lines) brought together ; the highest part supporting them ; and again bringing them under one head ; with three points (of intersection) ; of the same kind ; principal and subordinate ; of equal length. Thou hast the lines of the A. And when the teacher Zacchæus heard the child speaking such and so great allegories of the first letter, he was at a great loss about such a narrative, and about his teaching."

The three lines of the A are perhaps explained in the following passage from a fifteenth century MS. quoted by Sir John Rhys : " The three elements of a letter are ╱ │ ╲, since it is of the presence of one or other of the three a letter consists ; *they are three beams of light*, and it is of them are formed the sixteen ogyrvens, that is the sixteen letters. These belong also to another art seven (score) and seven ogyrvens, which are no other than the symbols of the rank of the seven score and seven words in the parentage of the Welsh language, and it is from them all other words are derived."—*Hibbert Lectures*, p. 268. (*Italics mine.*)

[3] The Italian for *ram* is *montone*.

Unique AH or A, and this prime radical may be recognised in its original simplicity in the English word *awe*, and in the surnames HAY and HAW. *Agha* is the Sanscrit for *Lord*; *arka* in Sanscrit means *Sun*, and also a *hymn of praise*. The Happy Land of PAN, the leader of the celestial dance and song, was ARCADIA or ARCADY, a name resolving into the "resplendent mighty A." A is the root of *age* and of the Sanscrit *ayus*, meaning *life*. It is also the foundation of names such as AHAB, AHAZ, HAYES, HAWES, and AARON; AARON in Hebrew means lofty or mountainous, and in Cumberland there is a mountain named AARON END. The High Pontiff of the Mayans was known as the *Cay*,[1] i.e. *ac ay*, the great A; KAY and GAY are English surnames; and *gay* is an adjective: *kay* is Teutonic for *rejoicing*.

In all probability *boa*, the Portuguese for *good*, was originally *bo a*, "Father A." *Oca*, the great A, is Italian for *goose*; *ana* was Chaldean for *heaven*; and *ana* was Sanscrit for *mother*. *Abu = bu a*? is Arabic for *father*; at the town of ABA there was a famous oracle of APOLLO; and Mount ABU in India is a celebrated place of pilgrimage. At about the middle of Mount ABU the followers of VISHNU, known as the JAINS, have erected a magnificent group of *five* temples.

The first letter of the Egyptian alphabet was *ahom*, meaning *eagle*, and the first letter of the Hebrew was *aleph*, meaning ox. *Alpha*, the Greek for A, must be a later form of *aleph*, and is phonetically *aleph a*. *Caliph*[2] or *Calipha*, as also *Cadi*, Eastern titles of authority, all mean the great A, Aleph, or Alpha; and the Saint's name, ALPHAGE,[3]

---

[1] *Queen Moo*, p. 19.

[2] Near TADCASTER in Yorkshire is ULLESKELF, *i.e.* ULLES-AKELIF? On the River DUDDON in Cumberland, near ULVERSTONE, is the Chapelry of ULPHA. There is another ULPHA in Westmoreland. Near PENRITH is ULFSBY or OUSBY.

[3] Canterbury includes the parishes of St Alphage and Patrixbourne.

is probably related. The Israelites lapsed into the worship of a golden calf ; the ancient Muscovites also worshipped a golden calf ;[1] and the word *calf* is seemingly a contraction of *ac-alif*, the great A. The Gothic for calf was *kalbo*, the Great Lord Father ; and the ALPS[2] and CALVARY seemingly owe their names to this same root.

Dr Taylor maintains[3] that the Hebrew *aleph* is identical with *eleph* of *elephant*, the greatest, most powerful, and foremost of all beasts. The Semitic for *elephant* is *pul*, which also means *king*. In the Old Testament[4] a certain King PUL is mentioned as entering into a league with King MENAHEM, *i.e.* Sole Eagle or Sole A ?

LE PLONGEON states that among the Mayas the mastodon was venerated as an image of the Deity on Earth, " probably because this pachyderm was the largest and most powerful creature that lived in the land."[5] Much to the perplexity of historians a representation of the elephant, " the symbol of power and wisdom,"[6] is to be found carved on one of the round towers of Scotland in company with a crucifix and a lamb. HIGGENS, who first supposed these symbols to be of Christian origin, subsequently wrote : " I now doubt [the modern date of the tower] for we have over and over again seen the crucified man before Christ. We have also found ' the Lamb that taketh away the sins of the world ' among the CARNUTES of Gaul, before the time of Christ ; and when I contemplate these, and the elephant of Ganesa, and the ring and its cobra, *Linga, Iona,* and *Nandies*, found not far from the tower . . ., I am induced to doubt my former conclusions. The elephant, the GANESA of India, is a very stubborn fellow to be found here.

[1] Payne-Knight, p. 147.
[2] Part of the Alp district is named the OBERLAND.
[3] *The Alphabet*, i. 169.   [4] 2 Kings xv.
[5] *Sacred Mysteries among the Mayas*, p. 64.
[6] *Bible Myths*, p. 117.

The ring too, when joined with other matters, I cannot get over."[1]

One of the wonders of the world is the stupendous shrine cavern of ELEPHANTA. This "oldest and most magnificent temple in the world" is described by Maurice as "neither more nor less than a superb temple of the Triune God."[2] The Indian GANESHA, represented either as an elephant or as a man with an elephant's head, is invoked as the vanquisher of obstacles by Hindoos of all sects at the outset of any business: the name resolves in *ag an*, the

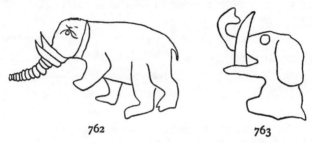

762   763

Great One ISHA. In the *Ganapati Upanishad* the God is addressed: "Praise to thee, O Ganesha! Thou art manifestly the truth; thou art undoubtedly the Creator, Preserver, and Destroyer, the Supreme Brahma, the Eternal Spirit. I speak what is right and true; preserve me, therefore, when speaking, listening, giving, possessing, teaching, learning; continually protect me everywhere."[3] The image of GANESHA is seen at the crossing of Indian roads and is placed by architects at the foundations of edifices. In ancient MEXICO the mastodon's head was similarly the principal and most common ornament.[4]

The incarnation of BUDDHA is said to have been brought about by the descent of the divine power called "the

[1] *Anacalypsis*, ii. 130.   [2] *Indian Antiquities*, iii. p. 9.
[3] *Hindoo Mythology*, Wilkins, p. 273.
[4] Le Plongeon, *Sacred Mysteries*, p. 97.

Holy Ghost" upon MAYA, a human mother, and this Holy Ghost or Spirit descended in the form of a white elephant.[1] Stow in his *Survey* speaks of *elephants* as *oliphants*, whence one may surmise the meaning of the English surname OLIPHANT.[2]

The German for *goat* is *ziege*, the "aged Fire," and the Sanscrit is *aga*, the mighty A. Our English *goat* is varied in the languages of Europe into *gat, goot, geit, ged, get*, and the radical of all these words is *at*, which is the Egyptian for *goat*. There is reason, as will be seen, to surmise that this syllable once meant the same as our modern English *heat* and *hot*.

ETNA,[3] the volcano, is a contracted form of *attuna*, the Phœnician for a furnace. The French for *stove* is *étuve*, and the syllables *et, at, ot*, etc., occur persistently in words relative to *heat* or things *hot*.

Just as *t* and *d* are interchangeable elsewhere, they here again vary. The early English for *hot* was *hoot*, the Anglo-Saxon *hat*; Dutch is *heet*; Swedish *het*; and Danish *hed*. The French for *warm* is *chaud*, and for warmth *chaleur*, the Ever-Existent, Everlasting Fire.

TAMMUZ was known as ATYS or ATTIS, and his alternative name ADONIS resolves, with a singular aptness to current opinion, into "warm Sunlight." *Aton*, the Aztec for *sun*, and *aten*, the Egyptian for *sun*, would appear to have originally meant the *hot one* or the "*hot 'un*"; and PTAH-HOTEP, one of the titles of the Egyptian PATAH, may perhaps be transliterated into "the Father Shining AH or A, the Hot Hoop."

The principal Fire Deity among the Japanese is ATAGO-SAMA. ATAGO may be understood as the "hot mighty O,"

---

[1] Doane, *Bible Myths.*
[2] Numerous remains of elephants have been found in Britain.
[3] Compare Christian name EDNA.

and the word SAMA is closely akin to SAMAS, the Babylonish Sun-God or Goddess, who was also known as UTUKI, *i.e.* the "Hot Great One" (?). The chief shrine of ATAGO-SAMA is at the summit of the high hill of ATAGO near KIOTO, and *hill* shrines are dedicated to him at all the chief cities of JAPAN. In the old state religion the God and fire were regarded as identical.[1]

The Japanese word *kami*, meaning God and anything godlike, is the same as KAMI,[2] the old name for Egypt. *Khama* is the Hebrew for *sun*, and *cam*, *kem*, and *can* are the Gypsy words for *sun*. In Sanscrit *khan*[3] means *sun*; in Hebrew *kham* means *heat*; and it is probable that the name KAMI or KAMIT applied to Egypt meant not "Black Land," but the "Land of the Great Hot Sun." The word EGYPT resolves into EJ-YP-TE, "the aged Brilliant Eye."

On the shores of the Red (*ured*) or "Fire-hot" Sea, which the Italians call *mar Rosso*, is the notoriously hot town of ADEN. *Adim* is the Sanscrit for *first*, and ADAM is believed to be the first ancestor of Humanity. ADON was the great Deity of the Phœnicians, and ADONAI is a mystic and poetic term for the Supreme Spirit spoken of as the *Monad*. *Monadh* is the Gaelic for *mountain* or *hill*, corresponding to the Welsh *mynydd*, and both these terms occur frequently in place-names.[4]

The Babylonish RAMMANU, BIR, or BIRQU, was known alternatively as ADDU, "hot brilliance" (?); ADAD, "heat of heats" (?); and DADU, "brilliant of brilliants" (?). In the language of the Romany or Gypsy *dad* and *dado* mean *father*, and are clearly the same as our English *dad* and *daddy*. The Celtic for *ancestors* was *gour dadou* and *tadou koz*, both

---

[1] Aston, W. G., *Shinto*, p. 44.

[2] Or CHEMI, whence the word *chemistry*.

[3] Compare Afghan title *Khan*. In Celtic the names KEAN and KENNY meant *vast*.

[4] Taylor, *Words and Places*, p. 326.

of which terms reflect the primitive belief that man's first Parent was "Daddy Great Fire" or "Daddy Great Light."[1] In the Gospels DIDYMUS is mentioned as another name for THOMAS.

The Celtic for *father* was *tad* or *tat*, the origin, perhaps, of the surnames TOD, TAIT, TADDY, all of which may be compared with the Egyptian symbol called the *tat*, *dad*, or *daddu*. The *Tat*,[2] a representation of four pillars, was the emblem of stability. It has recently been decided that the *tat* or *dad* also represented the spine or backbone (*buck bone*) of OSIRIS.[3] In the emblem herewith the letter A forms

764

the foundation to a flame-like tree,[4] spinal column, or Fire of Life. This rod or stem of JESSE may be equated with the *Ashera*, a phallic object mentioned in the Old Testament in connection with the worship of ASHTORETH. The *Ashera* was an upright stem or pole answering symbolically to the English Maypole. In Japan a certain sanctity still attaches to the central pillar or king-post of the house, known as *daikoku-bashira*. The *bashira* or Father ASHERA is connected

---

[1] The Celtic for *angel* is *el*, God. The French for ancestor is *aïeul*.
[2] Compare English *teat* or *dud*. *Tud* is Gypsy for *milk*, and in the same language *tatto* = *hot*, *tatcho* = *true*, and *tatchipen* = *truth*.
[3] Tirard, *Book of Dead*, p. 79.
[4] Osiris was believed to have been imprisoned in a tree trunk.

in the old Japanese rituals with a House-God named YABUNE.[1] The "Good YA" was once, no doubt, the same conception as the Hebrew YAH or JAH.[2]

In certain parts of SAMARIA the great god PAN was known as ASHIMA,[3] and in Persian mythology ARMAITI, the Great Mother, has a daughter—"the good ASHI"—whose function it is to pass between earth and heaven and bring the heavenly wisdom to mankind. In Sanscrit the syllables A-SI are equivalent to the Hebrew JAH and mean "Thou art": fundamentally the Sanscrit A-SI resolves into "Fire of the A."

Among European nations the ALL-Father was peculiarly identified with the Mighty ASH, and it is probable that the rowan and the mountain ash were originally held in veneration by reason of the globules of "holy seed," the "fructifying honey-dew," scattered over them in red clusters. Red was the colour of Love and of Blood, and Blood was regarded as the essence of life and the source of all human activity. The Latin for ash-tree is *fraxinus*, the "great Firelight"; the Icelandic is *askr*, the "blaze of the Great Fire"; the Danish and Swedish are *ask*; and the Lithuanian is *asis* = Isis. The white fragrant flowers of the ash-tree, which are like small hawthorn blossoms, grow in dense clusters and appear in June or Juno's month. The flowers have each *five* small sepals and *five* round white petals, and the serrated leaves of the tree have somewhat the appearance of small flames. "I know an Ash called Iggdrasil, a high tree, sprinkled with white moisture (thence come the dews that fall in the dales): it stands evergreen by URD's[4] spring. Thence come three maids, all knowing, from the hall that stands

[1] Aston, *Shinto*, p. 46.
[2] In 1 Chronicles ii. 27, BUNAH is mentioned as the brother of RAM; in Ruth iv. 19, RAM is mentioned as begetting AMMINADAB.
[3] Smith's *Bible Dictionary* (*Ashima*).   [4] Compare surname HURD.

under the tree."[1] These three maids, the familiar Trinity of Good Thought, Good Deed, and Good Word, may be compared with the three guardian Queens of King ARTHUR; and the name IG-DUR-AS-IL may be resolved into the "Great Enduring Light of God."

In fig. 765 the vital Urge, the rejuvenating Fire, is symbolised by an ear of bearded wheat or barley. The French for barley is *orge*, a word which, identical with *urge*, reappears in *burgeon*, an opulent and richly-bursting bud.[2]

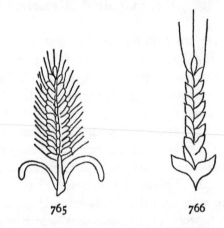

765 766

One of the Gnostic appellations for Christ, the Bread of Life, was "the Great Wheat-ear"; HORUS was entitled the Green Ear of Wheat, and the Ear of Wheat was a well-known attribute of ISIS, CERES, and other aspects of the Great Parent. It symbolised the spermatic power of the Creator and may be equated with the staff of life, the latter phrase being to this day proverbially applied to wheat.

In the vestibule of the British Museum there is a sculpture representing Mithra slaying the sacrificed BULL,

---

[1] From *The Edda*, W. Faraday, p. 29.

[2] Bud was originally spelled *budde* or *bodde*, and the Portuguese for *goat* is *bode*.

and the blood flowing from the wounded Bull is in the form of *three* wheat-ears.

An ear of bearded wheat figures on the coinage of the British King CUNOBELINUS, better known as CYMBELINE (A.D. *circa* 5). The capital of King CUNOBELINUS—BELENUS, the solar RAM, the great unique O—was COLCHESTER,[1] then known as CAMULODUNUM. Sir JOHN RHYS equates CUMHAL, the root of this name, with *himmel,* the German for *heaven* ; and *heaven* is the same as EVAN,[2] which was one of the titles of BACCHUS. The city of ROME, according to some accounts, was named after the Goddess ROMA, a daughter of EVANDER, the "enduring EVAN." ROMULUS, the alternative founder of ROME, is said to have instituted for the service of the gods an order of priests called CAMILLI or CAMILLÆ. CAMILLE is a French Christian name ; CAMILLUS was a Roman surname ; and in ITALY and MESOPOTAMIA there were people named the CAMELANI. In England and in Scotland there is a River CAMEL ; CAMMEL is an English surname ; and the same roots are responsible for CAMELOT, the wondrous city of King ARTHUR, which the poets describe as a city of spires and turrets piled picturesquely upon the slopes of a steep mountain.

The symbolic camel here illustrated has in every case its hump represented as a threefold or Holy mount—a fact that led me to investigate the connection, if any, between the word *camel* and CARMEL, the Sacred mount. In addition to Mount CARMEL in Palestine there is a CARMEL Point in ANGLESEY, and in SOUTH AMERICA there is an ALTA CAMELA.[3]

---

[1] PHRYXUS (*Furiksus*) is said to have flown to COLCHIS on the back of a golden ram. COLCHESTER was the capital of the TRINOBANTES.

[2] Compare names, EVAN, EVANS, LEVAN, and BEVAN or AP-EVAN.

[3] The ALTA here used may be compared with the British ALT and the Gaelic ALLTHA, meaning a steep place or mountain district, and used thus frequently in Scotland and Wales.

In *The Song of Solomon* the Bridegroom's head is likened to Mount CARMEL : "Thine head upon thee is like CARMEL ";[1] and in Micah the idea of CARMEL is coupled with that of a fruitful rod, or a spike of the staff of life : "Feed thy people *with thy rod*, the flock of thine heritage, which dwell solitarily in the wood, in the midst of CARMEL."[2]

The word CARMEL, according to the recognised authorities, means not only *circumcised lamb*, but also *harvest, vine of God—otherwise a garden or orchard—*and *full of ears of corn*.

Some Arthurian students identify CAMELOT with GUILDFORD, originally GILFORD, in SURREY. The Hebrew for

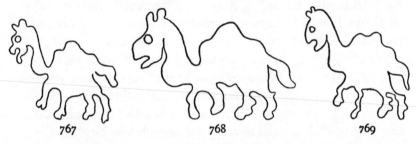

767　　　　768　　　　769

camel is *gimel*; and *gimel*, the third letter of the Hebrew alphabet, is believed to have taken its form from the camel's hump.[3] There must therefore have been some peculiar significance attaching to the camel's hump, and if GUILDFORD be equivalent to CAMELOT, we may perhaps rightly assume that GIL is a decayed form of *gimel*.

Among the place-names in the vicinity of Stonehenge is a GOMELDON ; *gamel* is Old English for *ancient*, and GEMMEL is a Scotch surname. In BABYLONIA there was a king, GIMEL SIN (2500 B.C.) ; he was deified during his lifetime, and after his death a temple in LAGASH (= "Lord Great-Ash " ?) was named after him.[4]

There is an Asiatic ox with a camel-like hump upon its

---

[1] vii. 5.　　　[2] vii. 14.　　　[3] *The Alphabet*, Taylor, p. 87.
[4] Jastrow, *Religion of Babylonia and Assyria*, p. 561.

shoulders and this sacred animal is known as the *zebu, i.e.*
" Fire Father."

The Israelites are said to have been guided through the
wilderness by a pillar of fire, and the idea of a flaming pillar
as the energising source of Being has been dramatically set
forth by Mr RIDER HAGGARD in *She.* " ' Draw near, draw
near ! ' cried AYESHA,[1] with a voice of thrilling exultation.
' Behold the Fountain and the Heart of Life as it beats in
the bosom of this great world. Behold the substance from
which all things draw their energy, the Bright Spirit of this
Globe, without which it cannot live, but must grow cold and
dead as the dead moon. Draw near, and wash you in those
living flames, and take their virtue into your poor bodies in
all its virgin strength—not as now it feebly glows within
your bosoms, filtered thereto through the fine strainers of a
thousand intermediate lives, but as it is here in the very
fount and source of earthly Being.' We followed her
through the rosy glow up to the head of the cave, till we
stood before the spot where the great pulse beat and the
great flame passed. And as we went we became sensible of
a wild and splendid exhilaration, of the glorious sense of
such a fierce intensity of Life that beside it the most
buoyant moments of our strength seemed flat and tame and
feeble. It was the mere effluvium of the fire, the subtle
ether that it cast off as it rolled, entering into us, and
making us strong as giants and swift as eagles. Nearer it
came, and nearer yet, till it was close upon us, rolling down
like all the thunder-wheels of heaven behind the horses of
the lightning. On it travelled, and with it the glorious
blinding cloud of many-coloured light, and stood before us
for a space, slowly revolving, as it seemed to us ; then,
accompanied by its attendant pomp of sound, it passed away
I know not whither. So astonishing was the wondrous

[1] Note the felicity of this name.

sight that one and all of us, save *She*, who stood up and stretched her hands toward the Fire, sank down before it, and hid our faces in the sand."

Of the same family as the golden *Laburnum* and akin to it in the splendour of its flowery cataracts is the tree we spell *acacia*, but pronounce *akashur*, the "Great ASHUR."

Acacia is said to be the Greek *akakia*, "the thorny Egyptian acacia," and its root is *akis*, a *point* or *thorn*.[1] The Thorn is a tree of spikes or spines, *spike* meaning also a *sharp point*, a *nail*, and an *ear of corn*; *spine* meaning also the *backbone*.

According to Rabbinical tradition, the burning bush upon Mount Sinai,[2] wherein the God of Israel appeared to Moses, was a *thorn* bush. In Egypt the thorn bush was associated with UNBU, and the *thorny* acacia was reputed to be the habitation of the mother-goddess NEITH. In Assyrian theology we meet with the *thorny* tree of light sacred to ASHUR, and in ARABIA the *thorny* lotus was consecrated to BAAL.[3]

The crown of *thorn* with which the Jews crowned Christ is said to have been plaited from the spiny shrub named *jujube* or *jujuba*,[4] a genus belonging to the natural order *rhamnaceæ*. The Holy Thorn of Glastonbury is termed the *sacra spina*, and the *jujuba* was known as *spina christi*. There is little doubt that in the childhood of the World all prickly or spiky things were regarded as symbolic of the darting, radiating, and piercing Fire, a conclusion which an analysis of the words *pur ik el*, *bur is el*, *es pin es*, *se pyx*, and so forth, will confirm. The Americans term the spiky burr of the Horse- or HORUS-Chestnut a *buck-eye*.[5] The symbolic

---

[1] Skeat.
[2] SINAI was alternatively known as HOREB and CHOREB.
[3] *Bible Folk-Lore*, p. 61.
[4] *Chambers's Encyclopædia*.
[5] The word was presumably carried across by the Pilgrim Fathers.

twig, spray, branch, *rameau*, or *virgo* here illustrated may be recognised as *Buckthorn, Bellacthorn*,[1] or Hawthorn—the thorn of the HAW or A.

It is evident that the axis of the Universe was conceived indifferently as either a fiery column, a pillar, a backbone, a spine, a spike, a nail, a torso, a trunk, a staff, a pivot, a spindle, an axle-tree, a rod, or a pole. In this universal character EROS, the God of Love or Attraction, the first

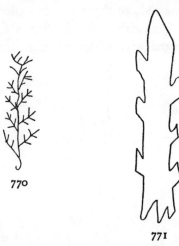

770

771

principle of animation, the father of Gods and men, and the regulator and disposer of all things, was worshipped under the name PRIAPUS—PUR-I-APUS. He was said to pervade the Universe, with the motion of his wings bringing pure light, and thence was called "the Splendid, the Self-illumined, the Ruling PRIAPUS.[2]

The rugged staff that occurs in heraldry in conjunction with a Bear had doubtless a similar signification. This torso, or rugged staff, is represented in fig. 771.

[1] There is a town of HACKTHORNE near ERMINE Street as it passes LINCOLNSHIRE.

[2] *Orph. Hymn.*

Lying south of WHITBY and SCARBOROUGH under the encroaching sea are the submerged remains of the once flourishing city of OWTHORNE.[1]   On the same coastline have also been washed away the ports of RAVENSROD and RAVENS-PUR.   *Rod* or *rode* once, as in Holyrood, had the secondary meaning of a cross.   *Spur*, the root of *sperm*, occurs in the names SPURR, SPURLING, SPURGE, SPURGEON, etc.; in the Irish SPERRIN Mountains ; and at SPURN Head, the site of ancient RAVENSPUR, where there is a so-called " BULL Light-ship."   The leg herewith, starred with a five-rayed *eperon* or *spur* and anointed with a descending streak of flame, is

772

seemingly a symbol of God, the Golden Spur, the Energising Sperm, Spark, Spurt, or Spirit.   The arms of MONA are the well-known trinity of legs; these three legs, "spurred and garnished OR," emerging from a solar face, are the arms of TRINACRIA or Three Angles, now SICILY.

Close to SPURN HEAD are the towns of PAULL, PATRING-TON, BARTON, BRIGG, HULL, and GOOLE, *i.e.* the Great YULE or WHEEL ?   Within the precincts of GOOLE is the township of ARMIN.

Layard alludes to an Arabian tribe, the YEZIDIS, who possess a highly reverenced symbol which they term MELEK TAOS or King TAOS.   The MELEK TAOS—" Sun-god, great shining light"—was the image of a peacock supported on a

---

[1] Willson (Beckles), *Story of Lost England*, p. 82.

stand resembling a candlestick, and it was carefully explained to LAYARD that this object was looked upon not as an idol but as a symbol.[1] Images of a bird upon a pedestal were found by BENT during his exploration of the prehistoric Temples of MASHONALAND,[2] and similar symbols have been

773

discovered in PHŒNICIA, EGYPT, and CYPRUS. The pillar or *betyle*—compare our *beetle*, Anglo-Saxon *bitela*—was the emblem of the universal AXIS, and the Bird upon the top may be described as a *pigeon*, the " Father Ever-Existent Sun," or a *peacock*. Nowadays this royal symbol is called a *sceptre*—originally *se pitar*, the "Fire Father"; and the English

774

sceptre is tipped with an IRIS or *fleur-de-lys*. The Maoris of NEW ZEALAND possess a greenstone pigeon which has been carried about by them for untold centuries during their multitudinous wanderings. This symbolic bird, called " the KOROTANGI," the "Great Fire-Hot Sun, the Ever-Existent"(?), used to be set up on a hill-top (in Maori language, *taumata* = *tum*, the hot A) and invoked as an oracle.[3]

[1] *Nineveh*, p. 188.   [2] OM-ASH-UNA?
[3] Cowan, *Maoris of New Zealand*, pp. 72, 73.

775

776

777

778

779

780

In the emblems herewith PAN, MON, or TUM is represented partly with the face of a Goat and partly with that of a Lion. As a symbol of the Sun the lion was, and is, a universal emblem, and the cause is probably traceable to the resemblance between the conventional solar face and the tawny, yellow, mane-surrounded face of Leo. The word *leo*[1] means "Everlasting O," and *leon*, *laon*, or *lion* may be resolved into "everlasting One." The Hebrew for *lion* is *laish*, the "everlasting Light," and the Persian *sher* may be equated with ASHUR.

It is customary to identify Christ with the "Lion of

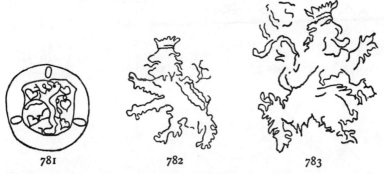

781   782   783

Judah," associated in Revelation with the Root of David.[2] JUDAH is said to have been the father of *five* sons,[3] and the sign *Leo* is the *fifth* in the Zodiac. In fig. 781 the Lion is identified with JUDAH, the "Ever-Existent Brilliant A," by *five* hearts, and figs. 782 and 783 are skilfully designed to represent the Living Fire.

In fig. 785, where realism has been sacrificed to symbolism, the head consists of a *lily* or *iris*. The mane forms *eight* lobes and the beard three v's or rays of Light. The tail represents a pomegranate, which in Hebrew is called a *rimmon*, *i.e.* RIMMON. The right hand is grasping the

---

[1] Compare LEOPOLD, LEOTARD, LEONARD, CLEO, etc.
[2] v. 5.   [3] 1 Chronicles ii. 4.

six arrows or lightnings of Divine Power, and the left hand holds a moon-shaped cresset or beacon light. The trident or three-forked spear—a familiar emblem of power —is an alternative form of the Cross.

A recumbent lion was the Egyptian hieroglyph for the letter L, and in INDIA, PERSIA, and apparently every part of the world, the lion is the recognised emblem of strength, courage, and the Sun. In MASHONALAND the

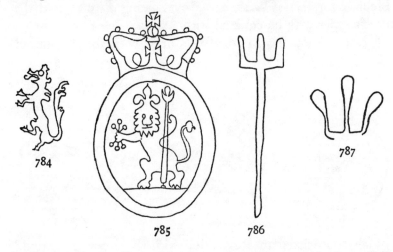

natives call the lion *Mondoro*, the "lone enduring O," and it is there worshipped as a good deity. BENT, describing a visit to the *Mondoro's* High Priest, who, like his Master, is also termed "the Mondoro," says : "Then we questioned him about the lion-god, and he gave us to understand that the Mondoro or lion-god of 'Mtoko's country is a sort of spiritual lion which only appears in time of danger, and fights for the men of 'Mtoko ; all good men of the tribe, when they die, pass into the lion form and reappear to fight for their friends. It is quite clear that these savages entertain a firm belief in an after-life and a spiritual world, and worship their ancestors as

spiritual intercessors between them and the vague *Muali*
or God who lives in Heaven."[1]

Once in twelve months a bullock and a goat are
sacrificed to the Mondoro; in the same district *bondoro*
is the native word for *manes* or ancestors.[2]

Overlooking the egg-shaped Temple of Great ZIMBABWE
in MASHONALAND—note the oval encircling fig. 785—is the
towering Mount BEROMA or VEROMA, and when the Portuguese first visited this part of AFRICA, it was then under
the rule of an Emperor MONOMATAPA. This name—"the
lone sun, the hot eye A"—is as full of interest as are other
African royal names, such as LUCERE, MANUZA, KHAMA,
CHAKA, PANDA, UMPANDA, and CHIPUNZA or CHIPADZI.

The word ZULU[3] is probably cognate with ZULA, a
place-name in CORNWALL, and the curious herring-bone,
mortarless, stone walls of ZIMBABWE are still being built
in certain parts of CORNWALL, notably near BOSCASTLE
and BOSSINEY. Bos—originally either *obus* or *bous*; both
bos and *bous* meaning *ox*—is a common prefix in Cornwall,
and it occurs sometimes as a suffix, as in the place-name
PROBUS[4] near PAR. On the River OUSE near BOSTON in

[1] *The Ruined Cities of Mashonaland*, p. 329.

[2] "A lion (Simha) was the mythical ancestor of Prince Wijaya, the
Aryan Conqueror of Ceylon, and the people who crossed over with him
from North India (543 B.C.) bore the name of Simhalese. The Ceylon
Chronicles bear witness that in the third century before Christ, when
Buddhism was introduced into the Island, the Great Monastery at
Anurādhapura was laid out in the shape of a lion reguardant. Later
the walls of the capital were ornamented with figures of lions, and the same
emblem appears in numerous sculptures in the sacred city, as well as in the
later capitals, such as Pollonnaruwa. The marvellous rock citadel, Sīgiri
(the Lion Rock), was shaped in the form of a lion. The national device
also appears on the gold coin of Parākrama Bāhu the Great (1164–97)."
—*Miscellanea Genealogica et Heraldica*, ser. iv., vol. iii., pt. viii., p. 371.

[3] ZULU is a shortened form of AMAZULU. The ZULUS are a branch of
the BANTUS. Compare British names BUNTY and BUNDY.

[4] *Probity* is *honesty*. "Honest" resolves into "shining light of the One,"
and the expression "honest as the light of day" is proverbial.

Lincolnshire is a place called WYBOSTON in the parish of
EATON-SOCON. On the USK (*usik* or Great OUSE) near
the WYE in the County of MONMOUTH is the town of
CAERLEON, *i.e. the seat* or *fortress of the lion*. The rock of
LAON, the stronghold of the later Merovingian kings, was
also known as LAUDUNUM. The place-name LAU or LEO,
as in LEIDEN—again the *Leo's Den*—and LEON, as in the
French LAON and LYONS, is always alternatively LUGUS, *i.e.*
Lord Great Ouse, Uz, or Light.[1] The lost land of LYONESSE
was alternatively termed LOGRIS, and the French LYONESSE
(now NORMANDY and BRITTANY) was originally one large
province called LUGDUNENSIS, divided like the Cross of St

788   789

George into *four* quarters, known respectively as LUG-
DUNENSIS PRIMA, -SECUNDA, -TERTIA, and -QUARTA. There
is a LEOMINSTER on the River LUG near SHREWSBURY, and
SHREWSBURY was known to the ancient Britons as PENG-
WERN. The Bird herewith is either the *Penguin*, a bird
of PAN? or it may be intended to represent the *Auk* or
Great Auk.

In Sussex there is a LEOMINSTER, containing the hamlet
of CROSSBUSH. LEINSTER (or LEONSTOWER), one of the four
provinces of Ireland (or URELAND), may be equated with
LEIDEN and LAUDUNUM; and LEINSTUR is next to MUNSTER,[2]

---

[1] "The name LUGUS," says Mr C. Squire, "still clings to the cities of
LYONS, LAON, and LEYDEN, all anciently called LUGUDUNUM."—*Mythology
of Ancient Britain*, p. 13.

[2] ULSTER="God's Tower"(?). Compare also ULLESWATER near PEN-
RITH, PATTER- or PATERDALE, BIRKFELL, and POOLEY.

MINSTER, or MINISTER, a tower or fortress of MINIS,[1] the Sole Light. The chief seat of APOLLO-worship was the city of PATARA ; the name CLEOPATRA resolves into *ac leo patara*, the Great LEO, the Everlasting O, Father enduring A.

LEO, like PIUS, the light of PA, and URBAN, the benign FIRE, is a conventional name assumed by the Popes or Papas. The crossed pipes herewith are the symbol of Christ, the Piper or Great PAPA.[2]

" The Father of the All," says one of the Gnostic writers, " is moreover denominated the ' Piper,' because that which is born is the harmonious Spirit (or Breath). The Spirit is likewise called the Father, and the Son begotten by the Father for the worship of the Perfect is not carnal, but spiritual. . . . This is the mystery of the Incomprehensible One furnished with innumerable eyes, whom all Nature longeth after in different ways. This is the Word of God."[3]

There is a SLAV fairy-tale related of one of the CARPATHIAN Mountains called the CARAIMAN, but which applies equally to MAN or PAN, the President of all mountains. It runs thus : " Long, long ago, when the sky was nearer to the earth than now, and there was more water than land, there dwelt a mighty sorcerer in the Carpathians. He was as tall as the tallest pine-tree, and he carried upon his head a whole tree with green twigs and budding branches. His beard, that was many yards long, was of moss, and so were his eyebrows. His clothing was of bark, his voice was like rolling thunder, and beneath his arm he carried a set of bagpipes, as big as a house. He could do anything he liked with his bagpipes. When he played softly, young green sprang up all round about him, as far as his eye could

---

[1] MINNS or MINNES is an English surname.

[2] In *Travels on the Amazon* Dr Wallace mentions the Great King Vulture—in Egypt the vulture was the symbol of maternal care—as " Sarcorhamphus papa " (p. 320). Whether this is the local or the scientific name I cannot say.   [3] See *The Gnostics*, King, p. 92.

reach ; if he blew harder, he could create living things ; but when he blew fearfully loud, then such a storm arose that the mountains shook and the sea shrank back from the rocks, so that more land was left uncovered.

" Once he was attacked by some powerful enemies, but instead of having to defend himself, he merely put the bagpipes to his lips, and changed his foes into pines and beech-trees. He was never tired of playing, for it delighted his ear when the echo sent back the sound of his music to him, but still more was his eye delighted to see all grow into life around him. Then would thousands of sheep appear on every height and from every valley, and upon the forehead of each grew a little tree, whereby the Caraiman might know which were his ; and from the stones around, too, dogs sprang forth, and every one of them knew his voice. Since he had not noticed much that was good in the inhabitants of other countries, he hesitated a long while before making any human beings. Yet he came to the conclusion that children were good and loving, and he decided to people his land with children only. So he began to play the sweetest tune he had ever yet composed —and behold ! children sprang up on every side, and yet more children, in endless crowds. Now you can fancy how wonderful the Caraiman's kingdom looked. Nothing but play was ever carried on there ; and the little creatures toddled and rolled around in that beautiful world and were very happy. They crept under the ewes and sucked the milk from their udders ; they plucked herbs and fruit and ate them ; they slept on beds of moss and under overhanging rocks, and were as happy as the day was long. Their happiness crept even into their sleep, for then the Caraiman played them the loveliest airs, so that they had always beautiful dreams.

" There was never any angry word spoken in the kingdom of the Caraiman, for these children were all so sweet and joyful that they never quarrelled with one another. There was no occasion for envy or jealousy either, since each one's lot was as happy as his neighbour's. And the Caraiman took care that there should be plenty of sheep to feed the children ; and with his music he always provided enough of grass and herbs, that the sheep, too, might be well nourished.

"The children knew nothing of reading or writing ; it was not necessary they should, since everything came to them of itself, and they had to take no trouble about anything. Neither did they need any further knowledge, since they were exposed to no dangers.

"Yet, as they grew older, they learnt to dig out little dwellings for themselves in the ground, and to carpet them with moss, and then of a sudden they began to say, 'This is mine.'

"But when once a child had begun to say, 'This is mine,' all the others wanted to say it too. Some built themselves huts like the first ; but others found it much easier to nestle into those that were already made, and then, when the owners cried and complained, the unkind little conquerors laughed. Thereupon those who had been cheated of their belongings struck out with their fists, and so the first battle arose. Some ran and brought complaints to the Caraiman, who in consequence blew a mighty thunder upon his bagpipes, which frightened all the children terribly.

"So they learnt for the first time to know fear ; and afterwards they showed anger against the tale-bearers. In this way even strife and division entered into the Caraiman's beautiful, peaceful kingdom.

"He was deeply grieved when he saw how the tiny folk in his kingdom behaved in just the same way as the grown people in other lands, and he debated how he might cure the evil. Should he blow them all away into the sea and make a new family ? But the new ones would soon be as bad as these, and then he was really too fond of his little people. Next he thought of taking away everything over which they might quarrel; but then all would become dry and barren, for it was but over a handful of earth and moss that the strife had arisen, and, in truth, only because some of the children had been industrious and others lazy. Then he bethought himself of making them presents, and gave to each sheep and dogs and a garden for his particular use. But this only made things far worse. Some planted their gardens, but others let them run wild, and then perceived that the cultivated gardens were the fairest, and that the sheep that had good pasture gave the most milk. Then the trouble became great indeed. The lazy children made a league against the others, attacked them, and took away many of their gardens. Then the industrious ones moved to a fresh spot, which soon grew fair also under their hands; or else they refused to be driven out, and long conflicts arose, in the course of which some of the children were slain. When they saw death for the first time they were greatly frightened and grieved, and swore to keep peace with one another. But all in vain—they could not stay quiet for long; so, as they were now loth to kill one another, they began to take away each other's property by stealth and with cunning. And this was far sadder to see; the Caraiman, indeed, grew so heavy of heart over it that he wept rivers of tears. They flowed down through the valley and into the sea; yet the wicked children never considered that these were the tears their kind father was weeping over them, and went on bickering and quarrelling. Thereupon the Caraiman wept ever more and more, and his tears turned to torrents and cataracts that devastated the land, and ended by changing it into one large lake, wherein countless living creatures came to their death. Then he ceased weeping, and blew a mighty wind, which left the land dry again ; but now all the green growth had vanished, houses and gardens lay buried under heaps of stones, and the sheep, for lack of pasture, no longer gave any milk. Then the children cut their throats open with sharp stones, to see if the milk would not flow out in a fresh place ; but instead of milk, blood gushed out, and when they had drunk that they became fierce, and were always craving for more of it. So they slew many other sheep, stealing those of their brethren, and drank blood and ate meat. Then the Caraiman said, 'There must be larger animals made, or there will soon be none left!' and blew again upon his bagpipes. And behold! wild bulls came into the world, and winged horses with long scaly tails, and elephants, and serpents. The children now began to fight with all these creatures, and thereby grew very tall and strong themselves. Many of the animals allowed themselves to be tamed and made useful ; but others pursued the children and killed them, and as they no longer dwelt in such peace and safety, many grievous and dangerous sicknesses appeared among them. Soon they became in all respects like the men of other lands, and the Caraiman grew more and more soured and gloomy, since all that which he had intended to use for good, had but turned to evil. His creatures, too, neither loved nor trusted him, and instead of perceiving that they themselves had wrought the harm, thought that the Caraiman had sent sorrow upon them out of wanton cruelty and sport. They would no longer listen to the bagpipes, whose sweet strains had of old been wont to delight their ears. The old giant, indeed, did not often care to play on his pipes now. He had grown weary for very sorrow, and would sleep for hours together under the shade of his eyebrows, which had grown down into his beard. But sometimes he would start up out of sleep, put the pipes to his mouth, and blow a very trumpet-blast out into the wicked world. Hence there at last arose such a raging storm that the trees ground, creaking and groaning, against one another, and caused a fire to burst out, so that soon the whole forest was in flames. Then he reached up with the tree that grew upon his head till he touched the clouds, and shook down rain to quench the fire. But all this while the human beings below had but one thought— how to put the bagpipes to silence for ever and ever. So they set out with lances and spears, and slings and stones, to give battle to the giant ; but at the sight of them he burst into such laughter that an earthquake took place, which swallowed them all up, with their dwellings and their cattle. Then another host set out against him with pine-torches, wherewith to set his beard on fire. He did but sneeze, however, and all the torches were extinguished and their bearers fell backwards to the earth. A third host would have bound him while he slept, but he stretched his limbs, and the bonds burst, and all the men about him were crushed to atoms. Then they would have set upon him all the mighty wild beasts he had created. But he swept the air together and made thereof an endless fall of snow, that covered them over and over, and buried them deep, and turned to ice above them ; so that after thousands of years, when their like was no more to be seen on earth, those beasts lay still, with fur and flesh unchanged, embedded in the ice.

"Then they bethought themselves of getting hold of the bagpipes by stealth, and carrying them off while the giant was asleep. But he laid his head upon them, and it was so heavy that men and beasts together could not drag the pipes from under it. So at last they crept up quite softly and bored a tiny hole in the bagpipes—and lo ! there arose such a storm that one could not tell earth or sea or sky apart, and scarcely anything survived of all that the Caraiman had created. But the giant awoke no more ; he is still slumbering, and under his arm are the bagpipes, which sometimes begin to sound, when the storm-wind catches in them, as it hurries down the Prahova Valley. If only someone could but mend the bag-pipes, then the world would belong to the children once more."

I have transcribed this tale almost verbatim from *Legends from River and Mountain*,[1] collected by Carmen Sylva from the folk-lore "associated with the mountains which surround her home among the pine-woods of SINAIA."[2] Judging from the vast antiquity of folk-lore in general, it is possible that this CARPATHIAN story may preserve one of the legends of PAN in a comparatively pure and primitive form. The emblems reproduced in figs. 790 and 791 are described by Mons. BRIQUET as *Cornemuses*. They appear to represent the inflated breath-bag of the cornemuse or bagpipe, and I conceive that whoever it may have been who designed them had heard and recognised the Pipes of PAN.

[1] Translated by Alma Strettell, London, 1896.
[2] Compare SINAI, SINODUN, etc.

790   792   791